W9-ANN-444

101
TOUGH CONVERSATIONS
TO HAVE
WITH **EMPLOYEES**

101
TOUGH
CONVERSATIONS
TO HAVE
WITH EMPLOYEES

A Manager's Guide to Addressing Performance,
Conduct, and Discipline Challenges

SECOND EDITION

PAUL FALCONE

HARPERCOLLINS
LEADERSHIP

AN IMPRINT OF HARPERCOLLINS

© 2019 Paul Falcone

All rights reserved. No portion of this book may be reproduced, stored in a retrieval system, or transmitted in any form or by any means—electronic, mechanical, photocopy, recording, scanning, or other—except for brief quotations in critical reviews or articles, without the prior written permission of the publisher.

Published by HarperCollins Leadership, an imprint of HarperCollins Focus LLC.

Scenarios 77, 78, and 79 previously appeared in slightly different form in *HR* magazine © 2016, 2018 Paul Falcone

Book design by Elyse Strongin, Neuwirth & Associates.

978-1-4002-1202-6 (eBook)
978-1-4002-1201-9 (TP)

Library of Congress Cataloging-in-Publication Data

Library of Congress Control Number: 2018966315

Printed in the United States of America
19 20 21 22 23 LSC 10 9 8 7 6 5 4 3 2 1

TO MY MOTHER, DOROTHY

For teaching me to listen openly, judge fairly,
and always look for the best in others . . .

CONTENTS

7. Lack of Requisite Skills   123

PART III: INAPPROPRIATE WORKPLACE BEHAVIOR AND CONDUCT

8. Sexually Offensive Behavior   143

9. Substandard Communication Skills 171

10. Personal Style Issues 189

11. Leadership Style Challenges and Career Management Obstacles 223

PART IV: CORPORATE ACTIONS

12. Corporate (Intentional) Actions   261

13 Corporate ("No Fault") Actions   295

14. Summary Offenses (Immediate Discharge) 315

15. Special Circumstances 329

PREFACE

Having tough discussions with your employees will always be one of the most daunting tasks that you'll face as a manager. As a general rule, the path of least resistance is avoidance, and how many of us haven't been guilty from time to time of allowing problems to go on, hoping they'd simply fix themselves? If you've purchased this book, you're probably someone who has faced this challenge on a number of occasions throughout your career, but you instinctively know that if you simply had the right verbiage and a strategic game plan in place, you'd be able to address minor problems head-on before they escalated into something far more serious.

Take comfort, dear reader, in knowing that you're not alone. And know that this book is designed and structured as a handy guide—and guiding hand—to walk you through some of the most common as well as the most serious employee challenges that you could ever come across in your career. My goal in writing *101 Tough Conversations to Have with Employees* is to be there by your side and walk you through these issues carefully and thoughtfully, all the while protecting you as well as your company from liability or unforeseen consequences.

Prior to publishing the first edition of *101 Tough Conversations to Have with Employees*, I wrote a book called *101 Sample Write-Ups for Documenting Employee Performance Problems: A Guide to Progressive Discipline and Termination*. The purpose of that book was to provide managers and corporate leaders with sample documentation to walk them through some of the most challenging minefields that exist in corporate America today: written warnings, workplace due process, and terminations for cause. This book is specifically meant to complement the *101 Sample Write-Ups* book, only from the verbal—rather than written—perspective. It will similarly focus not just on *what* to do but on *how* to do it, keeping in mind that people are sometimes fickle and difficult to predict.

The paradigm in *101 Sample Write-Ups* is to treat people with dignity and respect at all times, even through the discipline and termination processes. The paradigm focuses on two key areas:

▶ Documenting your affirmative efforts at proactively rehabilitating employees and "meeting them halfway" in terms of fixing the problem at hand
▶ Holding employees fully accountable for their actions and shifting the responsibility for improvement away from the company and to the employee, where it rightfully belongs

This way, if termination is the ultimate result, your documentation will show that those employees actually terminated themselves, despite your responsible efforts at helping them.

101 Tough Conversations follows those same principles in verbally addressing employee performance and conduct problems. As we all know, if we can address problems verbally and early on, then (in theory at least) there should be little need to move forward with a written warning or a termination for cause. And even when there is a need to move to formal documentation in the form of a written warning or an immediate termination, the record you'll have created via your verbal counseling or intervention will show that you have handled the matter respectfully, responsibly, and in a timely manner—and those are the key standards of workplace due process and fairness.

In addition, remember that performance interventions—whether verbal or written—have to be viewed as good faith attempts to encourage employees to change course and alter their behaviors. They're never supposed to be viewed simply as ways of "papering files" so that you have documentation on record to justify a dismissal. How many managers using this methodology have been pleasantly surprised by employee turnarounds once a formal intervention has been introduced into the equation!

Therefore, take heart: This operational field manual will help you skillfully address problematic employee performance and conduct issues in the workplace with a level of confidence and certainty that you might not have had up until now. After all, involved management is all about getting to the truly human concerns at hand, which are issues that may have been left unaddressed for far too long. And it's only in that mode of positive confrontation that you'll be able to simultaneously protect your company and allow your employees to take back control of their careers. That's what enlightened leadership is all about.

How This Book Is Structured

101 Tough Conversations to Have with Employees is structured in a simple format. Each of the scenarios is followed by a solution section that outlines a sample script that you might choose to employ under those particular circumstances.

Perhaps the idea of pre-writing a verbal communication sounds insincere or artificial. In fact, having a structured outline on hand to help you through these various scenarios will go a long way in helping you get into the appropriate mindset while remembering the key issues that need to be addressed.

In addition, many solutions are followed by a special note section that will remind you of any red flags that could come back to haunt you. For example, if you're speaking with an employee about a body odor problem and suspect that this may be the result of a medical condition, then the Americans with Disabilities Act (ADA) may be at issue. The ADA specifically sets forth that employers who *regard* workers as being disabled may have an affirmative obligation to engage in an "interactive process" with the employee to determine an appropriate accommodation. The special notes flag some key areas for consideration before you begin a dialogue with your employees.

All in all, expect *101 Tough Conversations* to address the most difficult conversations that exist in the workplace, along with tips and guidance on how to handle them professionally and with the utmost care. So grab a highlighter and your favorite pen, turn to the scenario that best matches the challenge you're currently facing, and outline the structure of the argument you want to make along with the salient points that you want to cover. Used correctly, this book will help you protect your company, guide and develop your employees, and catapult your leadership and management skills to new heights as you positively address the most challenging people issues that come your way.

ACKNOWLEDGMENTS

To my newest friends at HarperCollins Leadership—Jeff James, vice president and publisher; Tim Burgard, senior acquisitions editor; and Amanda Bauch, editor—thank you all for welcoming me to the HarperCollins family. I'm honored to become part of such an outstanding, world-class organization. And to my dear friends at AMACOM, who made the first edition of this very special book so successful—please know how much I appreciate our longstanding partnership and friendship.

To Winston Tan, managing principal of InTandem, LLC, a management compensation consultancy group in Spokane, Washington, and coauthor of our book *The Performance Appraisal Tool Kit: Redesigning Your Performance Review Template to Drive Individual and Organizational Change* (AMACOM, 2013): Your guidance on the tough conversations regarding compensation was as always helpful and insightful.

And to the finest legal team and legal minds in the business, who helped review select portions of this manuscript as it made its way through the various stages of review and development: Rich Falcone (no relation), shareholder and management litigation partner with Littler Mendelson, LLP, in Irvine, California; Jacqueline Cookerly Aguilera, partner, labor and employment and Kathryn McGuigan, of counsel, labor and employment, with Morgan, Lewis & Bockius LLP in Los Angeles; Frank Melton, principal and labor and employment attorney in the Los Angeles office of Jackson Lewis PC; and Christopher W. Olmsted, shareholder in the San Diego office of Ogletree, Deakins, Nash, Smoak & Stewart, PC.

I consider myself so fortunate to call you all friends, and I benefit tremendously from your wisdom and guidance.

INTRODUCTION
TO THE SECOND EDITION

101 Tough Conversations to Have with Employees could easily have been *1,001 Tough Conversations* or *10,001 Tough Conversations*—there are no limits to the challenges that senior leaders and operational managers face on a daily basis, and the breadth of issues can be daunting. Of course, no two employees or situations are alike. The purpose of this book, now in its second edition, is to help capture the nuances of effective leadership. Communication is a skill that can be honed and developed over time, and many would argue that it's the most critical skill of all for effective leadership and high levels of individual and team performance.

Yes, lists of rules are likewise helpful in providing guidance and structure to every manager's daily life and should be followed closely. Employee handbooks, policy and procedure manuals, collective bargaining agreements, and codes of conduct ensure consistent treatment and fair application of workplace rules. But people learn more from storytelling than they do from rules: Having a real-life context helps leaders place learning material in perspective, where they can filter those new ideas through a historic lens of what might work for them and for their particular communication styles.

No example in this book or any other will exactly replicate your reality at any given time. However, people tend to react in certain ways to particular situations, and one of the advantages I have to offer as an HR executive with thirty years' experience is a shortcut to predictable human responses to many of the examples in this book. The content wasn't concocted by an incredibly creative imagination full of "what-if" scenarios: this content *found me* on a daily basis every day of my career, whether I was working in companies large or small, for-profit or nonprofit, union or nonunion, international or domestic. People are people, and that basic fact won't change much across industries, geographies, or even international boundaries. This book is intended to help you navigate difficult conversations—from motivational to disciplinary—by providing insights into typical responses you'll encounter in the workplace.

Where do communication, effective leadership, and motivation usually fall apart? Once a manager starts sweeping things under the rug or leaves ongoing challenges unaddressed. As they say, the path of least resistance is avoidance, and it tends to be natural for human beings to hope problems fix themselves over time. And sometimes they do. . . . In the other 99 percent of cases, however, it becomes important to intervene and help guide your employees back on the right path. How you do that is what this book is all about, and it approaches that very topic from a coaching standpoint. Come across as a unilateral decisionmaker and disciplinarian, and you will likely kill the spirit that makes every team unique; present your ideas on the basis of selfless leadership with a spirit of growing and developing those you're fortunate enough to lead, and you'll quickly become someone's favorite boss, which is one of the highest honors the workplace has to offer.

Sure, it's much easier to reward good performance than to address problematic situations. But the workplace has plenty of room for both: recognition and appreciation as well as course correction, and at times even discipline and termination. Your responsibility as a leader is to create a work environment where people can motivate themselves, and the simplest way to do that lies in addressing employees professionally and respectfully while maintaining the highest standards of fairness and integrity.

Sometimes tough conversations result in general discussions about getting an individual or a team to course correct or tweak a particular practice to ratchet up performance or to provide a higher level of customer satisfaction. Sometimes those conversations have to address massive challenges like discipline, layoffs, and terminations. What's important in all cases is that people feel like they were treated fairly and with dignity and respect. A basic tenet of this book is that although you may have to deliver devastating news about terminations and intensely personal situations, you can still do that respectfully, professionally, and compassionately. That's the key to effective leadership communication: This book is intended to help you set high standards for your employees, hold them accountable, and in advance of a particularly challenging meeting, to role-play what that conversation might sound like, how an employee might respond, and how you can *hear* what that dialogue might sound like in your mind before it ever occurs.

What *101 Tough Conversations* isn't intended to do is create a word-by-word script for every difficult scenario that comes your way as an executive leader, operational manager, or frontline supervisor. As an author, I can't know your or anyone else's style—I can only know my own. Telling you how to have tough conversations with your employees is like trying to tell you how to have difficult conversations with your kids: So much depends on your own unique parenting style, your beliefs about the parent-child relationship, and the way you were parented yourself. So please view the material in this book as suggested approaches to common scenarios you'll encounter in the workplace. Customize them in your voice; infuse them with your personal style, creativity, and leadership beliefs.

Most managers would agree that people problems are what often keep them up at night. CEOs worry about employee performance, productivity, and innovation. Chief human resources officers are frequently concerned with turnover, employee satisfaction and engagement, and succession planning. Operational leaders at all levels focus on everything—output, quality, timeliness, and overall operational excellence. As social scientists who study the workplace will tell you, human capital performance is the primary lever that drives organizational success and distinguishes great companies from merely good ones.

My purpose in writing *101 Tough Conversations* is to help you master one of the most challenging aspects of effective leadership: communication, which includes setting expectations and holding employees accountable. Building your leadership muscle in this one critical area is the greatest investment you can make in your career. Communication is a natural skill and talent that can be honed over time—if you're willing to build muscle and confidence in this key area of professional and career development.

As a writer and teacher, I hope this book becomes an important step in your career growth and development. One thing's for sure, though— effective communication is likely the focal point that will benefit you most on your path to becoming the best leader and executive you can be. Thank you for allowing me to take this journey with you and share my experiences, in an effort to shortcut your road to mastery. It's a privilege I don't take lightly. I'm honored to be your mentor and coach through something as critical to your career success as becoming a skilled communicator, leader, and mentor to those who follow in your footsteps. Let's do this together, and allow me to be your "coach in a box." We're treading on sacred ground here, and there's nothing but opportunity ahead. Enjoy this second edition of a very special book.

Paul Falcone
Valencia, CA (USA)
June 2019

PART I

UNCOMFORTABLE WORKPLACE SITUATIONS

1

Common Managerial and Supervisory Discussions

Mediating disputes among subordinates, responding appropriately to requests for confidential information, and providing advice before a holiday party are all part and parcel of being a leader and manager. These oh-so-common conversations, however, can trip up well-meaning supervisors who may not be thinking through some of the possible ramifications of the advice they dole out.

Consider this chapter a crash course on Management 101. The tips and strategies here will help you to navigate common but potentially dangerous pitfalls that await you as a manager. Not only will these discussions help you lead more effectively, they'll also help your subordinates learn how to manage more effectively when they are placed into leadership roles.

SCENARIO 1

Establishing Your Leadership Brand

Why is this a tough conversation? We tend to think of tough conversations as confrontations, disagreements, and differences of opinion—places where we expect stiff resistance to our message. And for many of the examples that follow in this book, that will be the case. But sometimes tough conversations stem from setting expectations that may go against the grain or conflict with team members' experiences or beliefs. Whether you're a new hire assuming responsibility for a department, a recently transferred leader taking on new team members, or you simply want to reestablish the rhythm of your team, delineating who you are and what you believe in is a critical exercise. Discussing your beliefs about the Big Three—leadership, teambuilding, and communication—will go a long way in helping others understand who you are, what you believe in, and where the line can be drawn regarding unacceptable behavior.

The Solution

While it's acceptable to outline your performance expectations to the team—outstanding, knock-your-socks-off customer service, high achievement, accountability and reliability, and the like—it's more important that you discuss behavioral expectations. After all, that will help your team get to know the real you more quickly, and it will likewise help them understand your beliefs and values regarding your team's interpersonal relationships. Never underestimate the value of this "soft skill" in establishing behavior and conduct standards because, as your team will soon figure out, what goes for you goes equally for them. Reset expectations in your first week, paint a picture of what the experience of working with you will feel like, and ensure that all team members are pulling the sails in the same direction. Here's what a typical meeting might sound like; change the criteria below to meet your personal needs and leadership style:

> Hi, everyone, I've called this meeting to get us all on the same page going forward. Like every leader, I have my own ideas about what's important in a working relationship, and I want to share them with you right from the start, so we can discuss them and determine how they'll best apply to this particular group's needs.
>
> The first thing I'll share with you is that I always focus on leadership, communication, and teambuilding with every member of my department. I'll come back to these three themes over and over again, as they'll be the pillars that we build from. To start, leadership shouldn't be confused with management. Managing has to do with overseeing others' work, providing direction, and getting results through a team's efforts. Leadership, on the other hand, can come from an individual contributor as easily as it can come from a supervisor, manager, or director. Leadership, in that broader sense, means making yourself an indispensable member of the

team, going the extra mile to help, focusing on selfless leadership that puts others' needs ahead of your own, and balancing your career and professional needs with your work accomplishments.

My goal as the new director of licensing is to help you all build your résumés with solid achievements that can be linked to increased revenues, decreased expenses, or saved time. And those achievements that you can codify on your resume will transfer seamlessly to your LinkedIn profile as well as to your annual self-review, when it's time for the annual performance appraisal. I'm going to invite you right now to schedule quarterly meetings with me to discuss your performance, any roadblocks you're encountering, or classes or coursework that will help you build your résumé and prepare for your next move in progression—either here or elsewhere. I'd like you to make me your coach and mentor—not just your supervisor in that strictest sense—and partner with me to give our unit even greater firepower and lift as we move forward. But these meetings are optional—it's up to you to schedule these with me, for your own career development.

On the communications side, I believe in direct and on-the-spot feedback. I don't shy away from providing constructive criticism and am open to it myself. Trust in a group relationship stems from full transparency—no drama, workarounds, walking on eggshells, or anything of the sort—but respect for one another, a sense of friendly inclusiveness, and a willingness to apologize and make ourselves vulnerable, because vulnerability, in its healthiest sense, begets trust. In short, we're all responsible for creating a friendly and inclusive work environment, where all of us can do our best work every day. I hope to make the overall experience fun and filled with laughter, and above all else, I want to make sure that we all celebrate successes and enjoy a sense of recognition, and that we all appreciate the hard work and efforts that make our department stand out from our peers.

As far as teamwork, I expect you all to role-model, to be the first domino to help, to apologize, or to be willing to reinvent your relationship with your peers and with this company. I have the advantage of being a blank slate, with no baggage coming into the relationship. As far as I'm concerned, it's your first day with the company as well. Welcome. I'm looking forward to working with you and getting to know you better. I'm willing to help you stretch the rubber band and will have your back as you take careful and thoughtful risks in an attempt to perform at a higher level.

On the flip side, everyone, it's important that you know and hear what my hot buttons are and what can quickly make things go wrong. First, I expect us all to create a friendly and inclusive work environment where everyone can do their best work every day. Any perception that someone is attempting to quash that will be addressed immediately. Second, I intend to build our team relationship on trust and mutual respect. I don't do drama—I need to let you know that right up front—and I expect you all to admit mistakes, revamp the way we do things or get along with one another, and put others' needs ahead of your own—a concept known as "servant" or "selfless leadership."

Finally, I want to share the mantras I believe in: (1) Each to his own without judgment. (2) What you want for yourself, give to another. (3) Change your perspective, and you'll change your perception. (4) When in doubt, err on the side of compassion and assume good intentions. (5) Don't ever leave me flying blind: I don't mind if there are or will be problems; I just want to know which way to duck when it all hits the fan. I don't expect you to be perfect, and I don't believe that mistakes are to be avoided—I believe they're necessary and can be learned from. But here's the catch: They've got to be smart mistakes that are well thought out and discussed in advance.

We'll discuss these five concepts more as time goes on, but I find them to be a helpful framework within which to solve workplace problems and build relationships.

So that's me in a nutshell, being as transparent as I can about my beliefs and values.

I appreciate your meeting with me to discuss this, and as a next step, I'm planning to meet with each one of you to better understand your roles and what's important to you in our working relationship.

In my experience as an HR practitioner, less than 10 percent of corporate leaders set their expectations as transparently and honestly as the above example. But by putting your beliefs on the table from day one, you help minimize the drama that gets carried over from prior regimes, you make it safe for employees to reinvent their working relationships, and you create a structure to solve problems that can set high ideals while minimizing substandard performance or unacceptable behavior. Whatever values you espouse (relative to the ones shared above), create your talking points, meet with your team at any point in the relationship to establish or reestablish these values, and know that your goodwill will return to you in the form of increased loyalty, higher performance, and a greater level of acceptance and inclusion.

SCENARIO 2

Mediating Disputes Among Subordinates

Every line manager in corporate America has felt frustrated over employee tensions and unresolved conflict. And let's face it: There's typically more than enough work that needs to be done without involving hurt feelings, resentment, and that walking-on-eggshells sensation that makes you feel more like a referee than a supervisor.

With the critical need for retention of key talent, managers have to find ways to get their people "plugged in" again or else face premature turnover. The reality, though, is that your staff members will almost always take the path of least resistance with each other—which is avoidance—rather than address problem issues head on. As the manager, you must intervene in a mediating role to ensure that a lack of communication doesn't lead to performance problems or turnover.

Pretending that a problem doesn't exist or allowing staff members to work out problems on their own may be a safe strategy when a new interpersonal conflict first arises; however, once that initial frustration has festered, it becomes time to step in.

The Solution

When two of your staff members are at war, meet with each individual separately and explain how you intend to resolve the problem:

> Sam, I'm meeting with you one-on-one and will do the same with Christina once you and I are done. I want you to understand how together we're going to resolve the underlying tension that's become fairly obvious between the two of you.

First, I'll want to hear your side of the story, and then I'll share that with Christina when we meet. I'll then want to hear Christina's side of the story, and I'll share her feedback with you before the three of us come together as a group. This way everyone will know everyone else's issues, or the *what* of it all, and we can come together and focus on *how* to resolve it.

In short, we'll solve this in three meetings: Our meeting right now, Sam, is the first one. My meeting with Christina right after we're done will be the second one. I'll follow up with you after that and give you her feedback. Finally, we'll have a third meeting this afternoon where we can talk this out together. Again, everyone will know the issues, so there won't be any surprises, and we'll solve this like adults, maintaining each other's respect and dignity. Are you clear on how I'm planning on handling this?

Privately find out Sam's side of the story at that point. In your meeting with Sam, ask him why Christina may be feeling the way she does. Ask Sam what he'd like to see happen ideally in terms of his relationship with Christina, and then ask him what he'd be willing to change about his own behavior to elicit a different response from her in the future. Afterward hold the same meeting with Christina, learn her side of the story, and then share her perceptions with Sam.

The third meeting where you all come together is where the proverbial rubber meets the road. Understanding that employees may be nervous that a serious escalation may occur, set the ground rules as follows:

Okay, Sam and Christina, I've got two key ground rules that we all have to follow before we begin.

First, you shouldn't hold anything back. This is your chance to get it all out in the open, and if you withhold anything, then you'll have missed a golden opportunity to share your side of the story. You're not going to get another chance to readdress these pent-up issues and frustrations in the future. After our meeting today, I'm re-welcoming you both to the company as if it were your first day of employment. I'm also holding you both accountable for reinventing your working relationship from that point forward. Understood? [*Yes.*]

Second, everything that you share has to be said with the other person's best interests in mind and in a spirit of constructive criticism. There is no attacking and no need for defending in this meeting; this is really more a sensitivity session where you both get to walk a mile in the other's moccasins and hear firsthand how the other is feeling. Do I have your agreement on both of these ground rules? [*Yes.*]

Setting up a meeting with these qualifiers automatically deescalates feelings of angst or anger in the participants. It also gives you the chance to take a gentle approach to interpersonal issues that, like scars, sometimes run long and deep.

Special Note

During the group meeting, you'll sometimes notice that each employee will first address his or her concerns directly to you—the mediator. It will be as if the other person weren't even there. Third-person "he-she" discussions need to be changed into an "I-you" dialogue. To accomplish this shift in audience, simply stop the conversation as soon as one of the participants begins speaking about the other in the third person. Ask the individual to speak directly to the other person as if *you* weren't there. That may appear a little challenging for the participants at first, especially if emotions are running high, but direct communication works best. After all, you're helping them fix *their* problem.

In addition, you should encourage your two staff members to use the phrases "this is how I feel" and "can you understand why I would feel that way?" Feelings aren't right or wrong—they just are. Since perception is reality until proven otherwise, it's each individual's responsibility to sensitize the other regarding the existence of perceptions that have developed over time.

Knowing that guilt will allow for the assumption of partial responsibility for an imperfect situation, that element of accountability will serve as the seed of goodwill that helps heal old wounds. For example, if Christina feels bad about her relationship with Sam, shares with him why she feels the way she does, and admits that it takes two to tango and that she's part of the problem, then Sam will likely respond positively to the olive branch that Christina's extending.

Once you've pierced the heart of the combatants, so to speak, then the battle is won. You'll know you're there when they're talking to each other, agreeing that they've got a problem on their hands, and demonstrating a willingness to fix it. These kinds of management interventions aren't normally fact-finding investigations. Instead, they're sensitivity training sessions where goodwill and openness naturally heal the wounds associated with ego and principal.

Conclude the meeting this way:

Christina and Sam, you've both heard the other side of the story now. I'm not asking you to become best friends, but I'm insisting that you both demonstrate respect and open communication toward each other at work from this point forward.

I'll end this meeting with two questions. First, do I have your commitment that you'll view the other with goodwill and assume good intentions from this point forward? Second, do you both understand that if the situation doesn't improve and the workflow is negatively impacted in any way, my response next time may result in formal progressive discipline rather than a goodwill sitdown like this?

And voilà—you'll have given both employees their day in court, so to speak, where each vents and shares perceptions of the problem. You'll end the meeting on a constructive note where both agree to change their behavior. And you'll also create a healthy sense of paranoia where both realize that if the problem surfaces again, there may be a more formal management response—most likely in the form of a written warning. Congratulations! You've treated your warring parties as adults and held them accountable for fixing the perception problem on their hands.

Remember, no matter how much you care, you can't manage *their* differences. Only they can do that. Still, you can provide a forum for solving employee disputes that brings out the best in people. Establishing a culture of openness means confronting problems in an environment that's safe and that maintains the individual's dignity. It enhances your position as a leader and establishes your reputation as a fair arbiter of disagreements. There's no better formula for employee retention than treating people with respect, dignity, and a caring ear.

SCENARIO 3

Appropriate Responses to Requests to Speak "Off the Record"

Have you ever had an employee come up to you and ask to speak with you off the record? Many well-intentioned managers have been happy to grant their employees full access, without qualifying the nature of the issue up front, much to their later chagrin. In fact, you've got to be very careful about promising confidentiality before you know what the employee is about to divulge for one important reason: Certain issues, by their very nature, require immediate disclosure. You simply won't have the discretion to maintain confidentiality under any circumstances by the very nature of the topic, and your promise to do so may place you in a precarious position in terms of breaching a subordinate's trust.

Here are some real-life scenarios that innocent managers have inadvertently stepped into without realizing that they would have to disclose the information to the company's HR or legal department:

> John, I'm really concerned about Marlene. It looks to me like she's being harassed by her supervisor, and she's just not the type to make waves or formally complain. I feel so bad for her, but she'd die if she knew that I was telling anyone about this. Poor thing! She knows I've overheard his rants and shouting sessions, but I'm sure she thinks I'll keep it confidential. I certainly wouldn't want her to know that I mentioned this to you.

> Vic, I'm having a really bad day today. In fact, if anyone bothers me, I may be upset enough to really ruin someone's day (pulling a bullet out of his pocket and tapping it on his desk).

> Millie, not that it's my business, but it looks to me like Doris is moonlighting for our competition on the weekends. Don't say anything! I wouldn't want her to get in trouble or lose that extra income stream, but I wonder if she's feeding any of our proprietary information to our competitors.

The Solution

These scenarios point to the real-life danger—both to the company and to your own physical well-being—of promising confidentiality before you know the nature of the issue. That's because subordinates often don't realize what they're asking you to do when they request that you keep matters confidential before knowing what those matters are about. When someone asks you to speak off the record, respond this way:

> Laura, I'd be happy to speak with you confidentially, but it depends on the nature of the issue. I *can't* speak off the record if the subject has anything to do with one of three things: (1) harassment and discrimination, (2) potential violence in the workplace, or (3) a conflict of interest with the company. If what you're about to say has anything to do with those three things, then I've got an *affirmative obligation to disclose* the information and can't keep it confidential. So before you say anything to me, keep in mind those parameters and understand my obligation as a manager and officer of the company. That being said, do you still want to have a confidential discussion?

Yes, this may sound a little formal, especially if you know the employee well. Keep in mind, though, that you don't have the discretion to keep matters confidential that could negatively impact the organization. In addition, remember the low threshold used over and over again in harassment and discrimination cases: Once a supervisor or other member of the management team is made aware of a problem, then in the eyes of the law, *the entire company is deemed to be placed on notice.* That's an awfully large burden for you to bear if a lawsuit ignites based on the fact that you were the sole supervisor informed about a serious problem. It smarts all the more when the plaintiff's counsel then alleges that your being put on notice was the same as your company's CEO being put on notice.

Remember, you don't have the option of responding, "Well, I didn't say anything because the employee asked me to keep it confidential." That's the death knell for your case, and any experienced defense attorney (representing your company) will roll her eyes once she hears that and recommend that your company simply settle out of court. In short, you'll have no defense and will have provided just about the weakest excuse imaginable because "my employee asked me to keep it confidential" is an outright breach of your fiduciary responsibility to your company, and everyone but the most unseasoned and untested supervisor knows that. It's a sucker punch of the highest degree, and it's one that you'll want to avoid at all costs.

Likewise, after you've promised confidentiality to an employee, you don't really want to be the one who goes back to HR and divulges that the individual made a veiled threat of violence by tapping a bullet on his desk. Of course, you have to disclose that information for fear of workplace violence and in light of this threat to others' safety; however, the employee will know that you're the only person who knew of his "comment," and that could bode poorly for you in terms of protecting your own health and safety. Add this red flag to your management toolbox so that any time you're asked to talk off the record, you'll know how to respond up front.

SCENARIO 4

Inheriting an Employee with Disciplinary Problems

Incorporating employees from other departments is a fairly common occurrence in corporate America. Of course, hiring someone from another group who is looking for a transfer is one thing; being told that you have to now incorporate someone from another department into your team in light of restructurings and other corporate initiatives— especially if he's known to have performance or conduct problems—is quite another. And to make matters worse, you'll sometimes have a newly inherited employee join your group with a set of unrealistic expectations established by the former supervisor:

> "My boss promised me a 10 percent merit raise this year. Is that still on?"

> "I've been told I'll be promoted on my anniversary, which happens to be next month. What would you like my new title to be?"

> "Yes, it's true that I'm on final written warning for what my boss called substandard job performance, but she just didn't like me."

Remember, this is what you signed up for when you got into management! These individual challenges can often take up more of your time and cause you more angst than the whole cultural integration process of merging your new and old teams together. When one employee is a squeaky wheel, dedicate your time to hearing the individual's side of the story and tending to her needs, but promise nothing until you've had a chance to research the situation thoroughly and through as many sources as possible.

The Solution

What prior management promised in terms of promotions and large salary increases may in fact hold true because it's documented and because your human resources and finance departments have given prior approval. More often than not, though, you'll find that such claims are based on assumptions on the employee's part, so be sure and temper their ambitions while you look further into the matter.

Unfortunately, you may have the unpleasant chore of communicating to your new employee that former management, HR, and finance do not agree that this was a done deal, so the huge merit increase or promotion won't be happening this go-around.

> Gene, I researched your initial request regarding the promotion from assistant to coordinator that you feel you were promised. After speaking with Mark in finance, Carson in human resources, and Ashley, your former supervisor, I'm afraid that your proposed promotion never formally got approved. Ashley had every intention of making that happen, but as you know, without signed approval from the department, HR, and finance, the item remains on the wish list.
>
> Unfortunately, I won't be able to award a promotion now due to company budget constraints and the fact that our working relationship is untested. If you'd like to speak with Mark, Carson, or Ashley, you're more than welcome to do that. I can only tell you what they've shared with me and also let you know how I'm planning on handling the matter as your new supervisor. I'm sorry I don't have better news for you.

In cases like this, let the individual know exactly whom you spoke with, what they said, and why there may have been confusion. That being said, confirm that all parties are in agreement with the decision, and invite the employee to speak directly with those individuals himself if he so chooses. Just remember that you weren't part of that decision. You're simply communicating what was communicated to you, and you'll be open to evaluating the situation with a fresh set of eyes on a go-forward basis.

Sometimes it will be more than hurt feelings or disappointment that you'll be inheriting. Candidates who are transferred into your group on final written warning status for substandard job performance, attendance, or inappropriate workplace conduct may cause specific challenges. When that is the case, make copies of the written and final written warnings, share them with the employee up front in a private meeting, and talk about them openly. In most cases, it's best to get things like that out in the open and to discuss them rationally, adult to adult. You might open your meeting with the employee as follows:

> Michelle, I realize that there are typically two sides to every story, and the validity of the documents isn't in question: As far as I'm concerned, they're valid because they're in your personnel file with your signature. What I'm looking for now is how we reinvent our relationship and move forward, on one hand with a clean slate, and on the other with knowledge that these prior occurrences are real and to a certain extent "in play." Share with me how you'd recommend that we reconcile these two realities.

What you want to look for now is how the individual responds to those warnings. If she is very defensive and quick to blame others, you may have someone who fails to take responsibility for her own actions. In comparison, if she readily admits that she's made mistakes, assumes responsibility for her actions, and is committed to avoiding those mistakes in the future, you're halfway there. That's because people who readily admit that they were the cause of a *perception* problem—even if they don't agree with the facts—demonstrate a high level of business maturity and are much more prone to seeing the bigger picture and not repeating past mistakes.

Yes, these can be challenging scenarios that are sometimes forced on you, especially if you really like your current team and don't want the added responsibility of integrating others into the close-knit environment that you've worked so hard to cultivate. But don't underestimate the value of this opportunity that lies before you. You'll rarely be given such a chance to shine from a leadership development standpoint, your résumé will have a nice new juicy bullet point to discuss for years to come, and you may just find that today's most sought-after attribute—the ability to lead others through transition and demonstrate key leadership skills in a changing business environment—is a hidden strength that you can apply in any workplace situation that comes your way.

SCENARIO 5

Stopping Attitude Problems in Their Tracks

One of the most common challenges facing supervisors is dealing with employee attitude problems. You'll know you have this situation on your hands when you sense an entitlement mentality evidenced by rolling eyeballs, sighs, and antagonistic body language. Trying to stop such "silent" behavior is difficult because it's so easily denied by employees.

Frequently, supervisors tend to avoid confrontation associated with employees who "cop a 'tude" because the path of least resistance is avoidance and because the whole matter seems so slippery. After all, as a manager, you don't want to come across as touchy or overly sensitive. Still, the feelings of resentment linger and too often result in the employee being publicly shunned and isolated. Sometimes those pent-up emotions result in a public shouting match when some proverbial last straw is broken, and by then the situation is out of control.

The Solution

There are two key points to keep in mind when attempting to eradicate this all-too-common workplace problem. First, tell the person in private how you *perceive* her actions and how she makes you feel. Be specific and paint a picture with words so that the employee clearly understands the behaviors in question. Ask for her help in solving the perception problem that exists, and make a mutual commitment to hear that person's side of the story and better the situation. Second, avoid the term *attitude* in your discussion and replace it with words like *behavior* and *conduct*, which are much more neutral and objective. The word *attitude* is subjective and inflammatory and typically escalates disagreement by fostering feelings of resentment and anger. More important, courts have interpreted *attitude problems* as being mere differences of opinion or personality conflicts. It is therefore critical that you avoid that specific term in any of your conversations or disciplinary documentation.

When attempting to fix a communication problem that exists with one of your staff members, approach the matter by painting a picture with words like this:

> Lisa, I need your help. You know they say that perception is reality until proven otherwise. I feel like you're either angry with me or angry with the rest of the group. I may be off in my assumption, but that's an honest assessment of what you're giving off. I don't know if anything's bothering you or if you feel that I can be more supportive of you in any way, but please let me know if that's the case.
>
> Otherwise, though, understand that *you make me feel* embarrassed in front of other members of the staff when you roll your eyes upward and sigh then say, "Okay, I'll get it done!" Your body language is also confrontational when you cock your head back and place your hands on your hips.
>
> Do you feel it's inappropriate for me to ask you to complete your work on time? Should I even have to follow up with you regarding project completion deadlines, or should it be your responsibility to keep me abreast of the status of your projects? *How would you feel* if you were the supervisor and one of your staff members responded that way to you in front of others? Likewise, *how would it make you feel* if I responded to your questions with that kind of tone in my voice or body language? Wouldn't you feel that I was disrespectful or condescending toward you, especially if I did it in front of the rest of the group?

Notice the highlights in the paragraph above: "You make me feel . . . " and "How would you feel . . . " are common phrases that invoke feelings of guilt in others. Feelings aren't right or wrong—they just are. When combining such phrases with an opening statement like, "There's a difference in perception here," employees are usually much more willing to hear your side of the story objectively. After all, there are two sides to every story, and employees typically won't deny that they're partially responsible for the problem if it's presented in the right way. What they often want, however, is to be heard and to gain your attention as their manager. Therefore, seize this opportunity to fix the problem verbally by declaring a truce and listening with an objective ear.

Advice Before a Holiday Party or an Offsite Event

Sometimes being a manager is like being a parent. You've got to get "into your kids' heads" before an important family event to make sure they're adequately prepared and in the correct frame of mind because one careless comment or mistake could do some significant damage, both to themselves and to other family members. And how many times have we, as parents, thought about a situation involving our kids and gasped, *What were they thinking?!* How many times did our parents think that about us?

Of course, we're not expected to play the literal role of parent in the workplace, but like it or not, we're saddled with a similar sort of obligation in our roles as supervisors and leaders. Company holiday parties, picnics, and outside activities are meant to be fun and lively and a way for coworkers to get to know one another outside of the work setting. However, the damage that can be done by careless comments or inappropriate behavior may have exceptionally negative ramifications for participants who aren't thinking straight or who otherwise let their guard down (and for the whole company). After all, hearing about people who were fired after a holiday party because they got drunk and made inappropriate comments is not just folklore—it's alive and well in the business world today.

The Solution

Before embarking on a company-sponsored offsite event like a holiday party, meet with your staff to help them "get their heads on straight," especially if alcohol will be served at the affair. Your opening salvo might sound something like this:

> Hi, everyone. I wanted to call this short meeting in advance of tonight's holiday party.

'Tis the season, as they say, but I want to spend a few minutes with all of you discussing how to best handle yourself and what to do if you're placed in an uncomfortable or awkward situation for any reason. Also, note that alcohol will be served, and each of you will get two tickets, which will be good for a total of two drinks. That doesn't mean that you have to use them, though, and soft drinks may be the alternative of choice after you think about what I'm about to say.

Yes, holiday parties are meant to be fun and spontaneous. And yes, I don't want to spend so much time warning you all about potential inappropriate conduct at tonight's bash that I end up taking all the fun away before the party's even begun. But there are limits to what the company considers acceptable behavior at holiday parties, and people have been known to jeopardize otherwise healthy careers with just one night of indiscretion. In fact, people have even lost their jobs for losing their cool at a party. So before you head out to this holiday get-together, please be sure and keep these three rules in mind:

Rule #1—Employees are responsible for holding themselves accountable for all aspects of their conduct and behavior as if they were back in the office, and that's the standard you'll be held to. Unfortunately, many employees forget their manners at holiday parties by overdrinking or otherwise making fools of themselves. Then they sit back and wonder why they're being disciplined or terminated the next day because things got out of hand.

Rule #2—This is a *work-related* event—not a private free-for-all—and work standards need to prevail. So here's what we're doing to help all of you successfully navigate the temptation that lies ahead: First, we'll serve plenty of nonalcoholic beverages as well as foods that are high in protein, which slow the body's absorption of alcohol. Second, we'll collect car keys at the beginning of the party, and we'll stop serving alcohol early. We'll distribute car keys when you're ready to leave and after we've ensured that employees or their family members are sober. Finally, we'll have volunteer spotters and designated drivers assigned to monitor the party and, if necessary, to drive intoxicated employees home. The company will also arrange for taxis or even a hotel room should anyone become impaired by alcohol. Under no circumstances are you to drive while under *any* influence of alcohol.

Rule #3—If you find yourself in an uncomfortable situation because someone is acting like an ass, come and see me or one of the staff members from human resources. When it comes to inappropriate conduct and harassment, the fact that you're at a company-sponsored party doesn't mean that workplace rules no longer apply. If you're uncomfortable for any reason, excuse yourself and come and get me immediately—even if the person acting inappropriately is a member of the senior management team.

This is meant to be a fun event, but not all managers have these kinds of talks with their staff members in advance, and I want you to know that I'm here to help—as is human resources—if you need anything at all. Have a great time, make new friends, expand your network, and all that fun stuff. But don't do anything that would make you wake up tomorrow and moan, *Oh, no! What was I thinking?*

Yes, you're ending your presentation on a bit of an ominous note, but that's okay. If the last words that your staff hears you utter are words of caution and prudence, you'll have done your job. Don't feel guilty. They'll figure out how to have fun on their own without much help from you or anyone else. What's important is that your team is tight, sharp, and prepared to handle any situation that comes their way because of your thoughtful and proactive leadership.

2

Individual Appearance and Uncomfortable Workplace Dilemmas

his chapter isn't meant to be disrespectful, inappropriate, or in any way irreverent. It's just that these all-too-common workplace issues often get short shrift because they're simply too uncomfortable to deal with. The path of least resistance is avoidance, and managers often steer clear of confrontation—especially if they hope that the problem will simply disappear. But what are your responsibilities to your immediate subordinates and to the rest of the company when it comes to uncomfortable workplace situations? More important, what do you say to fix the problem without insulting or embarrassing the individual involved?

You've probably seen one of these variations on a theme before: Several of your staff members come to see you because a longtime co-worker has developed a body odor or a halitosis problem. Or perhaps an individual arrives at work with her hair in a mess, looking like she just got out of bed. Maybe a subordinate's face sports a new, prominent piercing or a visible tattoo is being shown off to make a statement. How nice it would be to pull out a policy manual that dictates management responses in instances like these. More likely than not, however, you'll need an ad hoc solution to the circumstances that you're facing.

SCENARIO 7

Bad Hair Days

Bad hair days may be a result of a new hair color, wild style, unkempt appearance, or just about anything else that people can do (or fail to do) to their hair. If an employee shows up at work looking like he's stuck a finger into an electric socket or otherwise presents some kind of shocking twist to what used to be a "normal" hairstyle, you might want to address the situation using some of the sensitive approaches outlined next.

The Solution

Publicly shaming or ridiculing an individual will only develop resentment and anger. The goal of any management response in situations like these is to ensure that the individual is treated with dignity and respect. So here's how we might address our first scenario, bad hair days, by making light of the situation and using a little humor:

> Leslie, come see me in my office for a few minutes. Here, I'll shut the door. I have to share something with you, and I don't want to hurt your feelings or embarrass you in any way. This is private, just between the two of us. Leslie, your hair—something's either happening too much to it or not happening enough. I thought it would be a good idea to address it with you quietly before anyone else addresses it with either you or me. What are you planning on doing with that (pointing to the coif)?

Typically you'll find some nervous shuffling along with an apology. "Oh Paul, I woke up and went to the gym and didn't have time to comb it out the way I normally do. I'll run to the restroom right now and fix it and make sure that I come to work dressed for work from now on—including my hair! I'm sorry about that. Did anyone else say anything? I'm so embarrassed!"

Okay, easy enough. But what if your employee looks at you like you're the crazy one and is very proud of her new follicular achievement? If you suspect your employee may take offense or if she doesn't respond well to a light-hearted approach, lower your voice and give your discussion a more serious air.

> Leslie, that's not the way you typically wear your hair. I respect people's right to adjust their appearance however they see fit. However, there are some parameters in the workplace that typically need to be followed for obvious reasons—clients' possibly

taking offense, the company's reputation, its perception in the business community. Do you feel it might be possible that someone could find your hairstyle a bit distracting or out of alignment with the overall image of our office?

Again, it's always better to lead the horse to water than to force it to drink. If the employee in this situation sees your logic and accepts your suggestive hints, then she'll assume responsibility for the problem and fix it. It's that simple. However, if you still sense resistance or an outright challenge, you certainly have the right to outline the company's expectations and directions.

Leslie, I'm sorry, but I'll have to disagree with you. I called you into my office in private so that we could discuss this quietly, and I wanted to handle the issue respectfully, adult to adult. However, if you insist that you have the right to wear your hair the way you're wearing it today, I'm afraid I beg to differ. If you simply won't wear your hair in a manner that's acceptable—the way you've typically worn it to work since you began here—then I'm afraid I'll need to speak with human resources (or senior management) to determine how to best handle this.

I'd like to outline for you, however, what my recommendation to HR will be. I'll suggest to them that you be allowed to take the rest of the day off with pay to determine whether you want this job and feel my request is reasonable or whether you'd prefer to no longer work here.

Either way, I'll respect your decision. However, you need to realize that if you're unwilling to present yourself in proper attire and appearance—which I know you know how to do since you've carried yourself that way since you began here—then I'll accept that as your resignation. Again, I want to speak with HR first before giving you the rest of the day off to rethink this whole thing, but I wanted you to know my initial stance on the matter. For now, please hold off on dealing with any customers until I've heard back from HR. I'll get back to you shortly.

Note that a "decisionmaking leave" like this is certainly not your only alternative. See the following three scenarios to identify other options in situations like these. Further, you're under no obligation to pay a nonexempt employee for the rest of the day. However, you may find that offering time off with pay is a smart move. It shows you to be a wise, patient, and nonjudgmental employer, and it creates a sense of guilt and self-awareness (rather than anger) in the employee. In contrast, if you choose to send nonexempt employees home without pay, then you'd simply dock the hours after they leave the office. (With exempt employees, you wouldn't dock them for a partial day's absence in a situation like this.)

In addition, notice how you've clearly laid out your expectations and calmly explained the outcome of the employee's actions. There's no need to rush to termination for failure to follow company policy (if you've indeed got this outlined in a dress code of some sort in your company handbook or policy and procedure manual) or for insubordination (for failing to follow a directive). Instead, allow the employee to make the decision to adhere to normal dress standards and remain employed or to simply resign. No drama, no fuss—just a calm and respectful response with clear expectations and outcomes.

Special Note

Before you place someone on a "decisionmaking leave," be sure and check with your human resources department or other members of senior management. After all, when it comes to matters that could result in termination, you don't want to assume all that responsibility by yourself. Instead, think of it as a hot potato that you want to share with others in management. So before you officially send your employee home to consider whether she wants to remain employed or to resign, make sure the appropriate parties are aware of your intended actions. This way, before you terminate anyone, you'll have gotten the appropriate levels of advance approval.

In addition, by getting these approvals up front, you'll be deemed to be working *within the course and scope of your employment*, which is important should your company ever be legally challenged over the outcome. Remember that when individual managers get entwined in lawsuits and are sued separately from the company, it's typically because they were deemed to have been operating outside the course and scope of their employment.

If this employee resigns at day's end based on principle, then so be it. No one on your management team will be shocked to learn of this outcome, and they'll all be united in fighting any claim for wrongful termination (or discrimination or harassment, for that matter) because they were involved up front in the organizational decision.

SCENARIO 8

Inappropriate Dress

Let's assume a female employee shows up for work in a blouse that shows way too much cleavage. This conversation, of course, would work just as well for a male employee who wears inappropriately revealing pants.

The Solution

As you saw in Scenario 7, the normal way to handle uncomfortable workplace situations is to call the individual into your office in private and relay your concerns discreetly. In the case of excessive cleavage, however, a male supervisor may want to invite a female co-supervisor to join the meeting to avoid perceptions of sexism or harassment. You might initiate your conversation like this:

> Phyllis, I wanted to speak with you briefly in my office about your workplace attire, and I invited Joan to join us. I don't mean to make you feel uncomfortable in any way, and truth be told, I'm a bit uncomfortable bringing this issue to your attention because it has to do with the amount of cleavage that you're showing in the outfit that you chose today. Again, I don't mean to offend you, but I'm afraid your choice and style of dress this morning might offend some of our clients. Could you help me find a solution to this?

A reasonable response on the employee's part might be, "I'm sorry, Paul, but I didn't think that this was too revealing. Do you really feel like this is an inappropriate outfit?" You might then respond, "Well, it looks fine when you're standing straight, but truth be told, Phyllis, when you bend over—which you do quite often as a teller—your cleavage becomes more prominent. I don't want to embarrass you in any way, but I don't want our customers to feel uncomfortable either. That's why I'd like your help in figuring out how to best handle this."

And the most logical conclusion would end, "Well, I don't have another business outfit here at the bank, so I'll need to go home and find something else. I could be back in forty-five minutes, and I'm sorry if my choice of clothes this morning made anyone uncomfortable." And voilà, the employee takes the hint and rethinks her wardrobe selection from that point forward. Happy ending!

But what about someone who challenges your gentle suggestion: "I feel this outfit is perfectly appropriate and shouldn't offend anyone. I'm sorry if you don't like it, but last time I looked, I don't believe we have a policy on the amount of cleavage that's allowed to be shown." With a challenge like this, beware: The worker may have an ulterior motive or may simply want to challenge you on principle. In either case, you'll need help, especially if you're a male supervisor dealing with this particular topic.

Let the employee know that you hear what she's saying but that you'd like additional input from your human resources department (or other appropriate department, like legal or administration). The employee could perhaps work on paperwork (but avoid meeting with customers) for the time being while you research more thoroughly. Assuming that your HR department approves, you're then free to instruct the employee to return home for the rest of the day with pay to rethink her commitment to the company. At that point, proceed by placing the employee on a decisionmaking leave, as outlined in Scenario 7.

SCENARIO 9

Body Piercing and Body Art

Assume that your customer service manager walks in one day with a new ring in his eyebrow and a metal post in his lip. After you gasp and think, *He can't service customers looking like that!* you again devise a way to position your message so that he arrives at that same conclusion himself.

The Solution

Try opening your initial conversation this way:

Michael, I need to talk with you privately about your fashion deci-sion. First, let me say that I don't mean to embarrass you in any way. I respect you as a person, and I don't mean at all to dictate what you do in your personal life. But I've got to ask you: Are you sure that you've given sufficient thought to your eyebrow ring and lip post in terms of how they might impact the customers that you service in our accounting firm? I guess what I'm getting at is that knowing that kind of look might alienate some of our cli-ents, would you be willing to remove them while you're at work? Or would you consider removing them whenever you have to deal with the public? What are your thoughts?

The value to this approach lies in its subtlety and reasonableness. Few companies have policies restricting facial hair on men or insisting that women wear dresses in the office. And even the major accounting firms' consultants now arrive at their consulting assignments in more of a casual dress mode than in the blue suit–red tie combinations of the past. Still, body piercing tends to result from epiphanies about what's cool, what's important in life, and what rights people believe they have over their own destinies. In short, it's not something to brush over lightly. If your conversation leads to some kind of compromise where the employee agrees to leave the hardware at home or to take it off whenever dealing with customers, then you'll have accomplished your goal. Employees who feel they've been treated respectfully and not simply been told what to do will almost always agree to some kind of modification that will please the company and allow them to main-tain their individuality.

If the employee, on the other hand, insists that he has the right to show off his new accoutrements to whomever happens to walk into the CPA firm that day, you again have the right to send the employee home to think about whether he wants to remain employed or to simply resign. As outlined in Scenario 8, you also have the right to move to outright dismissal if you feel you're left with no other choice. Just don't forget to obtain advance approval from human resources or qualified legal counsel.

SCENARIO 10

Inappropriate Tattoos

Eyebrow rings and lip posts are removable. Tattoos aren't (at least not for the sake of this conversation). How would you address the back-of-the-neck black widow tattoo that seems about ready to climb into the employee's hair? The phraseology may be different, but the strategy is the same: Discuss your concerns openly, listen to the individual's side of the story, and then look for some resolution or compromise that you can both live with.

The Solution

Initiate your conversation on a problem-to-solution level:

> Eileen, a few of the staff members brought to my attention that you'd gotten some new tattoos over the weekend. I respect the fact that you have the right to do body art, but as the nursing supervisor in the ICU, I'm a little concerned about how some of our patients might respond. In essence, you know that we're a little bit more of a conservative hospital, but that doesn't mean that we want people to act like robots and repress their individuality. I wanted to talk with you and see if there could be a way where your desire to express yourself has a minimal impact on the patients and their families who come to us for care. What are your initial thoughts about that?

Once again, the majority of people will offer alternatives that minimize the problem in the workplace: "Maybe I'll wear blouses with collars so that patients won't be able to see the spider tattoo on my neck." And there you have it—a reasonable approach begets a reasonable response.

Again, more likely than not, employees will respond reasonably to your request if your presentation is respectful and appreciative of people's differences. In fact, it's more the exception where employees don't respond favorably to such an understanding approach.

However, there can be an occasional instance where a subordinate chooses to make a stand over a new tattoo. If the employee totally refuses to engage in a dialogue with you, a decisionmaking leave as outlined in Scenario 8 may be appropriate. In addition, if you feel you have a legitimate business reason for insisting that the tattoo not be prominently exposed, you may be within your rights to terminate the individual. Again, this is not a protected category under the law, and most "at will" states will provide you with the discretion to separate employment. Always check with your company's human resources department or with qualified legal counsel before proceeding down that path.

SCENARIO 11

Halitosis (Bad Breath)

Suppose your subordinates meet with you en masse to complain that a coworker's bad breath is making the workplace intolerable. Breath odors typically come from garlicky diets or insufficient personal hygiene. Whatever the case, those coworkers shouldn't have to suffer through such challenges, especially if the issue simply stems from a coworker's choices about personal hygiene.

The Solution

As with all cases involving uncomfortable workplace situations, handle the matter respectfully and in private, remembering that your goal is to fix the problem without damaging the individual's self-esteem or creating unnecessary embarrassment. Here's how you might open up the conversation with your subordinate:

Dominic, I called you into my office because I wanted to speak with you about something. This feedback is a bit difficult to share, and I'm fairly uncomfortable right now, so I want to make this as straightforward and simple as possible: I believe you may have a problem with bad breath.

You know how most of us would appreciate it if someone told us that we had spinach stuck in our teeth or that our zipper was down just to save us from embarrassment? I see this as one of those conversations because even though it's difficult news to share, it's really in your best interests.

I know these things are usually the result of overindulging in spicy or garlicky foods, but is there something you might be able to do on your own to fix this perception problem that exists?

A reasonable response on the employee's part would be to apologize for the problem and ask if anyone else has noticed. In those circumstances, it's best to be honest, although you may want to deliver your message gently: "Yes, I'm afraid that I'm not the only person to notice this. A few of your coworkers came to me out of concern for you, not to get you in trouble. They were about as uncomfortable telling me as I am telling you. That's why I'm hoping we could agree that this is a fixable problem that we can address now that you're aware of it."

That caring approach will typically be all you'll need to fix the problem without a lot of drama. In matters regarding personal hygiene, employees will usually fix problems that are brought to their attention both out of embarrassment and peer pressure. If the problem surfaces again, it would be easy enough to remind Dominic of this initial discussion without having to say much other than, "It appears that the problem we discussed about your breath may have become an issue again. Will you be able to fix that for me?"

But if you're ever called to have this discussion for a second time, you'll want to add one more sentence to your closing statement: "Dominic, I want your commitment right now that we'll never have to have a conversation about this again." With that commitment in hand from the second event, you can probably rest assured that the matter will become a nonissue from that point forward.

A difficult conversation can make the difference between success and failure for a valued employee. Care enough to hold that difficult conversation. You have that responsibility to your subordinates who, for whatever reason, may not see the impact of their personal behaviors.

Special Note

If the employee volunteers that there's an underlying medical reason for the problem, ensure that the individual is provided the time and support to have the matter taken care of. The Americans with Disabilities Act is an antidiscrimination law that allows for "reasonable accommodations" intended to keep employees working via specific job protections. If you suspect the ADA may come into play, immediately consult with qualified legal counsel for guidance on how to handle the discussion going forward. The ADA carries the potential for liquidated damages, and as of this writing, disability discrimination remains one of the hottest lawsuits in the employment litigation arena.

SCENARIO 12

Body Odor from Lack of Cleanliness

Body odor is an uncomfortable issue to address because of the personal nature of the problem, but don't expect that the employee is even aware that it's an issue. If he were, there probably wouldn't be a problem in the first place. But some people pride themselves on defining a bath as jumping into a chlorinated pool, while other folks simply fail to apply deodorant consistently. At other times, it may simply be a case of too many wears before a wash. Whatever the case, an odiferous offender shouldn't upset everyone else in the department, and there are tactful ways of handling the matter professionally.

The Solution

You're best off opening your private conversation with the assumption that the individual isn't aware there is a problem. This way, even if he does know, he could pretend that he's being made aware of this problem for the first time and take appropriate measures to correct the situation. Here's a sample conversation launcher:

> Roger, I wanted to meet with you one-on-one in my office because I need to share something with you privately, discreetly, and with as much sensitivity as possible. You may not realize it, but it appears that you have a body odor problem, and it isn't merely a personal matter—it's a workplace disruption issue that I'll need your help to repair.
>
> I've had conversations like this with employees before, and usually they're not even aware that the problem exists. I don't mean to make you uncomfortable, but don't mind my asking: Are you aware of the issue, and if so, is this something you can take care of on your own?

Again, this is a fairly comfortable approach that avoids putting anyone on the spot. Assuming the individual is unaware of the issue to begin with, your putting him on notice should be all that's necessary to solve that odious challenge. You might offer Roger the option to return home with pay, freshen up, and then return to the office when he's ready. That's a fair and objective way of handling an uncomfortable workplace situation without drama or histrionics.

People with poor hygiene habits may be oblivious to how that can affect others in the workplace. Your conversation links the personal hygiene problem to a workplace performance matter, which places you on clear ground to address the matter as part of the individual's overall performance.

You might then choose to end the conversation on a positive note:

Roger, listen, I'm here to help in any way I can. If you'd like us to set up a fan in your office, or if you'd like to change your schedule so that you could take breaks throughout the day to have time to freshen up, I'd be very supportive of that. Just let me know whatever I could do to help, okay? If you wouldn't mind, though, I'd prefer not to have to address this with you again because it's a bit uncomfortable for me, so is this something you feel you can fix on a go-forward basis?

And that little segue out of your conversation will allow the employee to dash out of your office, run home to shower, and then make sure that he never has to hear those horrible words from anyone else again for the rest of his career!

Special Note

If the employee begins to offer reasons for his body odor that go beyond mere hygiene (for example, medical issues), stop him before he goes into too much detail. You don't want much information as to the cause of his body odor if it's anything more than failure to use the appropriate amount of soap. Instead, let Roger know that if he needs to seek medical treatment for a health-related condition, he should take time off to go to the doctor as soon as he can get an appointment. And if your company offers an Employee Assistant Program (EAP), provide him with an EAP brochure so that he can call them and get the appropriate resources that he needs to solve the dilemma.

If accommodations will be necessary, you'll receive them from the physician or medical facility in the form of a doctor's note. Doctors' notes should immediately be shared with your corporate human resources team or with qualified legal counsel for an appropriate company response.

Finally, if the employee's offensive body odor continues and it's not linked to a medical condition as far as you're aware, inform him that coming to work unclean or unkempt is unprofessional and disrupts productivity. You can then place him on verbal notice that if you have to address this matter again with him, disciplinary action may follow.

Appropriate disciplinary action in a case like this would most likely be in the form of a first written warning. The nature of this infraction, especially if it has anything to do with obesity, will not lend itself to more progressive forms of discipline like immediate termination or even a final written warning for this first documented offense. Of course, this will depend on your company's progressive discipline practices, but this is probably not a good time to accelerate or skip steps in that process.

SCENARIO 13

Body Odor from a Suspected Medical Reason

Unlike in Scenario 12, odors may sometimes come from chronic medical conditions like obesity or colostomy bags. These conversations are not necessarily something your employee can physically control. In addition, the Americans with Disabilities Act (ADA) may govern these matters, so how you address them may be more than workplace sensitivity: It may be a matter of law.

The Solution

Now that I've gotten your attention, proceed this way:

> Joan, I need to make you aware of a situation that has come to
> my attention, and I'll need your help to solve it. A few of your
> coworkers came to me out of concern for you, but also out of

concern for themselves. Apparently, there is an odor coming from your desk area that makes it difficult for them to do their work. The odor is described as being a combination of sweat and urine, and apparently this is the third time that they've noticed it. It's happening about the same time every month, and they've asked me to address it with you. You don't need to share any specifics with me regarding the cause. I'd rather you address some possible solutions with me so that I can help.

If the employee identifies some underlying cause for the medical problem, refocus her comments on the effects of the issue rather than its causes. Under the Americans with Disabilities Act, you're not obligated to accommodate a disability that you're unaware of, so the fewer details you have, the less you have to formally "accommodate." At that point, ask her how she could resolve the matter: "I trust that you understand how this could be a problem." A typical response on her part might be, "Well, I'll make a doctor's appointment for tomorrow and see how this can be solved."

Special Note

First, a caveat about the ADA: As a civil rights–oriented anti-discrimination law intended to bring disabled workers into the workplace and to keep disabled employees in the workplace, its intentions are more than admirable. It is not a "leave statute," per se, but has become more and more associated with one over time. However, the law itself was written loosely and provides plaintiff's attorneys with lots of room to argue its merits and applications to the workplace. In addition, a number of states have their own interpretations of the ADA, many of which are even more employee-friendly than the federal version. Add the fact that remedies can include punitive damages, and your company could face serious legal exposure.

In addition to defining a disability as a physical or mental impairment (or record of such an impairment) that substantially limits one or more major life activities, the ADA also covers individuals who are "regarded as having" an impairment. In other words, even if no disability technically exists, a plaintiff's lawyer could argue that you, the employer, *regarded* the employee as having a disability and that your company was therefore governed by the act.

Finally, in preparing for any workplace discussions with your employees regarding physical or mental conditions that may be governed by the ADA, remember that the law does not merely prohibit discrimination against the disabled. It imposes additional affirmative obligations on employers to accommodate the needs of people with disabilities and to facilitate their economic independence.

Medical intervention may be the only practical direction in which an employer can lead an employee under these circumstances. Just be sure and close your conversation this way: "Joan, you just take care of yourself. If you need time off, or if your doctor recommends any special considerations that we can help you with, just let us know. We're all concerned about you and want to make sure you're okay."

Practically speaking, you'll have demonstrated care and compassion to an employee in need of your help. Legally speaking, you'll have begun the process of fulfilling your obligation under the ADA to engage in an "interactive process" with the employee to determine an appropriate accommodation, if one is applicable, resulting in a work environment that enables the individual to be comfortable and productive. Well done!

3

Cultural and Social Differences

Today's workforce is the most diverse in history. We work at a time when many of us take for granted the fact that men and women of various ages, ethnicities, and religious beliefs work side by side every day, and for good reason: As a society, we've become a lot less judgmental and open to other people's differences. On a more practical basis, we've learned that diversity in the workplace is a profitable business practice.

This positive trend has been due to the gradual expansion of our tolerance and acceptance levels—not to close a blind eye to others' differences or to pretend that they don't exist. Instead, as a working society, we've come much closer to living by the mantra "Each to his own without judgment." However, because differences still persist, there's always an underlying concern that someone may take offense at others' behaviors and turn that perception of unfairness into a claim of discrimination or harassment.

Multiple generations in the workplace, as well as foreign languages in the hallway and on the shop floor, are great examples. On the one hand, it's wonderful to see four generations of Americans working side by side: Traditionalists, Baby Boomers, Millennials, and Gen Zers can learn from one another, pass along wisdom, and ensure a smooth transition of talent from a succession-planning standpoint. Yet most seniors will attest to the fact that ageism is alive and well in the American workplace and is felt nowhere more than in the job-finding process. Similarly, many historians and economists teach that the United States's historical approach to welcoming foreign talent to its shores is one of the three pillars that accounts for America's wealth and progress over the past two centuries. Along with abundant natural resources (including ocean access on both coasts) and its Declaration of Independence, founded on ideals and values from the eighteenth-century European period of Enlightenment, America's ability to attract and retain the greatest global talent has created a nation of incredible wealth and opportunity. Yet tensions and resentments continue to plague the workplace when foreign languages are heard and English-only speakers assume that their coworkers are talking about them behind their backs (well, actually, right in front of them).

This is all part of the American experiment. We endeavor to recognize the strengths and advantages of our differences and even celebrate them via our formal diversity and inclusion efforts, yet tendencies to focus on our differences and assume ill intentions abound. And that's okay—Every workplace finds its own challenges and looks to "heal wounds" that from time to time stem from preconceived notions or assumed differences. Your role in leadership, however, takes on an especially important significance when tackling matters that relate to these and other common workplace challenges. Following are some discussion formats that will help you address common cultural and social challenges that emerge when certain sensitivities are lacking, miss awareness, or fail to create and sustain a friendly and inclusive culture.

SCENARIO 14

Euphemisms like "Honey," "Sweetie," and "Doll"

Sometimes male executives feel that they're acting warmly and benevolently toward female subordinates by using euphemisms like "honey" and "sweetie," especially when those subordinates are as young as their grandchildren. And sometimes it's gentlemen from the South who may be visiting northern climes who wish to share their charms with members of the opposite sex. Although sometimes it's women who feel they can take the liberty of using diminutives with men while batting an eye and getting all "cutesy." In reality, whoever is using these epithets may not realize that they may be coming across as condescending and offensive.

What should you do if a subordinate puts you on notice that the "old-timer" executive vice president's comments are rude and out of touch? Well, before you respond, "That's not my job. The division president needs to fix this, as she supervises the executive vice president (EVP), so I'll politely inform the president so she can get involved," know that such simple solutions don't always work in the "C suite." First, the president may have a reputation for avoiding confrontational issues like this. Second, you may be aware that the president dislikes the EVP, and this may give the president political fodder to damage the EVP (which you may not want to happen).

Of course, it would probably make sense to bring the employee's complaint to HR so that they can address the situation. However, if your company doesn't have someone in an HR capacity or if that's not a reasonable option under the circumstances, it may fall upon you to deliver the news upward. (After all, who said tough conversations only happen with your subordinates!) In cases like this one, diplomacy and goodwill are critical, and occasionally delivering bad news up the line is one of your responsibilities as a manager and a leader.

The Solution

In delivering this kind of message to the EVP (let's call him Fred), you've got to make sure that you're respectful and appreciative of his intentions on the one hand while informing him of the liability that can be created on the other. You'll also want to tactfully remind him that the subordinate (we'll call her Linda) brought the matter to you in good faith and that no form of retaliation is permissible for Linda's having come to you for help. Your conversation with EVP Fred might sound like this:

> Fred, I'd like to ask your help in solving a situation that came my way today. Is now a good time to talk? [*Yes.*] Great. Here's what was shared with me: I know you've known Linda for a long time and that you enjoy working with her. She feels the same way about you, and she came to me feeling very uncomfortable about something that she didn't know how to handle.
>
> I know you're both comfortable with each other, and no one wants that to change, but truth be told, Fred, she's a bit uncomfortable with you referring to her as kiddo, honey, and sweetie. She told me that it pretty much hurts her feelings when you talk to her that way because it minimizes her role here in the office.

In fact, that's probably something that I should keep in mind, too. I get very comfortable with the staff here sometimes because we've all been working together for so long, but I have to be careful not to get too comfortable with the staff, so I'm pretty much going to eliminate those cute little phrases when I speak with others. Would you be okay joining up with me in that little endeavor?

This is clearly a "walking on eggshells" approach, but hey, Fred is indeed an EVP, and you certainly don't want to be shot just for being the messenger. However, Fred may push back a bit and respond, "Nonsense. I've known Linda since she started here, and if she can't take a little bit of humor, then maybe she's in the wrong company."

Sigh. Your work is just beginning. In case you sense resistance to the practical and objective advice you've given, continue this way:

Fred, I beg to differ. I love working with you, she loves working with you, and no one wants that to change. But you've got to be careful for one very important reason: You're low-hanging fruit in litigation land. If anyone ever wanted to make a claim of sexual harassment or hostile work environment, one of the first things that would be called into question would be your vocabulary.

If you only refer to female employees using these diminutive euphemisms—and let's face it, there are no similar terms for male colleagues—the burden will be on you to explain why that seems to be your state of mind. And as an EVP in this company, you're a natural target because you've got the deepest pockets personally as well as the CEO's loyalty more than anyone else.

I'm not asking you to change your personality or your friendly, warm, and outgoing disposition. But I do feel that you're potentially setting yourself up for future heartache, and you know that a judge or jury wouldn't give much merit to your argument that "We always spoke that way to each other." Truth be told, once an employee puts you on notice that she's not comfortable, you pretty much have to oblige because you wouldn't want a record to show that you were told about the problem but refused to deal with it.

Oh, and there's one more thing, Fred. She came to me concerned and not knowing how to handle the situation. What's important, though, is that she came to me in good faith. I don't think this is that big an issue personally, and I hope you agree. But we can't do anything that could appear to be retaliatory for her having come to us with a good faith complaint. Retaliation is a separate animal in the law's eyes, and we certainly wouldn't want to burden ourselves with something that serious over an issue that's so easy to fix. Do you agree with me? If you don't, let's keep talking this through because it's a smart business practice, and I'm ready to keep convincing you if you'd like to keep our discussion going!

This example illustrates how to gently address a topic that could make the perpetrator angry, even though it has such a simple solution. The same approach will work for the gentleman visiting from the South who's trying to "charm" the ladies or the woman who's batting her eyes and acting cutesy. Emphasizing that the complainant simply wants the behavior to stop is key. If additional discussion is required, point out the low threshold for hostile work environment claims and how such salutations could be used as evidence of bias in a jury's eyes. Finally, remind the individual that anything resembling retaliation for a good faith complaint is a serious, separate infraction and must be avoided at all costs.

SCENARIO 15

Speaking Foreign Languages in the Workplace

Are you permitted to create a workplace rule stating that all employees must speak only English? It depends: Although no federal law specifically supports or prohibits English-only rules, states have determined that it can be illegal to prohibit employees from speaking in a foreign language at work (as it may constitute national origin discrimination in violation of Title VII of the 1964 Civil Rights Act). Therefore, it's best not to create any hard-and-fast rules without gaining appropriate legal counsel first.

One of the more balanced interpretations taken by certain states is to allow employees to speak with each other in a foreign language during breaks and meal periods, while requiring them to speak English during the normal work shift. This reasonable approach allows coworkers to converse in their own language during their free time, while permitting management to supervise and maintain control and safety during the regular shift.

Let's look at a scenario that occurs all too often in the workplace: A group of employees at your company speaks Tagalog with each other, leaving the non-Filipino staff members feeling isolated and out of the loop. One of the English-speaking employees complains to management that the Filipino staff members may be talking behind her back, possibly laughing at her and other members of the staff, or hiding something that could be work-related.

The Solution

Let's assume that your state permits limiting foreign language discussions to breaks and lunch periods. In that case, knowing that you have the right to address the situation with the group of foreign-language speakers, you call a meeting with them as follows:

> Hi, everyone. I've called this meeting today because an employee on staff came to me concerned about your speaking Tagalog with each other during business hours. I wanted to enlist your help to see if we can arrive at a reasonable solution together.
>
> Let me open up this dialogue with two thoughts: First, I respect the fact that you may want to speak Tagalog with each other because you're more comfortable that way. The second point, though, is equally important: As you might imagine, your speaking Tagalog together may leave others feeling alienated and isolated, and it can come off as being cliquish and exclusive (as opposed to inclusive).
>
> Our state law says that a balance can be struck: Workers who prefer to speak in a foreign language can certainly do so; however, it should be reserved for breaks and meal periods. During the rest of the workday, the company has the right to instruct its workers to speak English.
>
> I feel that's a reasonable approach since management wants to be able to ensure that communication is open, expectations are transparent, and all employees feel included. That's especially important since we've been put on notice that others may be feeling isolated. Can I count on your support to move forward in that new direction?

It's sometimes tough to balance workers' needs and their rights to speak foreign languages in the workplace with the company's right to ensure that safety and open communication are maximized at all times. This approach acknowledges the staff's desire to speak in their native tongue and retain a sense of camaraderie while demonstrating the business needs to restrict that foreign language to rest and meal periods.

Special Note

Be especially careful about this particular issue in the workplace. The American Civil Liberties Union (ACLU) has argued that English-only rules in the office stem not from true safety and management concerns but from bigotry and anti-immigrant sentiments. And because national origin discrimination challenges based on English-only rules have seen significant increases with the EEOC in the past few years, it's best to vet this particular issue with qualified counsel before addressing your group.

This is an area where you may want to have a written record or email documenting your approval to launch into this particular discussion with your staff members. Otherwise, you may find yourself in the case law books defending what circumstances, if any, justify English-only rules without creating a hostile work environment and other claims under Title VII.

SCENARIO 16

Inappropriate Displays of Sexually Explicit Material

At first glance, you may be wondering why this topic isn't found in Chapter 8: Sexually Offensive Behavior. If the next example were clear cut—man hangs naked picture of a *Playboy* centerfold on the wall of the shop floor—then you'd be right: This would be found in the chapter on sexually offensive behavior.

However, what constitutes an "inappropriate display" of "sexually explicit" material is often controversial. Is a Victoria's Secret brochure or *Sports Illustrated* swimsuit edition out of bounds? How about a mother who proudly displays a photo of herself breast-feeding her newborn child? What if a male employee frames a photo of his scantily clad wife on his desk? Is that offensive? Would it make a difference if she were in a two-piece versus a one-piece bathing suit—especially if one of your coworkers believes in a religion that insists that women be covered from head to toe?

Clearly, impropriety may be in the eyes of the beholder—which doesn't help you all that much if you're asked to make the uncomfortable call about a subordinate's breast-feeding photos. To determine the appropriate way to respond, much will depend on the nature of the display as well as the number of complaints you receive and from whom. As is often the case with touchy workplace matters, when in doubt, speak with your company's human resources department or legal counsel first.

For the sake of this example, let's take the breast-feeding incident because it's clearly uncomfortable to address (especially if you're a man or a mother yourself), it's not *sexually explicit*, per se (even if you can see almost the entire breast), and the possibility of highly offending the mother is great. Now there's a good example!

The Solution

When potential workplace discussions tie your stomach in a knot, always go back to the Introduction of this book to review your strategy. That's where you'll find a few key tips to outline your game plan: First, we know it's not what you say, but how you say it that counts. Second, we'll want to rely on guilt rather than anger to get our point across. Finally, we know that the word *perception* is our key to helping others see our point of view, even in the most uncomfortable workplace situations. Therefore, you might want to proceed with your employee Phyllis as follows:

> Hi, Phyllis. I wanted to meet with you because I'm going to need your help, goodwill, and patience to solve a little challenge that's come our way. Before we begin, though, please know that this is a bit uncomfortable for me to discuss, and if I turn red at any point, I'll ask for forgiveness in advance. That being said, as the department head, I have to address something with you that's important, although I intend to do it as delicately as possible and with the utmost respect.

Umm. The photo of your breast-feeding Ashley that's now become your desktop screensaver. . . . Well, I'm afraid that it's made some of your coworkers a bit uncomfortable. I haven't seen it myself, but I have to respect the fact that others find it to be totally natural and beautiful, of course, yet a bit too explicit. In fact, I was told by more than one person that they're not quite comfortable coming into your cubicle at this point.

The people who asked me to address this felt very badly and really were uncomfortable asking me to intervene. Of course, we're all happy for you and for little Ashley, it's just that that particular display shows off a bit more of you than others expected to see. Under the circumstances, would you consider no longer displaying that particular photo as your screensaver and maybe using a picture of the baby instead?

Again, the challenge in a case like this is that breast-feeding is indeed fully natural and absolutely beautiful. That being said, not everyone chooses to have children and many prefer to keep those kinds of images outside of the workplace. Your approach here is caring and sincere, and people will typically respond in kind. That same approach would work with the gentleman who displays photos of his wife on the beach in a bikini or who leaves copies of the *Sports Illustrated* swimsuit edition on his coffee table.

In short, it's not up to you to dictate what's right or wrong. It's simply a matter of sharing the *perception* that people may be uncomfortable or even offended by the material. It would be difficult for an employee to respond, "Well, people shouldn't feel uncomfortable simply seeing pictures of me breast-feeding my newborn/the swimsuit edition of *Sports Illustrated*/the newest Victoria's Secret catalog on my coffee table." People will typically "get" that others may be offended and, out of respect for others' concerns, remove the screensaver or magazine and replace it with something else.

If you're challenged by someone who insists that she has the right to display a breast-feeding photo or a revealing photo of her husband in a Speedo, then don't rush to judgment. If your first conversation results in defiance (after all, some people are just *like that*), then let the individual know that you'll want to look into this further with the help of human resources or general management. You'll likely find that before you have to readdress the issue with the individual, she'll come to you and confirm that she's thought about it and agrees to remove the photo.

Even if that doesn't occur, let a third party (typically HR) come in and lay down the law. Since you have to continue supervising this individual, it's best if you're not viewed as the unilateral disciplinarian and decisionmaker. Once that third party confirms that the image or magazine needs to be removed to avoid a possible hostile work environment claim, then there will be little room for discussion or debate.

Of course, if you have to have that discussion yourself (and don't have the luxury of having an HR representative present to deliver the message), then be sure and let the employee know whom you spoke with and what that person recommended. It's also a good idea to invite the employee to speak directly with that person herself if she so chooses.

SCENARIO 17

Lack of Understanding of Multicultural Differences

Working side-by-side with foreign-born citizens here on temporary visas or with green cards sometimes poses challenges for U.S.-born workers. Differences in communication styles, mastery of English, and varying customs and norms sometimes clash in the workplace. And no wonder: America may pride itself on being the world's melting pot, but with that accolade comes occasional differences of opinion and worldviews.

The Solution

With so many competing and conflicting styles, norms, and expectations, what's a worker to do? Let's say that someone in your information technology (IT) department seems to have ongoing difficulties with a coworker from India who's here in the United States on an H1-B visa. The American worker complains that the Indian employee often shows up to meetings late and rarely tells his clients no, leading to additional, unplanned work. In addition, the Indian employee lacks a sense of urgency in getting things done and shows no remorse when delays become necessary. The Indian worker, in comparison, feels that his U.S.-born counterpart is abrupt, and on occasion, downright rude.

Knowing that these two coworkers come from different parts of the world, and acknowledging that you're arguably no expert on Indian business norms and protocols, it's best to first meet with each individual privately and acknowledge your own limitations. If the American worker, Peter, initiates the complaint against the Indian employee, Raj, then after listening to Peter's issue, meet with Raj as follows:

> Raj, Peter met with me today because he said he's been experiencing ongoing issues between the two of you. Specifically, he said that you're often too slow in responding to clients' requests, you appear not to worry about delays in your work, and you can't seem to tell anyone no. As a result, he feels frustrated that the two of you aren't getting all of your work done on time and then doubly upset by the fact you're taking on additional work when you can't complete the initial workload on time. Is there some legitimacy to his claims, and if so, is there something we could do to solve this together?

Don't be surprised at this point if Raj acknowledges some of those perception problems but also attributes them to differences in cultural norms and expectations. He may inform you at that point that in India, saying no directly to others is considered impolite and harsh. He might also tell you that business is typically conducted at a much more leisurely pace with less focus on meeting deadlines and more focus on building relationships.

In a situation like this, you'll soon find that Peter was probably spot on in terms of the problems he's complained about. Then again, it's very difficult to find qualified IT professionals at many US companies these days, which is why your company agreed to sponsor Raj's H1-B visa in the first place.

Your meeting with Raj should then go on to explain the expectations at your company. "No" and "not right now" are legitimate responses to ad hoc requests that could throw off your department's production schedule. Reporting to meetings on time or early is an absolute requisite to success. And meeting deadlines is tied to department budgets, so knowing the pressure that your department faces in terms of controlling overhead costs should clarify your expectations of Raj in this particular business environment.

When you then call both parties into your office to negotiate and mediate an agreement, your opening statement might sound like this:

Peter and Raj, I've called you together so that we could solve, as a team, the issues that were brought to my attention. Peter, I met with you on Wednesday when you asked to meet with me because you were frustrated with a number of issues regarding Raj. Specifically, you told me that Raj had difficulty telling clients no, which was increasing your workload. You were also frustrated that Raj reported to meetings late and had a very casual attitude about pushing back deadlines.

Raj, I then met with you to share Peter's concerns with you, and you shared with me some of the different expectations that exist in India in terms of telling clients no, arriving late to meetings, and expecting delays. It was important for us at that point, Raj, to discuss the expectations that we have at our company and in our department toward these very same issues, and you agreed that it was reasonable to meet the expectations that were outlined.

Specifically, you said that from this point forward, you would be very careful about politely telling clients no, and you said that if you felt uncomfortable doing that, you would refer them to Peter. Is that correct? [*Yes.*]

You said that you would be more diligent about reporting to meetings on time and that you would ensure that project delays were more the exception than the rule. You also committed to letting Peter know in advance any time a project looked like it might not be completed by the target deadline. Is that a fair assessment of what we discussed? [*Yes.*]

Good. Then let me ask you this, Raj: Is there anything else you'd care to discuss with Peter while we're here together—any concerns, questions, or recommendations you'd like to share with him and me? [*No. I think we just had different expectations.*]

Okay then, Peter. You've heard what we've discussed and now agree to. Is there anything else you'd like to share with Raj while we're together right now? [*No. Just that I hope that you don't mind that I originally went to Paul for help because I really didn't know*

how to handle this. But I'm very much looking forward to con-
tinuing working together, especially now that we've got these issues
out of the way.]

And voilà! The "confrontation" didn't have to be confrontational at all, and your ability to gently reeducate Raj in terms of your department's expectations after hearing his side of the story led to a reasonable agreement to adjust his way of looking at things.

PART II

JOB PERFORMANCE CONCERNS

4

Performance Transgressions

Performance transgressions occur when employees fail to meet established production or output guidelines. Underperforming salespeople, analysts with excessive error rates in their calculations, and customer service representatives with an inordinate amount of complaints all fall under this category.

Unlike behavior and conduct infractions like theft and embezzlement, which may justify immediate termination for a first offense, performance transgressions usually require that workers receive workplace due process in the form of written warnings and decisionmaking leaves or unpaid suspensions, as outlined in your company's policy manual and in accordance with your organization's past practices.

Decisionmaking leaves typically last one day and are paid: They represent a once-in-a-career benefit that allows employees to rethink their commitment to the company and decide whether they wish to resign or reengage. Unpaid suspensions, in comparison, typically dock workers anywhere from one day's pay to one week's pay. They contain a "shaming element" because workers must explain to their family why their pay was docked. Whenever possible, look to shift your unpaid suspension practice to a paid, one-day decisionmaking leave as it treats workers like adults and appeals to people's sense of guilt rather than anger. Decisionmaking leaves are typically much more effective at achieving true employee turnarounds.

The typical first step in such interventions lies with verbal counseling or sensitivity sessions as outlined in this chapter so that your workers are aware of their errant performance and understand what they need to do to fix that perception problem. Failure to make necessary improvements after verbal intervention will lead to a written warning which, if violated, leads to a final written warning, and so on. When it comes to progressive discipline, keep in mind that each attempt to address an ongoing performance problem adds a more serious or progressive element to the process, until the employer concludes that it must terminate the individual for cause. The progressive discipline process ensures that your company acts reasonably and consistently and documents the effects of the worker's unwillingness or inability to do the job adequately.

Your verbal counseling and subsequent documentation accords employees with workplace due process: They learn of their problematic performance, are told what they need to do to fix the problem, and are given a reasonable amount of time in which to do so. Should your company later be sued for wrongful termination, you can demonstrate that, despite your good faith attempts to better the situation, you were ultimately left with no choice but to terminate the substandard performer for cause. In fact, you will very likely be able to argue that the employee terminated himself despite your proactive attempts at rehabilitating him.

And it all begins with verbal interventions, sometimes known as verbal counseling or verbal warnings. Let's look at some of the more common scenarios that you'll face as a supervisor in corporate America today.

SCENARIO 18

Lack of Quality, Detail, or Efficiency

Most workers are judged in terms of both their quality and quantity. Of course, people lean more one way than another in almost every case: Some are "production hounds" who master large volumes of work, while missing details on occasion. In comparison, others cross every *T* and dot every *I* in paying extreme attention to detail, but sometimes sacrifice speed for accuracy. Both styles are necessary, assuming that the individual doesn't get too sloppy or go too slowly. Let's assume we've got the former problem on our hands: an employee gets lots of work done but pays scant attention to the quality of his work. What's the best way to address that type of problem at the verbal, or initial, stage?

The Solution

When you're faced with a subordinate who is becoming sloppy, starting to lose paperwork, forgets to follow up with you, or otherwise demonstrates poor judgment in performing her job, it's time to jump in both feet first and bring this issue to her immediate attention:

Denise, we need to talk. I'm concerned about what I'm starting to see in terms of the work quality coming from your desk. Here's what things are looking like from my vantage point: I see that you have too many work orders open on your desk, which means that you're not closing these up in a timely and efficient manner like you historically have.

Your work area is cluttered with equipment that needs repairing and spare machine parts. You've always kept a very organized work area, so I'm not sure what's changed. However, we found an unopened Repair Work Order inside a completed folder, which means that the new work order was misplaced. In addition, in the past few weeks, I've had to redo the work you had attempted— unsuccessfully—to repair yourself, which leads to an inefficient use of my time.

So tell me what's going on from your viewpoint, Denise. [*I'm sorry. I must not be paying attention.*] I'd say. Okay, I'm glad you see the issue, which is an important first step. Now the question is how do you want to fix these ongoing problems that you've been experiencing? [*I don't know. I'll certainly try harder.*]

That's a good start, but I want to hear specifics. I just gave you three issues: too many work orders on your desk, a sloppy work area, and repair work that was left unfinished. I'd like to hear how you're planning on bettering each of those three problem areas specifically. Tell me what you have in mind. [*Okay, well, as far as having too many work orders open on my desk at any given time, I'll be sure and . . .*]

Good, Denise—I think those are all good plans. I have no reason to doubt that you won't meet these performance expectations now that I've brought them up to you. The only question I have left is what do I do if you fail to meet the terms of your own commitment to me right now? [*I guess I'll have to be written up.*]

Yeah, I'm afraid there will have to be disciplinary consequences. Refocus, reengage in your work, and please don't take any of this for granted. And let me know how I can help. I want you to continue to be successful here, and I certainly would prefer not to have this kind of discussion with you in the future, but it's up to you, Denise. This is all within your control. Do I have your commitment that you'll do everything within your power to improve the situation at hand? [*Sure, Paul. And again, I'm really sorry.*]

Okay, that was not an easy conversation, especially with someone you like and who had done a solid job for you over the past year or so. Still, Denise is an adult, and as such, you have every right to hold her accountable for fixing this problem. After all, she has the tools and the know-how, and more important, she has the track record. If she fails from this point forward, then she's failed herself. Your job then will be to simply reflect her lack of commitment and lack of focus in the form of a written warning, which may ultimately lead to a termination for cause.

SCENARIO 19

Lack of Quantity or Speed

Slow or inefficient production is the reciprocal of the previous scenario. If an employee demonstrates a slower-than-expected pace in the office or fails to produce work in a timely manner, then you'll need to address your concern candidly and up front. Whatever the reason, you have every right to "look under the hood" and find out where the individual is coming from. The clear issue, however, is that if the employee isn't able to improve his performance speed and volume, a written warning may soon follow. Therefore, be very clear about your expectations and offer guidance to help him pick up the beat and shift gears to a higher speed.

Let's assume that you have a human resources assistant in your department who is responsible for entering new hire and termination information into your database. You find that new hires do not get processed on Mondays, their first day of hire, which is also their day of orientation. As a result, payroll doesn't receive its necessary information until Tuesday and sometimes Wednesday. This has gone on for a few weeks, and it's time to hold a conversation with your departmental assistant to resolve the problem.

The Solution

Your initial conversation should inquire about the individual's self-analysis of the problem; from that point forward, you can lay out your expectations as follows:

> Don, I wanted to follow up with you regarding your role in processing new hires. How do you feel that's going? [*Well, not very well because I'm overwhelmed and have no one else to help me.*]
>
> Oh, I didn't realize that you felt overwhelmed by that. Tell me more about it. [*Well, there's so much information that needs to be entered into the system—names, addresses, Social Security numbers, W-4 information, and the like—that I feel like I need someone's help.*]
>
> Who would you propose helps you with this? [*I don't know—anyone.*]
>
> And what is it specifically that's leaving you feel overwhelmed and underresourced? [*Everything. It's just too much work for one person.*]
>
> Well, that's problematic to hear because as an HR coordinator, that's pretty much your primary job responsibility. Entering new hires into the system on the day of orientation as well as terminations would account for the majority of your job responsibilities, correct? [*Yes.*]
>
> Then if that's your key role within the department and you don't feel like you could keep up with the volume, how do you propose that we fix that? [*I don't know. I'm hoping you could tell me.*]
>
> Okay, Don, here's how it looks from my vantage point. Now, admittedly I may not have the whole picture, so you'll have to help me fill in the blanks here, but if we had eight new hires earlier this week and you weren't able to process all eight, I'd have to wonder about your speed in processing the information. As far as I understand it, if your primary responsibility is data entry and you're not being asked to constantly step away from your desk to

help others who may be interrupting you, then there's something wrong with the whole picture here.

For example, entering the data that you mentioned in your example just now shouldn't be overwhelming. It's actually very basic. Typing in names, addresses, and Social Security numbers shouldn't take more than a few minutes. Doing that for eight new hires in the day should be doable within a few hours, at most. Why would you feel that is overly demanding and requires additional hands to support you? And why wouldn't you be able to complete that on Monday so that Payroll has all the information it needs to enter these new hires into the system? [*Well, it's just so overwhelming, that's all.*]

Do you have any other reasons other than "it's overwhelming"? [*No, not offhand. I'd just like someone else in the department to support me.*] Okay, doing what, Don? What would you expect them to do? [*Help me with the data entry.*]

Well, I'm afraid that this conversation is going in circles, and you're not giving me much of anything concrete to justify assigning other staff members to help you or for allowing the data entry not to be complete by the end of day on Monday.

Here's what I'm going to suggest: Give this some thought tonight and meet with me tomorrow to let me know if you could think of any additional suggestions to correct the situation at hand. I'd be very open to listening to anything that you have to offer.

Shy of that, however, I'm afraid that since this is one of your essential job responsibilities, you'll have to give some thought as to whether this role is a good fit for your talents.

That's because, barring other compelling reasons that you can share, I'm afraid that if the problem doesn't fix itself, our next response will be in the form of a written warning. And that could lead to your being terminated for cause. Please see me tomorrow and let me know what you think of, because I'd be very happy to hear your suggestions and input. I'll be available whenever you're free.

Of course, Don may come back with other legitimate issues: The paperwork isn't done properly 80 percent of the time, so he has to go back and collect all the correct data from the candidates. Or maybe the computer system keeps locking up when it goes on overload. If those issues turn out to be legitimate, your discussion will lead to a simple and agreed-upon solution.

It's not uncommon, however, for employees to have excuses that are more self-imposed or fabricated than based in reality. When that is the case, just understand that they're probably not geared for this particular opportunity and place that option on the table. A written warning leading to a possible termination for cause may be the only viable option to move this person out of that role, unless he self-selects out of the role by choosing to resign, which is good for him and even better for the company (sparing you the need to continue with progressive discipline). Resignation allows the employee to save face and maintain control over his career, rather than feel that he's getting boxed in and managed out systematically with no further recourse.

Of course, if you have any concern that this individual might perceive your counseling as a threat of some sort, and you suspect that he might try to attribute your comment to some protected status (like his age or race), speak with human resources or with qualified legal counsel first. It never hurts to have that advanced discussion before sitting down with an employee whom you suspect may be looking to place blame on others when the problem clearly lies with him.

SCENARIO 20

Substandard Customer Satisfaction

Customer service—whether internal or external—is the glue of goodwill that fosters communication and trust in any organization. External customer service keeps members of the public—consumers, customers, and clients—coming back time and again to frequent your business, regardless of tantalizing offers from your company's competitors. Internal customer service keeps the machinery of your organization well oiled as staff employees support their coworkers who have questions about how to get the work done in the most efficient manner possible.

Customer service takes work: After all, employees can only get so far on charm. And if you simply translate *customer service* into "solving others' problems with a cheery disposition," you'll communicate a message that when others are in need, you can provide them with a solution. Sometimes that solution is found in providing accurate information, sometimes it's found in fixing something that's broken, and at other times it's simply a matter of lending a caring ear to someone who needs to vent. Whatever the case, excellence in customer service distinguishes world-class from mediocre delivery, and that level of delivery easily translates into your company's profit margins.

When challenged by someone who demonstrates apathy or a lack of commitment toward others' needs in the customer service process, seize the opportunity to educate the individual on the importance of this one trait that will influence her career more than just about anything. After all, it's all about communication in the world of business, and loyal customers—internal or external—are the greatest source of job security and career advancement available.

Creating a culture of service and hospitality is no easy task, and the stakes are high in a world where fierce competition is the norm. Companies typically compete on product, price, and service. And although product and price may vary greatly, service must remain paramount to maintain a competitive advantage. When faced with an individual who fails to see eye to eye with you regarding this crucial workplace factor, don't be shy about making your concrete expectations clear.

The Solution

Assuming that your head of the hotel concierge desk has suddenly lost interest in exceeding the guests' expectations, your sit-down meeting might sound something like this:

> Anne, we need to talk. I called this private meeting with you because I'm suddenly sensing a difference in your approach to working with our guests. When you started with us last year, you would leap tall buildings in a single bound to help anyone who needed something. I was so impressed not only with the energy you displayed but also with your selfless attitude. Your energy and smile were infectious, and I teased you on more than one occasion about your smile being our greatest asset and how it increased your "face value."
>
> Now I'm sensing a totally different Anne: someone whose energy and willingness to help are palpably lower, someone who's not smiling or generating an energy that exudes confidence, and a

person who, quite frankly, appears disengaged from her work and mildly bothered by the guests.

That's my initial impression, anyway. Now tell me your side of things. [*It's true that I've got a lot on my mind lately, and I'm afraid that my home life is bleeding over into my work life. I'm sorry about that, Paul, and I never intended that to happen.*]

Okay, fair enough: I understand that such things happen sometimes. I guess my question to you is, are you willing and able to turn that trend around? [*Yes.*]

So when faced with that type of perception problem, Anne, how would you recommend turning things around? [*I'll be more mindful of our guests and do my best to reenergize myself so I can return to the old Anne.*]

Thank you. Those are very good answers. Let's talk about specifics. I want you to keep a few things in mind about customer service. And I'm not just talking about our hotel or this particular job: I'm talking about your entire career. Nothing is more important—nothing—than the perception you create for guests, coworkers, and, most important, your supervisors. Anyone willing to go above and beyond excels in their career because, well, people just like being around them. So if you ever sense that you're in a slump for any reason, think objectively from a career development standpoint about how you could improve and "plug back in" to that zone that you know so well.

Next, speaking of career development, remember that your most unhappy customers are your greatest source of learning. It's easy dealing with nice and happy people: The challenge in your job and mine is "getting inside their heads" and figuring out how to defuse a problem. That's the most creative part of your job, and it, more than anything, will help you stand out as a rarity among your peers.

Finally, remember that this job—and a career in management in any company—should be about selfless leadership. As you grow and develop in your career, understand that it's not about power: *Power* is one-sided where you get to do whatever you like just because of who you are. Instead, it's about *strength*—helping others get what they want through you. And that strength is what you could provide others who may be hotel guests, subordinates, or family members. Your goal is to help them be the best that they can be. That's what it means to lead a life well lived. That's the secret to it all. Apply it to everything and everyone you come across and you'll find that everything you do will be easier and more enjoyable.

Okay, I didn't mean to get too lofty there, but give it some thought. I have a lot of faith in you and see so much potential. Just don't lose sight of the bigger picture, whether it's your career, the company's profitability and well-being, or your overall sense of self. You have so much to give—and so much to gain from your giving. I'm glad we had this talk. Come see me any time you feel like you need a reminder, okay? [*Okay, thanks Paul.*]

Sometimes these minor challenges give us opportunities to bond with those we work with. Applied selectively, such discussions help you connect to your subordinates at a much deeper level, and the bond of trust and respect that forms at moments like this—when you lift the employee up when she's feeling bad about herself or about her life—is a gift that may never be forgotten.

SCENARIO 21

Lack of Sales Production

Sales is always where the rubber meets the road at any company. Successful sales executives often earn a lot of money, but the sales force in many industries is marked by excessively high annual turnover, sometimes in excess of 100 percent. The key to successful intervention will always lie in early monitoring and follow-up. Whenever you notice that activity or production results are lagging, you'll need to step in quickly to assess and correct the situation; otherwise, a written warning or outright termination may be right around the corner.

Let's assume that a recruiter in your search firm appears to be having difficulty reaching her production numbers. You know as the supervisor that it's the *activity* leading to those numbers that's the problem—not the production numbers themselves (which tend to take care of themselves as long as the underlying activities are sound and in place). The recruiter is aware that she's having difficulties and is starting to doubt herself, so you sense that it's time to step in for a little pep talk.

The Solution

Understanding that you generally have a lot of discretion to discipline and terminate salespeople—after all, the billing numbers are either above a minimum threshold or they aren't—you realize that you can do a lot more good by focusing this headhunter on improving her numbers rather than by yelling at her or putting her down. Your pep talk might sound something like this:

Candy, I wanted to meet with you in private because your billing is starting to concern me. I assume you've noticed the problem over the past two months as well. [*Yes.*]

Okay, tell me where you're coming from and what you think the problem may be stemming from. [*I can't seem to find good candidates for any of the searches I'm working on right now, and it's so frustrating. They look great on paper but don't seem to ultimately fit the client company's exact hiring criteria.*]

I understand. That's nothing I haven't seen before, so why don't you diagnose it and tell me what you think the problem is. [*I just seem to be having a run of bad luck.*]

No, don't give yourself that out. It's too easy. I really want to hear you diagnose this situation as if you were me. What would you say if you were the sales manager in this situation, speaking with a recruiter who may be losing sight of the fundamentals? [*Gee, I don't know.*]

Okay, but what would you say if you did know? (Smile) [*Well, I'd guess I'd say I'm not making enough outbound calls and I may not be qualifying the candidates well enough up front.*]

Good—that's a great start. What else would you say? [*Maybe I don't understand the nature of the search or what the company's key needs are in finding the right candidate.*] Bingo! You've just hit all three key issues that I'm concerned about: the volume of your calls, your ability to screen candidates effectively, and your understanding of the client company's needs in terms of using our firm to conduct the search. See, you asked all the right questions just as well as I would have!

Now that we know the issues, how do we get to the answers? [*I'll increase my outbound calls to sixty-five per day rather than fifty just to help me get out of this rut. I'll also speak with the*

*client company again and make sure I've got a thorough under-
standing of their key needs in filling this position, and I'll target
my recruiting efforts and candidate profiling more thoroughly as
a result.*]

Excellent. Now you know the *what* of it all. Here's my next
question:

How are you going to achieve those specific things? Talk to me
about the specifics of your game plan. That's where this stuff all
gets fun.

If you've noticed that most sales talks have to do with leading your
employees to the right questions as well as the *what* and *how* of their
answers, you're understanding how pep talks in sales work best. *Telling*
a salesperson what to do will actually do very little; *asking* a salesperson
to self-assess and diagnose the situation will work much better for one
very simple reason: No matter what field of sales you're in, the sales
function itself is very simple and straightforward—make money!

Wise sales managers in all industries know that it's actually difficult to control the making of money and "cash in" itself: What is
controllable, on the other hand, are the *activities* that lead to those
production dollars. Always focus salespeople on what they can control: the volume of their calls, their product knowledge, and their
ability to qualify and close prospects. The answers are there and they
know them. They just need gentle reminders at times to help them
refocus and reenergize.

SCENARIO 22

Failure to Follow Through, or "Dropping the Ball"

Initially diagnosing a problem is a critical trait that all workers need to
excel at their jobs. However, more often than not, problematic issues
can't be solved on the spot and require follow-up. When employees
drop the ball and fail to follow up, there's twofold damage to your company: First, the task at hand won't be solved, at least without angst and
drama on the part of the person who requires help. Second, a record
may be made that shows the company was officially put on notice, and
nothing was done to remedy the situation.

In most cases of "dropping the ball"—a technician fails to follow up with customers after a repair is made or someone forgets to mail concert tickets to a customer's home—the damage is limited to inconvenience and a bit of embarrassment. However, when it comes to medical professionals failing to inform patients of problematic test results or staff attorneys missing deadlines that jeopardize the timely filing of a lawsuit, the results can be disastrous.

Of course, you retain the discretion as an employer to determine the appropriate company response in these scenarios. In the case of the medical professional or lawyer, the appropriate company response may be in the form of a final written warning (even for a first offense) or even a summary dismissal. Assuming the situation doesn't rise to that level of seriousness, an initial conversation with your employee emphasizing the importance of follow-up is certainly warranted.

The Solution

Let's take an example from the "people" realm of business. Assume that one of your HR managers is in the cafeteria having lunch when an account executive stops by to say hello. When the HR person, Brett, asks how things are going, the account executive, Roland, responds, "Well, truthfully, I'm under a tremendous amount of pressure from my boss who's hitting on me." Brett gulps and replies, "Wait—is this something serious? Do you need me to get involved?" And Roland responds, "No, that would be the worst thing. I can certainly handle it myself, but I'll be sure and let you know if I need anything. Thanks and enjoy your lunch."

Brett scratches his head wondering what that was all about, but he wisely tells you, his supervisor, about the incident just to make you aware of the situation. You thank him for the heads-up and ask him to follow up with Roland in the next day or two to get more details.

A few days later, you casually ask Brett how his meeting went with Roland, and Brett sheepishly responds that he'd forgotten to follow up. Your conversation with him under those circumstances might sound like this:

> Brett, that's a problem, and let me tell you why: Once an employee puts someone in human resources on notice that he's being "hit on" by his boss, it could be a serious sexual harassment situation for the company. Now I know that Roland was fairly casual about

it all, and I know he told you that he didn't require any help with the matter—at least, not at this point.

Still, there's a very important reason why I asked you to follow up with him. Can you guess what that is? [*To make sure that the situation wasn't more serious than he made it sound at first?*] Yes, from a practical standpoint, I would agree with that. But there's an even more pressing issue: Once an employee puts HR on notice, even casually, of a possible harassment claim, then the hourglass is officially turned over and the race is started. We have to get back to him before he gets back to anyone else outside the company, or else we could be seen as being remiss in our duties. [*How do you mean?*]

That account executive, Roland, told you on Tuesday that his boss could possibly be hitting on him, right? [*Yes.*] It's now Thursday, and you haven't gotten back to him, right? [*Yes.*] Then what if he went to an attorney last night and complained of sexual harassment? The attorney would ask if he'd put anyone in the company on notice, and he would have responded, "Yes. I told HR." Then the attorney would ask, "Did HR do anything about it?" And he'd say no. And that record is where the trouble begins.

So even though Roland casually told you about a "minor problem" while you were at lunch in the cafeteria, and even though he specifically told you that he didn't need your help or want your involvement, *the company* is still on the hook for not having done anything. I know that may not sound fair, but that's the record that was created by your not having followed up with him. Do you get it? [*Oh, now I see what you're saying.*]

Okay, I should have impressed upon you more the importance of all this when you first told me about it. And I also should have given you this little story so that you understand how making a particular record is so critical to what we do. The worst kind of record to make, though, is no record at all and no follow-up due to thoughtlessness or oversight. Do you understand the sense of urgency now in following up with these kinds of issues immediately? [*Yes.*]

Good. So what are you going to do now? [*Call Roland.*] I agree. When will you do that? [*Right this very instant.*] Excellent—lesson learned. Let me know what he says after you've spoken with him. I want all the facts: who, what, where, when, why, and whether there were any witnesses. If he still doesn't want your involvement, then call me. I'll come into your meeting and review the matter with the both of you. Okay, I'll wait to hear from you.

Well, that conversation should have gotten Brett's heart beating! Whenever possible, explain your message in the form of a story or a cause-and-effect scenario. That will help your employees recall the information much more readily because people tend to remember stories a lot more than rules.

5

Policy and Procedure Violations

Violation of company policy has many faces, including personnel, computer, security, and safety applications. Companies often have different approaches toward policies in general: While some organizations publish policy and procedure (P&P) manuals, employee handbooks, and code of conduct ethics statements, other companies choose to forego documentation if at all possible, in an attempt to retain total discretion to handle violations and breaches on a case-by-case basis.

Most employees would argue that they prefer to have handbooks and P&P manuals so that they understand a company's rules and guidelines. It also benefits companies to publish such documents in an effort to consistently accord workplace due process. If employees clearly know what's expected of them and nonetheless violate a documented policy, then the employer (theoretically) has a much cleaner termination to defend.

Of course, that's not always the case. Sometimes documentation provides workers with opportunities to circumvent the rules because there are loopholes embedded in them. Many employers reason that certain workplace rules are self-evident, so documenting the rules becomes redundant and unnecessary.

Whether or how much your company chooses to document specific policies, worker violations can expose your organization to all sorts of liabilities, from personal injury to lost revenue to legal exposure. In addition, failing to punish rulebreakers may establish a company *practice* that in turn arguably establishes a *precedent*. If you choose, for example, not to terminate Employee A for violation of a company policy and later choose to terminate Employee B for violation of that same policy, a claim of discrimination or retaliation from Employee B's attorney may be sustained.

In short, you often don't have the luxury of waiving discipline or termination in cases of serious policy violations. Therefore, it becomes critical that you look at such violations not only on the individual merits of the case at hand but also on each case's precedent-setting value. Once you've established that big picture mindset, your decisions in terms of properly responding to policy and procedure violations will become clearer.

SCENARIO 23

Failure to Adhere to Safety Rules

Companies often post safety rules on shop floors because federal and state laws require their prominent display. Many workers in heavy industry face life-and-limb risk if they violate safety policies, and intense training programs and certification requirements often become the norm to prevent serious injury or even death. However, even if your company isn't engaged in that level of hazard or danger, conducting safety training, including fire drill exercises and injury-reporting procedures, makes sense—both in terms of complying with the law, ensuring worker safety, and mitigating legal damages should an injury occur.

Let's assume that a light industrial worker is responsible for wearing a hairnet, safety glasses, and gloves while working on a particular piece of machinery. You happen to walk by one day and notice the employee is wearing none of the above. Your initial reaction is to call the employee out in front of his peers and berate him for not wearing the appropriate equipment. You may likewise reason that a formal written warning is in order. However, this is very atypical for this particular employee, so you choose to call him into your office in private instead to find out what's going on. (Good thinking!)

The Solution

In your meeting, you learn that George was actually leaving the floor at the end of his shift when he realized he left his safety goggles atop the machine. You happened to see him just at the moment he climbed the ladder to pick them up. George apologizes and confirms that he knows that he's not supposed to do that: He's never compromised safety before and always wears his equipment religiously. Nevertheless, you have an obligation to sit him down and remind him of the company policy as well as the critical need to avoid any exceptions.

George, I hear you. I know that's atypical. I've never seen you violate a safety policy before, which is why I was so shocked to see you up on that ladder without your ponytail in a hairnet and without your goggles and gloves on. And I realize that my walking by at that particular moment was bad timing from your perspective, but let's not look at it that way.

Truth be told, we work around so much machinery every day that we take it for granted. It's kind of like when we fly on an airline and pay no attention to the attendant who reviews the safety rules at the beginning of the flight. Just so you know, I *always* listen to those attendants' presentations! And I always take safety rules seriously—there's just too much at stake if you're not paying attention or if your mind is elsewhere, even for just a minute. Therefore, let's look at my walking by just now as good timing for both of us.

First, you realize that if your hair were to catch on moving equipment, it could possibly result in death—no kidding—death. I know we haven't had any serious incidents or accidents since you've joined us, but machinery is machinery, and it doesn't discriminate if someone's hair gets caught. It just pulls them right into the gears.

Second, remember that the restraints, pullbacks, and those two-hand devices are all for your safety, George, and you've got to make sure you're familiar with how to use them. If there were ever an emergency, you wouldn't have time to think. You'd be working off pure adrenalin, so knowing how to use standard safety equipment has to become second nature.

Third, those eye goggles are lifesavers. I've seen someone splashed in the face by hot oil. The burns eventually blistered, scabbed over, and became minor scars, thank goodness, but the liquid splashed squarely across her goggles, and she would have lost her eyesight.

In addition, George, I want you take the opportunity to remind your coworkers about these same safety policies. You never want to live through the guilt of seeing someone suffer from a serious injury, especially if it was simply because that person wasn't paying close enough attention or was taking their work for granted. Occasional reminders are healthy because this is serious stuff. Will you make that commitment to me for the good of your team? [*Yes.*]

One final thought: I know you're not a supervisor yet, but I want you to view this from a leadership perspective. Here's the first lesson: There will be certain times when you won't have the discretion *not* to discipline someone for a safety infraction. That could set a dangerous precedent, and if you don't discipline one person for a safety infraction, it could be difficult to discipline someone else.

Yes, there are mitigating circumstances but generally speaking, when it comes to safety infractions, we've all got to have a zero tolerance approach for the sake of the company. It's all about the record you're creating, George, and you've always got to keep that bigger picture in mind. Can I count on you to do that? [*Yes.*]

And with that shared simple reminder, you'll have sensitized George to an important responsibility, for himself, his coworkers, and the company. Simple as this talk may seem, don't underestimate its importance as an occasional reminder of putting safety first. And what a great opportunity to let George know that you're thinking of his career as well as his safety.

Although you can safely assume that he'll walk away from your conversation feeling educated and empowered, any future incidents will most likely require a written warning—even for something as minor as picking up his goggles off the machinery without his other safety equipment on.

SCENARIO 24

Excessive Personal Telephone Calls

"Do companies actually have to pay for phone calls? I thought they were free!" Such was the logic of a college intern who called his mother every day of his internship—in Lithuania! Yes, adults young and old often forget (or may never have known) that companies have to pay for *all* phone calls made by employees on their monthly bills. They also fail to realize that the company phone bill can track every individual call back to the phone line where it was generated—and to the person who sits at that desk. So when the supervisor found out from the department head that a college intern generated $1,150 in personal phone calls in one month, well—let's just say the internship ended.

The Solution

College interns may have an excuse—they're too inexperienced to realize how this all works and they just don't get it. But what about full-time workers who see the company phone on their desk as a resource to avoid generating excessive cell phone charges of their own? You might want to proactively instruct your group to avoid any personal phone calls by distributing a short memo or including the following message in your next staff meeting:

> Everyone, one of the items on today's meeting list is personal phone calls. There are two important aspects of personal phone calls that I'll need you all to keep in mind. First, company phones are only to be used for company business. Barring any emergencies, all personal phone calls should come from your cell phone. Remember that we receive monthly itemized phone bills, and if we see repetitive calls made to personal phone numbers, you can be subject to formal progressive discipline. So please don't put me in the uncomfortable position of having to have that kind of discussion with you. Fair enough? [*Yes.*]
>
> Good. The second issue has to do with your cell phones. I realize that they're your personal possessions and don't belong to the company. However, you've got to be careful not to use them excessively during the workday. Limit your personal calls to your

breaks and meal periods, and understand that it is highly inappropriate for you to be seen on your cell phone during the regular business day. I realize that you wouldn't be using company equipment, but you also wouldn't be doing your job, and that's a serious issue, as I'm sure you can all understand. Do you all get my logic and reasoning behind these two rules? [*Yes.*] Okay then, does anyone have any questions? [*No.*] Good, then let's continue with the meeting's agenda.

An ounce of prevention is worth a pound of cure, and making this statement up front eliminates any confusion or misunderstandings right from the start. Now what about someone who has either used the company phone for excessive personal phone calls or who makes excessive personal calls using her cell phone? Well, it depends on how you define the word *excessive*. If the individual's phone bill shows scores of personal phone calls during the month, then your response should be in the form of a written warning. Depending on your company policy and practice, you can also require reimbursement.

On the other hand, excessive may be just a few too many calls during the day on the cell phone, and your response will more likely be in the form of a verbal counseling session that may sound like this:

Wanda, we need to talk. I called you into my office because, with all due respect, you've got a perception problem on your hands. That perception is that you're on your cell phone during the workday while you should be doing work. It isn't excessive at this point, but I'm concerned that this could become a slippery slope. If I allow you to make personal phone calls on your cell phone during the day, then others will assume they have that same right, and we'll lose a large chunk of our productive time in the office.

Therefore, I'll need your support in helping me fix the problem. With the exception of emergencies, will you commit to me to limit the use of your cell phone to breaks and lunch periods? [*Okay.*] Thanks. I'm not punishing you here: I just want to increase your level of sensitivity to how this looks. I don't expect anyone on staff to, in effect, take breaks during the middle of their shifts by calling family members or friends to chat. That's really what breaks and meal periods are for. Can you see my concern, and does it sound reasonable to you? [*Yes.*] Thanks for your support on this. I know it's an easy fix, but I wanted to make sure you understood my logic in asking you. How's everything else going on your desk?

That was nice and easy and without any drama. Our "perception problem" approach makes it easy to deliver a fairly straightforward message without any hesitation or angst. As a supervisor, you should never feel guilty for asking someone to do her job. Just use yourself as the baseline: If you wouldn't make personal calls during your normal shift, then don't be shy about asking your subordinates to follow your lead.

SCENARIO 25

Excessive Time Spent on the Internet

The internet has certainly made our lives easier. You can buy books, airplane tickets, computers, and more with the click of a button. You can gossip on blogs, share videos of family members, look up long-lost high school friends, and watch your favorite TV shows without getting out of your seat. And since company internet connections often allow unrestricted access, the temptation to engage in non-work-related activities can be too much for some people to resist.

The Solution

You might want to proactively remind your group to avoid excessive personal time on the internet by distributing a short memo or including the following pep talk in your next staff meeting:

Everyone, one of the items on today's meeting list is excessive use of the internet for personal reasons. There are two important aspects of personal internet usage that I'll need you all to keep in mind. First, the company internet connection is to be used for only company business. All personal online activities should be limited and minimal, and if you have to go online for personal reasons, please restrict your usage to your breaks and lunch periods. Remember that if you're nonexempt (hourly), however, I'd like you to be up and away from your desk during your rest and meal periods.

Of course, there can be exceptions to this expectation of leaving your desk for your breaks, but you'll need to get them approved each time, and I certainly don't want those exceptions to become a habit. Is that clear and does that sound fair? [*Yes.*]

It's always safest to ensure that nonexempt staff members physically leave their desks during their breaks and lunch periods. If that's not the case, they may feel inclined or obligated to pick up a ringing phone or do other work while they're officially at lunch, and that can invalidate their lunch period in the eyes of the law. If you choose to grant someone's request to spend personal time on the internet during a break or lunch period, just make sure that it's the exception and not the rule.

Good. There's one other thing. I don't want to sound like Big Brother here or anything, but remember that we've got filters on employees' systems and can turn them on if we suspect that someone is either spending excessive time on the web for personal reasons or visiting inappropriate websites. Again, I don't have time to do that, so I don't want you to become paranoid, but if I have reason to suspect that there's abuse, one call to the IT department will typically show me everywhere you've visited on the internet and how long you remained there.

And that's allowable, everyone, because just like when it comes to your desks and lockers at work, you don't have what's known as a reasonable expectation of privacy when it comes to your email or the internet. Those things are all considered company equipment, and the company has the right to inspect and review them at any time.

Therefore, a good rule of thumb is to close out any site that's not work-related as soon as you're done. Don't leave it open and minimized in the tray at the bottom of your screen. Do you all understand the rules and what's expected of you? [*Yes.*] Okay, then let's continue with the meeting's agenda.

Once again, an ounce of prevention is worth a pound of cure, and making this statement up front eliminates any confusion or misunderstandings right from the start. Now what about someone who abuses the system by spending too much time on the internet for personal reasons despite your prior coaching session? That depends: If you advised the staff a week ago, then you've got fair grounds to proceed right to a written warning. If it's been a year or so since your pep talk or if you've never given them advance notice of your expectations, then you might simply assume that the individual made inappropriate assumptions about her right to access the internet for personal reasons during the business day. Under those circumstances, your verbal counseling might sound like this:

Sarah, I need to talk to you about the time you're spending on the internet. First of all, I'm only sharing my impressions with you, so there's no need to be defensive about this or to feel a need to justify yourself. Just understand that, generally speaking, when I walk by your desk, I'm not surprised to see the internet up and rolling with commercial sites onscreen. Now you may feel that you're getting all your work done and that you spend very little time on the web, and that may be the case. But from my vantage point, you may have a perception problem on your hands. What I mean is that others may notice the same thing that I do—namely, that you're spending lots of time viewing personal interest pages during the workday.

Now before I go any further, let me ask you, is it possible that this "perception" issue that I've become aware of could be true? [*Yes, but I . . .*] Okay, again, I don't mean to interrupt you, but you don't have to defend your actions. I'm just giving you some subjective feedback based on what I've been noticing lately, and I want to sensitize you to the fact that others may be under the same impression.

As they say, perception is reality until proven otherwise, and I wouldn't want you to ever have to defend yourself or your overall job performance because someone comes under the impression that you're doing personal errands on company time.

Oh, there's one other thing, Sarah. Employees don't realize that our company—in fact, all companies—can track their employees' visits to the internet. The filtering software can tell us where someone's been, how long they've remained there, and more. I'm not telling you this to make you paranoid, but it's something that you should be aware of. At this point, is it safe for me to assume that you'll limit your internet access during the workday to business-related research only and limit your personal time spent on the internet? [*Yes.*] Good, then I think we're fine here. Thanks for meeting with me to discuss this. How's everything else going on your desk?

That very nice and professional one-on-one talk will likely be the only verbal intervention you'll ever need to make record of, as perception problems like this are easily fixed. However, if you ever again suspect that Sarah is spending an excessive amount of time on the web or visiting inappropriate websites, simply speak with your data security administrator in the IT department to activate those filters.

SCENARIO 26

Unauthorized Use of Company Equipment and Facilities

Employees sometimes take for granted the fact that your company has to buy supplies and equipment for its facilities. They think little of taking home notepads, pencils, rulers, and even (heaven forbid) computer monitors and printers. While the latter is theft and would likely result in immediate dismissal, few companies think termination would be appropriate for taking home a staple remover.

Okay, that's fair enough, but what about an employee who develops a habit of overnighting packages to his son's college dorm two states away? How about someone who comes to your facility with friends on a Saturday night to play cards or to watch a football game on the corporate big screen TV? Or what about a worker who expresses an outrageous personal opinion to a national radio shock jock—using a corporate email address that has your company name in its domain? You can only imagine when the shock jock says, "And Paul from XYZ Company has the gall to say. . . ." Oh, employees seem to find the darnedest ways of getting themselves into scraps now, don't they?

The Solution

Yes, these are all moments where you, the supervisor, sit back, shake your head, and ask, "What were they thinking?" But people will be people, and that's why you chose a career in management anyway, right?

Let's look at the example of the employee who sends overnight packages to his son in Denver. Boy, those are expensive! And the company won't know the difference anyway, will they? Well, it's true that the individual may not be caught, but if he is, you've got options: You can formally discipline the employee with a final written warning letting him know that if he *ever again* sends personal care packages using the company's overnight service, he'll be immediately terminated. You can also research all the packages he's sent to the Denver campus and hand him a whopping bill for those expenses that would be immediately payable. Or you might simply have a discussion with him (assuming this is a first or early offense) letting him know why using the company's package delivery service for personal benefit is a no-no.

Here's what your conversation might sound like in this last case:

Gary, we've got a problem on our hands. The folks in the mailroom let me know that they discovered that you had sent a personal package to your son at XYZ College in Denver. Is that true? [*Yes, I'm sorry to say it is.*]

You realize that's wrong, don't you? [*Yes, I do. I'm sorry, Paul. I was in a rush to get a package to my son via overnight delivery, and I should've told the mailroom folks what I was doing. I also realize that I should have paid for it, and I'll go back to the mailroom and pay for it right after our meeting.*]

Well, I think that would be appropriate under the circumstances, Gary, but the bigger issue I'm scratching my head over is your judgment. You know how expensive it is to send a letter via overnight express, never mind a package. And I'm sure you realize that those things are checked every night as the mailroom employees do their inventory. What made you think that it would go unnoticed? [*Honestly, I just wasn't thinking and I'm sorry for that lack of discretion.*] Fair enough—apology accepted. Understand something, though, Gary: Under other circumstances, we could pursue progressive disciplinary action, even for a first-time offense. This type of behavior can be construed as stealing, which would subject you to immediate termination. And even if the company chose not to go that far, we could issue a final written warning for a first-time offense, which is clearly something you wouldn't want on your record.

Here's where you have to be careful: Employees sometimes take things at work for granted. Not major things usually, but little things that can add up over time. Soon an entitlement mentality develops where employees feel the company *owes* things to them in exchange for all their hard work and sacrifice and, well, let's just say that's not a healthy view of reality. We pay for pencils here just like you pay for them at home, so taking anything from this house to bring home to your house can be viewed as stealing. Do you see my logic here? [*Yes.*]

Okay, we don't need to beat a dead horse, then. I think my message is pretty clear on this one. But this advice I'm giving you isn't just for our company—it's for your entire career. Successful careers can be derailed by not thinking things through, and little, seemingly harmless acts by employees can have them on the unemployment line before they know it. I wouldn't ever want to see that happen to you, so consider this a career coaching sensitivity session just to help you keep the proper perspective on things. Okay? [*Okay, Paul. Thanks.*]

Again, your company may have strict policies and practices in terms of how to handle first-time events like this one, from immediate termination to allowing the matter to slide altogether. What's important in most cases is that you intervene early and sensitize the employee to how harshly matters like this can be treated under other circumstances or in other companies. You're certain to make Gary think twice before taking something like that for granted again.

SCENARIO 27

Wage and Hour Challenges—Failure to Adhere to Rest and Meal Periods

Wage and hour challenges pose a particular threat to most employers, regardless of size. Plaintiff's attorneys that pursue class action or collective action wage and hour claims take advantage of technical or complex provisions in the law that are sometimes difficult for employers to comply with or fully understand. Whether pursuing rest and meal period violations, unpaid overtime, paycheck or pay stub errors, exemption misclassification, off-the-clock work, independent contractor misclassification, or other issues, such claims can have potentially disastrous effects on a company's bottom line. Further, as a general rule, companies will not be indemnified against wage and hour claims through any of their insurance policies because the liability is too big and uncontrollable for insurers to underwrite, so it's critical that you avoid looking like "low-hanging fruit" to a potentially aggressive plaintiff's attorney. An example of a good place to start: ensuring that your nonexempt workers are provided with rest and meal periods and use both.

The Solution

To safeguard against falling victim to an unforeseen wage and hour challenge, regularly talk about timekeeping expectations with your nonexempt employees (whether salaried or hourly). Don't make this a "read it for yourself in the employee handbook" type of passive leadership communique. Instead, openly discuss your concerns and recommendations, make sure your nonexempt employees have a voice in asking questions, and whenever possible, create a record of ongoing dialogue. Remember that wage and hour rules are established by the federal Fair Labor Standards Act, administered and enforced by the US Department of Labor, and vary by state and local government, and in some states, by industry wage orders. If that sounds confusing or daunting, you're getting the point. Ensure that you have clear instructions from management or from qualified legal counsel to share with your salaried or hourly nonexempt employees, and then set your expectations accordingly. Here's what your group discussion might sound like:

Everyone, I called this meeting to discuss timekeeping and hours-of-work rules. First, I want to emphasize to all of you in this room that I take this seriously and want to set my expectations clearly: If you're a "nonexempt" or "hourly" employee, we want you to take your rest and meal periods consistently and without exception, unless an emergency gets in the way.

As nonexempt employees, you're scheduled to take two ten-minute rest periods during a regular eight-hour workday in addition to a thirty-minute meal period (or "lunch break"). I'm meeting with you all today and plan to continue to bring this topic up from time to time because this is about fairness and respect: Laws were created to help guide your time throughout the day and to ensure that you have breaks and lunches at certain intervals. It's the right thing to do for our employees, and yes, it insulates our company from liability as well. But it's important that this becomes part of our culture, part of who we are, so that we all know how to handle and manage our time going forward.

First, while I want to make sure that as a unit, we're aware of the rules and abide by them, we also need to continue our focus on customer service and engagement. Both the rest and meal period rules, as well as our commitments to customer service, have to find a healthy balance with one another.

Second, I'm calling this meeting to remove any guilt associated with taking your rest and meal periods. There's no guilt involved in any of this. If you're a nonexempt or hourly employee, these time restrictions are built into our daily program by law, and I want to assure you all that I respect you enough to ensure that you're benefiting from wage and hour rules that were intended to grant you a well-deserved break from the action throughout the day. In other words, I don't want any of you engaging in what I call "on-duty rest and meal periods," where you're constantly interrupted and awaiting and expecting that interruption at any given time.

Third, I hope that a natural outcome of a meeting like this is to increase communication with your immediate supervisors. When you work overtime, you need to gain your supervisor's advanced approval because of the expense involved. I know you know that, but I also want to emphasize that if you suspect that you won't be able to take your two ten-minute rest periods or your thirty-minute meal period without interruption, you need to inform your supervisor as well. I've had this talk with your supervisors already, and they're aware of my expectations across the board. Surprises should be rare: I expect both supervisors and staff members to engage in ongoing dialogue throughout the day about a lot of things, but exceptions to your rest and meal period breaks, where truly necessary, must be included in that list.

Fourth, from a technical standpoint, our job in management is to pay you for all hours worked. To do this, you're required to clock in and clock out at the beginning and end of the workday and before and after your lunch period. Does anyone have any questions about the clock-in and clock-out rules? [*No.*]

Good. I'm here if you do, and you can always speak with your immediate supervisor or human resources or payroll if you have particular questions about how timekeeping and rest and meal periods work.

Fifth, you're required to take your meal and rest breaks every day. Do I have your commitment that you'll do so? [*Yes.*] Thank you. Do I have your commitment that you'll never work off the clock and that you'll record all time worked under all circumstances, with no exceptions? [*Yes.*] Do I likewise have your commitment that you'll always gain your supervisor's advanced approval before working overtime or skipping meal or rest periods, unless there's an emergency? [*Yes.*]

Okay, final point for this meeting. You're not allowed to work off the clock. I'm serious, you guys. For example, we won't ask you to arrive early to perform necessary preparations for work or to stay late to perform duties such as "closing up" after punching out. Am I clear? [*Yes.*] And what would happen if we found out that you were working off the clock? [*We'd be disciplined?*] You're getting it!

You can expect me to raise this issue from time to time, to ensure that you're all living up to your commitments. I also need to hear from you if anyone is not consistently adhering to these rules. As a reminder, supervisors have to ensure that nonexempt employees take their breaks, and supervisors are not permitted to allow hourly employees to do uncompensated work off-the-clock. That's a strict policy violation, and I need to know about it ASAP if that ever occurs.

Keep up the great work you're all doing, know how much we appreciate your hard work and efforts every day, and know that I'm here to help you if you run into any challenges. Thank you all for your commitment to make our company a better place, and always remember to come from a place of thankfulness, appreciation, and gratitude in all that you do. We're all fortunate to be working as part of a strong and unified team in such an excellent company. Now go out there and make our organization a better place.

Okay, you don't have to be quite so rah-rah in your closing—I just threw that in for good measure! But you get the idea: keep your teams focused on that same key message. It makes for happy and healthy workers. It also keeps plaintiff's attorneys away because your prioritizing this message will surely be repeated by the troops, and lawyers tend not to pursue companies where the workers are quick to proclaim, "Oh, we talk about wage and hour issues all the time, and the management team continues to remind us of how important they are."

SCENARIO 28

Working Unauthorized Overtime

Wage and hour claims often show up in the form of class action lawsuits and can literally cost your company millions of dollars. While you appreciate employees who demonstrate flexibility and a willingness to work whatever hours are necessary to get the job done, that selflessness can eventually become a liability for your company if the individual involved is *nonexempt* (i.e., covered by the overtime provisions of the Fair Labor Standards Act).

Nonexempt workers typically are entitled to two breaks and a meal period during a normal business day. If they habitually choose to forego their breaks and remain at their desks to work during their meal periods, it can come back to haunt you big time as an employer. Here's how that scenario typically plays itself out: Stellar hourly employee works through breaks and lunches on a regular basis. Employee eventually falls out of love with his supervisor, is terminated for cause, and retains the services of an attorney to sue your company for wrongful termination.

The scenario isn't over yet, though. The plaintiff attorney typically looks to pursue punitive damages from your company, since that's where the "real money" is made, and she asks the prospective plaintiff (your ex-employee) leading questions about harassment, discrimination, and retaliation. In addition, she asks questions like, "Did you or any other nonexempt workers on staff regularly work through your breaks and meal periods or work overtime without being paid for it?" The plaintiff-to-be actually defends the company and says, "Well yes, a lot of us did. But in my case, I willingly did that—the company never asked me to."

And voilà! That's all it might take for the initial makings of class action wage and hour claims to take root. Remember, the wage and hour board will not consider whether overtime was authorized; the fact that the employee worked the overtime without remuneration is all that counts to substantiate a claim for back wages.

The Solution

You typically wouldn't want to discipline someone for working diligently through their breaks and lunches or for working unpaid overtime at shift's end. Human nature will make you want to demonstrate appreciation and goodwill for the employee's loyalty and extra efforts. However, you really don't want to become known as a company that expects its nonexempt employees to work through their breaks or engage in unpaid overtime on a regular basis. That could land you in legal hot water with a particularly expensive price tag.

Even more, if you suspect that a disgruntled employee may be particularly litigious, realize that she may be setting the company up by working through rest and meal periods while putting in unpaid overtime hours after work. In such cases, you need to step in and stop this behavior. Depending on the nature and severity of the offense, your response may be in writing (in the form of a written warning) or, more likely for this type of infraction, via a verbal counseling session, which might sound like this:

> Margie, we've got to talk. I saw you clock out at 5:00 p.m. last night, which is your regularly scheduled time off. And I thought you had left to go home because I was leaving at the same time. However, when I got in this morning, Janet Swenson, the evening supervisor, told me she saw you working until 8:00 p.m. She was very complimentary and commented on how diligent and responsible you must be to put in those kinds of hours. I asked her if she'd seen you doing that before, and she mentioned that she had seen you working late nights a few other times as well.
>
> It's funny, though—I don't remember seeing any entries in your time sheets for three or four hours of overtime on any given night. [*Oh, Paul, I didn't want you to have to worry about paying me overtime. I know there's a cap on overtime expenses, and I didn't want you to have to worry about it. Besides, having quiet time to catch up on my work after hours helps me stay totally on top of my work, and I actually enjoy the peace of mind it gives me to be ahead of the game.*]

Well, as much as I appreciate your dedication, Margie, and I understand what you're saying about having quiet time to get your desk in order, I'm afraid that as a nonexempt or hourly employee, you have to be paid for any overtime that you do in excess of a certain threshold.

In our case, if you work more than forty hours in a week, you have to be paid at time-and-a-half. Period. No questions asked. [*But I don't mind, really . . .*]

No, no, I'm with you, Margie, but let me explain a bit further. It's not about the employee's willingness—that's not the way the wage and hour commission sees it. Whether or not the overtime was approved is not at issue; rather it's simply a matter of whether the employee worked the overtime or not. And it's not just about overtime after hours. You also have to make sure you take your breaks and lunch periods on a regular and consistent basis, which is why I ask everyone to get up from their desks and get out for fresh air every day. Not only is it healthier for the employees, but it stops anyone from picking up the phone during their lunch break and taking calls or doing any other work.

In fact, some companies discipline employees who work unauthorized overtime. It can be that serious. Now that's clearly not the case here, and I want you to know how much I appreciate your work ethic and your willingness to put the company's needs ahead of your own. But seeing that *we wouldn't want to do anything that could appear to be in violation of overtime rules*, I'm hoping you'll accept this constructive criticism in the positive spirit in which it was meant. [*Yes, okay, if that's the way you'd like me to handle it from now on.*]

Great—thank you. Oh, there's one more thing: We'll pay you for the three hours that you worked last night. And I want you to look up the additional hours that you've worked in the past so we can pay you for those as well. Just commit to me that we won't have any more surprises when it comes to overtime work from this point forward, and I'll be a happy camper. [*Okay, Paul, you got it.*]

You made your point, explained the business rationale for your request, and treated the employee with dignity and respect, so job well done. One more note, though: Pay special attention to the language "we wouldn't want to do anything that could appear to be in violation of overtime rules." That's a much more benign and safer thing to say than "We wouldn't want to violate the law" or "We wouldn't want to be sued for breaking the law." Be careful not to use language that could unwittingly instill in the employee's mind that the company could have violated any law or otherwise be sued for its actions.

SCENARIO 29

Off-Duty Conduct and Moonlighting

Moonlighting is always a questionable topic in the workplace. On the one hand, every company wants its employees focused solely on its business needs. And of course, there's always that risk of breached confidentiality. On the other hand, many employers understand that workers need to make ends meet and consequently don't want to stand in the way of their employees' desire to work two jobs. In fact, many managers would agree that such a solid work ethic is very admirable.

Only you can tell if moonlighting presents a significant conflict of interest to your company. For example, if you're one of the few chemists at Coca-Cola who has the secret formula for what makes a Coke a Coke, there's no question that split loyalties to different companies would be out of the question. On the other hand, if you supervise individuals who are engaged mostly in manual labor, there's little reason to believe that their participation in jobs at other companies could somehow compromise your business interests.

Therefore, we'll leave the propriety issue of moonlighting up to you. In our example, we'll assume that moonlighting is allowable at your company as long as it doesn't hinder the individual's work performance on a day-to-day basis. That's a reasonable standard of expectation for most employers, so let's have a look at someone who's working late-night shifts after putting in a full nine-to-five day at your firm, only to appear the next day acting worn out, grouchy, and prone to errors.

The Solution

Again, realizing that there is a balance to strike between privacy (i.e., what someone does in his private time away from work) and company performance standards, you might want to open your conversation this way:

> Pierre, we need to talk. I wanted to call this private meeting with you to ask you to gauge how you're feeling in general and how satisfied you are with your own performance these days. [*I'm fine. Why do you ask?*]
>
> Do you notice any difference between your performance over the past month and your historical work with us over the past two years? [*No, not really.*]
>
> Well, there's a significant difference, and it's not only been noticed by me but by a few others who were kind enough to give me a gentle heads-up. You're well-liked here at the company, Pierre, but you've got a perception problem on your hands: You look exhausted, and you're giving off the impression that you're unfocused and "out of steam."
>
> I've also heard that you may be moonlighting at night. Specifically, I heard that you've been working a 6:00 p.m. to 3:00 a.m. shift on Mondays, Wednesdays, and Fridays at another company during the week. How close am I in terms of having accurate information? [*Well, that's correct, but that's something I do in my private time and really shouldn't have anything to do with . . .*]
>
> Let me stop you, Pierre. I'm not looking to get in the way of your ability to earn extra money at night, so there's no need to defend yourself. I know that it's difficult to make ends meet, and I respect that. However, as much as our company doesn't look to interfere with the off-duty and personal interests of its employees after work, your current activities may be interfering with your work here with us.
>
> Let me give you an example: We haven't had much overtime to give out lately, but what if we needed you tonight? Would you be available to continue on beyond 5:00 p.m.? [*Yes, I told the other company that may happen from time to time.*]
>
> Fair enough. But here's how your performance looks from my vantage point: You're yawning, drinking lots of coffee, and it's evident that you're not getting enough sleep. In terms of "harder" facts, you haven't completed two of your last sixteen jobs. We got a complaint today that you didn't check in with the Jones tenants when you were done, and it appears that you left the

work area untidy. That's not like you, Pierre, and I'm afraid these split obligations may place your role with us in jeopardy. [*Okay, I understand, but I still need the second job.*]

That's your call, and I'll respect whatever decision you make, just as I'll ask you to respect ours, whatever the outcome. Our simple rule is this: We expect your performance to remain at the historical level we've seen, and we expect you to be available for last-minute overtime when necessary. Whether you're working two jobs or not isn't the issue, and I won't worry about that from this point forward. But I am expecting you to assume responsibility for the perception problem you've developed over the last month and ensure that your work here isn't compromised for any reason.

Also, I've got to remind you of a few things: First, again, although I won't mandate that you give up your nighttime position (or even reduce hours), I expect you to report to work in the proper physical and mental condition at all times. Second, you're not permitted to conduct any work for the outside organization on company time or using company equipment, including phone calls or emails. Third, none of the work that you perform with the outside organization can pose any type of conflict of interest with our company, either in terms of shared confidential information or taking business opportunities away from our firm. Do I have your commitment to abide by those rules? [*Yes.*]

Okay then, Pierre, I'll hold you to your word. Remember those three expectations, though, because we can't have any violations of those agreements. Fair enough? [*Yes.*]

Good for you. You investigated and confirmed that the moonlighting was occurring. And you informed the employee of your company's expectations in terms of focus and performance in the role, availability for overtime, and most important, conflicts of interest that could arise from serving "two masters." Make sure you jot down what you've discussed, and be prepared to move to formal progressive discipline in the form of a written warning should Pierre's work performance deteriorate further. You've done about as much as you can in light of the fact that your company generally allows for moonlighting. At this point, it's up to Pierre to manage his time and priorities appropriately, now that he has a clearer understanding of the company's rules and expectations.

6

Excessive Absenteeism or Tardiness and FMLA/ADA Issues

E xcessive absenteeism and tardiness can be particularly difficult to address. First, some facts: A July, 2013 *Forbes* article titled "The Causes and Costs of Absenteeism in the Workplace" suggests that excessive absenteeism is costing US companies $14 billion annually. That's $3,600 per year on average for hourly and $2,600 per year on average for salaried workers. The numbers may sound astonishing, but anyone in a leadership role in corporate America knows how difficult it can be to manage attendance and tardiness challenges, especially in light of laws like the Family Medical Leave Act (FMLA) and Americans with Disabilities Act (ADA), in addition to workers' comp–related leaves of absence.

While no one solution exists to a problem so grand in scale and so pervasive throughout the workplace, a practical and common-sense approach will always work best. Before we get there, though, it's important to understand the caveats and challenges inherent to this particular workplace challenge. The law is changing constantly in this area, and it's critical that you check with qualified legal counsel to ensure that your attendance policy is up to date and that your disciplinary methods and procedures are compliant with federal, state, and local leave laws. These laws protect employees who need time off from work due to their own sickness or health condition, to care for a family member, or for other protected reasons.

The samples that follow in this chapter will help set forth your strategy for dealing with workers who appear to abuse the company's attendance, tardiness, or FMLA policies and practices. However, a "one-size-fits-all" approach won't work when administering corrective action and potentially terminating workers for these particular work-place infractions. The landscape has changed drastically in this area, and several states and cities have enacted "paid sick leave" laws that protect workers who are absent or tardy pursuant to these laws. It's critical that you proceed with caution before disciplining and especially before terminating workers for excessive absenteeism, tardiness, or FMLA abuse.

Next, some historical perspective: Beginning with the passage of the ADA in 1990 and the FMLA in 1993, substantial limits were placed on employers' abilities to terminate workers under existing attendance control policies. The limitations became more restrictive with the recent passage of paid sick leave laws in multiple states and cities, which has made it more difficult for employers to hold workers accountable for abuse of paid time off or sick leave policies.

The result has been limits on disciplining employees for unscheduled absences. For example, employers may no longer require doctors' notes or specific advance notice under many paid sick leave laws, and "patterns" may not be established just because someone takes off on the Friday before a holiday, provided the employee uses paid sick time pursuant to one of these paid sick leave laws. Make sure that you check with outside counsel to redraft your current attendance policy and your proposed disciplinary procedures if your state or city is subject to paid sick leave statutes.

Further, ensure that your employees who manage leaves of absence know how to distinguish between pure unscheduled absence occurrences and time off from work that may otherwise be protected by the federal ADA and FMLA laws (and similar state laws) and by your state's or city's paid sick leave laws. Ensure that your leave of absence team understands how to calculate, track, and notify employees about paid sick leave under these statutes. And train your frontline leaders, so they understand that when legally mandated paid sick leave is involved, they may not have the discretion to discipline workers for attendance infractions as they might have done in the past.

An employee's absences may trigger your obligation to engage in the interactive process, to determine if the employee needs a reasonable accommodation such as a leave of absence under the ADA or other applicable laws. If an employee has not made such a request, you should consider having a conversation to determine if the absence is due to an underlying medical or family health issue protected by these laws. Not only courts, but state and federal agencies like the EEOC, are tracking these issues and are likely to rule in favor of employees where a leave of absence would be a reasonable accommodation.

Finally, expect a lot more press about paid sick leave and other issues relating to employee rights, such as minimum wage, gender pay parity, prior pay, background checks, and parental leave. While these matters may fluctuate depending on the administration in Washington, DC, and the administrative climate in various states and localities, these types of laws will continue to evolve and confound even the best-intentioned employers. It's crucial for employers to stay current and well-advised on these rapidly evolving laws.

The first place to look when addressing excessive, unauthorized absenteeism is your company policy. Many companies place caps on annual sick leave allowances; others refuse to write a policy for fear that the documentation will limit their discretion in dealing with employees on a case-by-case basis. Your decision to implement a policy should depend on the frequency of worker absenteeism relative to industry and geographic standards.

In addition, setting policy can be challenging because employers need to determine the parameters of the program:

▶ Will it measure actual days or incidents (i.e., an uninterrupted series of days off from the same sickness or injury)?
▶ Will a no-fault or an excuse-based system be more effective?
▶ Will a rolling year or a calendar year serve as the optimal performance measurement time period?

Beyond the nuts and bolts of your written policy, your past practices must also be closely examined. If you're inconsistent in the application of your organization's rules, a judge or arbitrator may determine that your actions could justify a claim of wrongful termination, discrimination, or retaliation from a terminated worker.

How much sick time off is considered excessive (assuming no paid sick leave laws are in play)? There's no easy answer, but a reasonable juror may typically consider one sick day per month, or twelve days a year, as a threshold. More than that and it's likely that the discharge will be sustained; less than that and a plaintiff's attorney may be able to convince a jury that your decision to terminate was premature and possibly pretextual.

Fixing the problem can be accomplished in three steps:

1. Review your organization's written policy with the help of legal counsel to ensure that you'll be able to retain the most discretion in managing this thorny issue.
2. Review your organization's past practices (for example, all of the disciplinary actions and terminations related to unauthorized absence in the past two years) across departments, divisions, and locations. Account for inconsistencies in prior decisions. Remember that you retain the discretion to change a policy or practice by notifying employees in advance and in writing. You're not obliged to perpetuate a problem once you discover that changing the rule or practice could make things better. Simply follow a rule of reason: If employees are given advance notice of the organization's changed expectations, they should be held accountable for meeting the new standard from that point forward.
3. Document substandard performance consistently. The documentation itself should begin like this: "Maintenance of good attendance is a condition of employment and an essential function of your job. In order to minimize hardships that may result from illness or injury, our company provides paid sick time. However, periodic sick leave taken on a repeated basis or evidencing a particular pattern may be viewed as abuse of the system. It is your responsibility not to violate the company's sick leave policy to receive sick leave pay."

Note that many paid sick leave laws affect an employer's ability to ask for information relating to the need for sick time off. Therefore, while an employer should be attentive to any abuse of the sick leave policy, the company must balance that with restrictions placed on the employer by state and local laws. In addition, many states have privacy laws prohibiting employers from asking workers to reveal specifics about their injury or illness.

List the dates and days of the week of the actual incidents like this:

YOU HAVE INCURRED FIVE INCIDENTS OF UNSCHEDULED AND UNPROTECTED ABSENCE IN THIS ROLLING CALENDAR YEAR:

Friday, October 11, 2019
Monday, October 14, 2019

Friday, November 22, 2019
Monday, November 25, 2019
Monday, December 23, 2019

In addition, document the negative organizational impact that re-sulted from the individual's unauthorized absenteeism, which might look something like this:

This number of incidents has disrupted the workflow in our unit and has caused the department to incur unscheduled overtime because others have had to carry the extra workload. In addition, a temporary worker had to be assigned to your area so that the deadline for the Vanguard project could be met.

Finally, if your policy does not spell out the specific number of in-cidents that could lead to termination, include general consequential language like this:

It is imperative that you minimize any future occurrences of un-scheduled, unauthorized absence. Failure to provide immediate and sustained improvement may result in further disciplinary lan-guage, up to and including termination.

On the other hand, if your company policy spells out the number of incidents of unscheduled, unauthorized absenteeism that will result in dismissal, include that specific consequential language in the written warning instead.

You are now being placed on notice that according to company policy, if you reach seven incidents of unscheduled and unau-thorized absence in the rolling calendar year, you will receive a written warning. A ninth incident of unscheduled, unauthorized absence in the rolling calendar year will result in a final written warning. A tenth incident will result in your immediate dismissal.

Patterning time off around weekends and holidays poses an ad-ditional challenge to you as an employer. If you look at the previous example, you'll note that all of the five days of unauthorized absence occurred on a Monday or a Friday. The definition of a *pattern* is a frequent, predictable, and observable employee action that repeats itself over time. When employees take more than 50 percent of their time off around weekends or holidays, then a pattern may be established. Just remember that this 50 percent rule isn't a legal definition; it is a reasonable company rule that you may wish to establish. Further, to the point made above, if a state- or city-mandated paid sick leave event is involved, or if the leave otherwise looks to be protected by FMLA or ADA laws, then counting those Friday and Monday incidents may not be permitted in attempting to establish and demonstrate a pattern.

Patterning in this author's opinion is a separate infraction from unscheduled absenteeism and should be handled separately in the written warning. Simply create two headings in the written warning itself:

Issue 1: Excessive, unscheduled, and unauthorized absenteeism
Issue 2: Patterning incidents of unscheduled, unauthorized absenteeism around regularly scheduled time off

Under this second heading, you might step up the consequence language like this:

All five incidents of unscheduled, unauthorized absence occurred on either a Monday or a Friday. You have therefore demonstrated a pattern of taking time off around your regularly scheduled weekends.

If any other patterns appear in the next year in terms of how you take time off—that is, if you regularly take unscheduled and unauthorized days off either before or after weekends, holidays, or vacations—you will be subject to further disciplinary action up to and including dismissal.

In addition, human resources will be notified of every additional occurrence of absenteeism from this point forward in order to provide you with additional support. Finally, you are now formally notified that any further occurrences of unscheduled and unauthorized sick leave must be substantiated by a doctor's note. The doctor's note will not excuse the absence but will be necessary to return to work.

Note that in many jurisdictions, employers may institute a policy requiring a doctor's note verifying the illness from employees who use a certain number of sick days in a row. In jurisdictions mandating paid sick leave, the general rule is that you should not ask for a doctor's note justifying the leave until the jurisdiction's minimum paid sick leave has been exhausted. With these progressive discipline tools in hand, you should be successful in minimizing further incidents of "patterning" because most employees will avoid this perception problem once it's been brought formally to their attention.

There's one more key issue that you must be aware of when disciplining employees for excessive absenteeism. In certain cases, the Family Medical Leave Act (FMLA) and the Americans with Disabilities Act (ADA), as well as similar state laws, hinder your ability to discipline effectively. These statutes could expose your organization to punitive damages should you run afoul of their rules. This leads many employers to avoid confronting excessive absenteeism for fear of facing a lawsuit.

Still, a little knowledge will go a long way in shedding some light on statutes like the FMLA. Does a doctor's note legitimize excessive absenteeism? More important, does it mean "hands off" any employee who relies on a doctor's note to substantiate his own or a family member's illness? These are difficult questions and will depend not only on the FMLA but also on the ADA and the laws of your state and city.

What's important to remember when looking at the FMLA's reach over your company's attendance management program is that FMLA-related leaves apply only when an employee or family member has a serious health condition. The following are considered serious health conditions for purposes of FMLA:

1. Inpatient care in a hospital, hospice, or residential medical care facility
2. An episode or chronic condition that requires an inpatient hospital stay
3. Continuing treatment by a healthcare professional
4. A period of incapacity of more than three calendar days

Other physical and mental conditions may be covered as well. Check with your manager or human resources department for additional information.

More often than not, employees who take sick time don't meet the threshold of having a serious health condition. For that reason, the FMLA may have little impact on your decision to document excessive absenteeism in the form of progressive discipline or to ultimately ter-minate an employee who violates your company's absenteeism control policy.

On the other hand, doctors' notes may preclude you from taking any adverse action (including progressive discipline or termination) against an employee for two reasons: (1) if the medical condition is a "disability," the employee will be protected under the ADA and similar state statues, and (2) in jurisdictions mandating paid sick leave, doc-tors' notes generally need not be provided to the employer until the employee has exhausted the minimum paid leave required by statute.

Moreover, in certain states, medical certifications cannot identify the condition being treated. A doctor's note may only tell you the date of the condition's onset and its estimated duration—no more. As a result, de-termining if an FMLA-qualified "serious medical condition" or an ADA "disability" is the cause may be difficult. When in doubt, speak with legal counsel about your rights when you suspect that doctors are padding an employee's file and allowing the individual to take excessive time off. Scenarios like this need to be handled on a case-by-case basis.

SCENARIO 30

Excessive Unscheduled Absence: "No-Fault" System

A "no-fault" attendance control system does just that—it looks beyond the reasons for incidents of unscheduled absence and simply counts the number of occurrences. No-fault systems assume that people will need to be out from time to time and establish numeric thresholds that violate the policy. For example, a hospital may set its no-fault system as follows:

▶ Five incidents of unscheduled absence = verbal warning
▶ Seven incidents of unscheduled absence = written warning
▶ Nine incidents of unscheduled absence = final written warning
▶ Tenth incident of unscheduled absence in a rolling calendar year = termination

The idea behind this kind of system is that it's fair and consistent in its treatment of employees and does not ask for employee justification (as would be the case in an excuse-based system). Conversations with employees governed by a no-fault system are simple and straightforward; what becomes important is that you provide them with a copy of your company policy so that they understand the consequences of future incidents of unscheduled absence. However, no-fault policies can run afoul of federal, state, and local leave laws that prohibit employers from taking any adverse action against employees for certain types of health-related leaves.

The Solution

In a program like the one just outlined, it's best to meet with employees well before they reach the fifth incident. Let's assume that an employee reaches a third incident of unscheduled and unauthorized absence in the rolling calendar year. It would make sense to have the following conversation:

> Hi Rudy, I just wanted to check in with you today in light of yesterday's absence. Are you feeling all right and is everything okay? [*Yes—I just didn't feel well yesterday.*] I understand. I thought this would be a good time to review our attendance policy just as a reminder. As you know, our company has a no-fault attendance control policy, meaning that we don't ask employees to justify or give details about the reasons for their unscheduled absences. We respect that people get sick from time to time, as do their family members, and we don't want to invade anyone's privacy.
>
> However, this is your third incident in the rolling calendar year, and I'm not sure if you're aware how our policy works. At our hospital, we've structured the attendance control policy to allow for four incidents of unscheduled absence in a rolling calendar year without triggering any formal company response.
>
> Therefore, on the fifth incident, you'll receive a formal verbal warning. On the seventh incident, you'll receive a written warning. And on the ninth incident, you'll receive a final written warning. A tenth incident in the rolling calendar year would result in your termination. Here's a copy of the written policy so you can review it. Were you aware of how our policy works, and do you have any questions? [*Actually, I didn't know, so thanks for telling me.*]

Of course. Let's talk more about that, though. I know it's intuitive that companies don't want employees to take unscheduled days off due to illness, but we get that it happens sometimes. Just so you're aware, though, when someone calls in at the last minute, we've got to scramble to get coverage. We either have to redistribute duties for the day so that coworkers can cover for the missing person, or we have to call a temp agency or registry to send someone over, which we rarely get to do because of budget constraints.

I'm telling you all this because I don't want you to take any of this for granted—not that you are, but sometimes people assume that those first four days are "freebies." When that happens, it becomes an issue of *entitlement*. What I'm here to tell you is that employees aren't *supposed to* take them off. They certainly can if there's an illness involved, and I don't want you to misinterpret what I'm saying here to infer that I expect you to come in to work sick. But I don't want you or anyone else on staff to consider those days like extra vacation days. That's not what they're meant to be, and as you might imagine, coworkers can get a little miffed over time if they feel like they're continually being asked to cover for a peer. Could you see how that might happen? [*Yes.*]

Great. Also, if there's some reason you can't show up reliably to work, let's talk about it now. [*There's no other reason.*] Then I hope you're feeling better, and I'm glad you're back. Thanks for meeting with me, and let me know if you need anything or if I can help in any way. [*Thanks.*]

It's interesting how a simple talk like this can go a long way in sensitizing the employee to the fact that you're aware of the absences, tracking them, and holding everyone accountable for being at work with very little exception. Moreover, given that these types of absences may be "protected" under federal or state disability laws, you'll have provided this employee with an opportunity to discuss the reasons for frequent absences, which may lead to the "interactive process" or other accommodations required by the ADA and similar state laws. Many workers do view sick days like vacation days. Once you've outlined your concerns and shared the policy with even one employee, you'll be surprised how few incidents occur in your group from that point forward. They do talk with each other, after all.

SCENARIO 31

Excessive Unscheduled Absence: "Excuse-Based" System

In comparison to a no-fault system, an excuse-based system actually looks at the reasons behind the incidents to determine if discipline is warranted. Those reasons are typically documented in the written warning itself if it comes to that. And the reasons behind the absences are certainly up for discussion in terms of counseling the individual if excessive, unscheduled, and unauthorized absenteeism appears to be a pattern.

The Solution

Here's how you might handle a typical conversation with an employee if your company adheres to an excuse-based attendance control system:

> Jamie, we need to talk about yesterday's absence. Although this hasn't risen to the level of formal progressive discipline, I'm concerned that the number of absences and the reasons for them are becoming problematic.
>
> Yesterday morning at 7:30 a.m., you called to tell me that you wouldn't be able to come to work. I asked you why that was the case, and you told me that you were obligated to attend a family-related function. If that was indeed the case, you could have advised me in advance of the time you needed to be away from work so that I wouldn't have had a last-minute scramble to reassign work to the rest of the staff. Just so you know, I ended up doing the majority of the work on your desk myself, which stopped me from doing my regularly scheduled work, and now I'm behind a day as well.
>
> On May 13, you also failed to report to work without prior notice. When I called you at home at 9:00 a.m., you said you were feeling sick and had overslept. We understand people get sick, and it wouldn't have been a problem if it had only happened that once, but I had previously reminded you and the other members of the staff that if you were ill, you still had the responsibility to contact the company receptionist by 7:00 a.m. so that we could get a temp in to cover your desk. Because you hadn't called in at 7:00 a.m., a half day's productivity was lost.

And back on April 25, you failed to report to work without notice. I asked you why you were out when you returned to work the next day, and you told me you didn't have a "good reason" but that it wouldn't happen again. I didn't pursue the matter any further because that was your first incident of unscheduled absence, and I believed you when you assured me that it wouldn't happen again.

Clearly, I'm a little frustrated here, primarily because I don't know exactly what's going on at your end. However, I'm concerned that this may be becoming an issue of entitlement. It's important that I remind you that employees aren't *supposed* to take sick days off. They certainly can if there's an illness or other legitimate reason involved, but I don't want you or anyone else on staff to consider those days like extra vacation days. That's not what they're meant to be, and as you might imagine, coworkers get upset if they feel like they're continually being asked to cover for a peer. Can you see how that might happen? [*Yes.*]

Okay, then I won't beat the issue into the ground. Just know that three incidents of unscheduled and unauthorized absence in a three-month period, only one of which has a reasonable excuse, really concern me. I expect everyone on our team to hold themselves accountable for all aspects of their and the department's performance. Do I have your commitment that you'll assume responsibility for improving the situation from this point forward? [*Yes.*]

That closing line becomes very important in a situation like this. After all, Jamie is now cognizant of the fact that you're aware that she let you down on April 25 and, more important, that you haven't forgotten. You've increased her sensitivity to unscheduled absences, and you've done it very nicely—but the point has been driven home. You'll likely experience a significant reduction in Jamie's unscheduled absences from this point forward.

SCENARIO 32

Patterning Excessive, Unscheduled Absence Around Weekends

As defined earlier, a pattern is a frequent, predictable, and observable employee action that repeats itself over time. When employees take more than 50 percent of their time off around weekends or holidays, a pattern may be established. It's worth sensitizing a subordinate to the fact that you're aware that the occurrences often happen on Mondays and Fridays.

The Solution

After you've discussed the issue of excessive incidents of unscheduled and unauthorized absence, it's time to add the following language to your discussion regarding the potential patterning that you're starting to see. Once an employee realizes that you're onto that particular little factoid, the problem typically fixes itself.

Sarah, now that we've discussed the quantity of incidents, we've got to discuss the quality, so to speak. Yes, I look at the number of unscheduled absences. But I also look to see when they're occurring on the calendar. In your case, two of the three incidents happened on a Friday or a Monday, and that's a separate problem.

The way we look at it, any time an employee takes more than 50 percent of unscheduled time off around weekends and holidays, we may have a pattern problem on our hands. In your case, 66 percent of your incidents occur on either end of your regularly scheduled time off. That's an additional problem and is considered a separate infraction, as far as I'm concerned.

Yes, three incidents won't trigger anything formal at our company in terms of a disciplinary response. And two of three incidents occurring on Mondays or Fridays may be pure coincidence. But I need you to become very sensitive to this issue as well. In short, I need you to fix both areas. Can I count on you to do that? [*Yes.*] Good. Thanks for meeting with me and agreeing to fix this issue.

And voilà—mission accomplished! Once an employee experiences this sit-down and commits to fixing the problem, the patterning problem should stop immediately. Now, of course, you may have a sick employee who shows up to work on Monday morning out of fear of having one more of these "talks" with you, but hey—you can just emphasize that "if you're really sick we want you home getting better, not getting other people sick here. But it's only for when you're really sick, not for creating long weekends." At least then you'll be part of the solution and have a better handle on what's going on staffwise.

SCENARIO 33

Rolling Calendar Year Maneuvers

Many companies employ a rolling calendar year when it comes to their absenteeism control policies. In comparison to a calendar year, which simply runs from January 1 to December 31, a rolling calendar year goes backward from today's date. So if today is May 13, 2019, the rolling calendar year goes back a year to May 14, 2018.

As you might guess, some employees game the system. They pattern their time off around the calendar year, so that when one date falls off the calendar from a year ago, they take a new day, always conscious of staying below a fifth incident (or whatever number would trigger a first, formal warning). These "gamers" think they're getting away with something—until you sit them down and let them know that you're on to their game.

Note that in a union environment, your ability to enforce a policy that limits such calendar gaming may be restricted. That's because if the collective bargaining agreement spells out a five/seven/nine/ten system, you may not be able to reinterpret the rules and censure employees for taking new days when old days roll off the rolling calendar. In addition, your ability to limit gaming may be prohibited if an employee has accrued paid sick leave pursuant to a state or city law and is using that bank to cover the absence. In either scenario, you can still appeal to the employee's sense of responsibility and commitment, but you may not be able to formalize any disciplinary action. Here, we're assuming the employee in question is at-will and working in a jurisdiction that does not have state or city mandated paid sick leave.

The Solution

Here's how your conversation might sound:

> Wes, now that we've discussed the number or quantity of inci-
> dents, we've got to discuss the quality, so to speak. Yes, I look
> at the number of unscheduled and unauthorized absences. But I
> also look to see when they're occurring on the calendar. In your
> case, you seem to be taking time off whenever a prior incident
> rolls off the rolling calendar year.
>
> Here's how I came up with that. When you took the day off yes-
> terday, May 13, I noticed that you also had an absence on May 13
> of last year. So now that it's one year later, we can't count the May
> 13 incident from last year toward the five incidents necessary to
> receive a formal warning. Therefore, in essence, the day that one
> incident fell off the calendar, you immediately took another day.
>
> Now I'm not accusing you of doing this on purpose or of
> gaming the system. I realize that this may have totally been by
> coincidence. But you've got to be careful here: If you create what
> looks like a pattern, taking an unscheduled and unauthorized day
> off any time an older incident falls off the rolling calendar, it will
> be a problem and it won't work for me.
>
> I'm not unreasonable, but if I sense that an employee is
> gaming the system and taking off new time once older dates have
> fallen off the radar screen, then that will be considered a separate
> offense from the number of unauthorized days off.
>
> I'm sure if you were the supervisor, you wouldn't want people
> on your staff who report to you working within the system this
> way. Again, I'm not accusing you of anything. But I don't want
> you to cause problems in your career because of a perception
> that you're the kind of employee who might take advantage of the
> goodwill built into the system. I wanted to heighten your aware-
> ness because it could get in the way of an otherwise successful
> career with our company. Can you understand why I'd want to give
> you that heads-up? [*Yes, I understand.*]

Once again, you'll have proactively addressed a pending problem
situation by sensitizing a subordinate to how behaviors might appear
to others. Congratulations again, Ms. Supervisor—job well done!

SCENARIO 34

Excessive Tardiness

Regular attendance and punctuality are expected of all employees. Workers are expected to commence and end their work on schedule, meaning that they've not only clocked in by 8:00 a.m. but that they're at their workstation and ready to begin work at that time as well. Arriving late or leaving early poses significant problems for your company, and both fall under the definition of *tardiness*. As most employees know, repeated incidents of tardiness may result in disciplinary action, including possible discharge.

When documenting problems relating to excessive tardiness in the form of a written warning, it's important that you list the arrival (or departure) times of the individual so that the appropriate record is made. In the following example, the expected starting time is 8:00 a.m.:

Date	Arrival Time
Friday, February 15, 2019	8:17 a.m.
Thursday, February 14, 2019	8:22 a.m.
Monday, January 14, 2019	8:06 a.m.
Wednesday, January 9, 2019	9:30 a.m.
Wednesday, December 5, 2018	8:04 a.m.

Of course, if you have an electronic timekeeping system, there will be no dispute as to the time of clock-in. However, if you measure this manually, make sure the employee knows at the time of occurrence that you've marked down a late starting time so that he can't later argue that you mistakenly jotted down the wrong arrival time.

It's true that many good, hardworking people are occasionally late. However, habitually late workers cause serious problems to both productivity and morale. After all, an employee who is habitually late can have a demoralizing effect on other staff members who arrive to work on time. Worse, lateness tends to be infectious: Before you know it, others will start seeing that there is no consequence for such behavior. Finally, be aware that tardiness caused by an unforeseeable illness may be protected under state and city paid sick leave laws. Many of these statutes permit employees to use sick leave in small increments (e.g., two hours), allowing employees who show up late to work to apply accrued paid sick leave to the time off.

Of course, the key question is, where do you draw the line on tardiness? And how do you select one person to discipline for *habitual* lateness when you don't discipline others for *occasional* lateness? Ah, isn't management fun?

The Solution

Generally speaking, if a person is ten or more minutes late more than four times in a given month, it may be time for a gentle chat. Assuming the employee's overall performance is acceptable (with the exception of this one little issue), your conversation might sound like this:

> Mark, I enjoy having you on our team, and I'm impressed by the consistent work that you do. I've got one issue that I'll need your help with, though, and I'm wondering if you could guess what that is. [*My tardiness?*] Correct! I'm glad you see it, too. I don't want to make too much of an issue over this, but I do get concerned if occasional lateness turns into habitual tardiness, and I don't want this to become a slippery slope. Is this something that you can fix now that I've brought it to your attention? [*Yes, and I'm sorry I made you have to have this talk with me.*]

And that should be all that's necessary to fix this minor problem before it becomes more progressive and pronounced. Now what about the employee who already demonstrates habitual tardiness? How do you address his situation once the problem is noticeable to others, possibly causing them to feel resentful? In such cases, try a discussion like this:

> Rebecca, I enjoy having you on our team, and I'm impressed by the consistent work that you do. I've got one issue that I'll need your help with, though, and I'm wondering if you could guess what that is. [*My tardiness?*] Correct! I'm glad you see it too.
> One of the things you need to understand is that although your work product and customer service are very strong, your ability to get to work on time makes up a significant part of your overall

performance as well. And I'm afraid that your being late four times in the last two weeks has been noticed by others and may be negatively affecting morale. *That's why I'll need to ask you to take a whole new approach to timeliness and assume full responsibility for fixing this part of your overall performance.* Can I count on you for that?

[*Well, other people come in late too. I don't mean to place blame or get others in trouble, but are they going to be held to this same standard?*] Yes and no. First, Rebecca, there's a difference between occasional and habitual lateness. I'm not an ogre about these things: I realize that occasionally someone may be running late for whatever reason. But in my mind, that's one day a month, not four days in two weeks. Your tardiness is now becoming habitual, meaning that I have seen you arriving to work ten to thirty minutes late every few days.

In short, treating situations like these *consistently* is key here, not necessarily treating all situations *the same.* So, yes, I will remind everyone to cut down on any unnecessary tardiness, and that message will be one of the talking points at our next staff meeting. But I'd like *you* to focus on your performance right now. Does that sound fair? [*Well, okay.*]

Good. Then will you make a commitment to me to avoid future incidents of lateness to the best of your ability and to assume responsibility for the perception problem that's been created? [*Yes.*] Thanks—I appreciate your willingness to help here.

Tardiness typically fixes itself after a gentle talk. Just remember to distinguish between occasional and chronic lateness when talking with repeat offenders. You'll find that one talk does it all when dealing with this particular workplace topic. If a written warning needs to follow because the behavior doesn't change, however, then refer to the date of this conversation in your written warning to demonstrate that you've accorded the employee with workplace due process. If necessary, depending on jurisdiction, this will also demonstrate that you are not basing the adverse action on any time off protected by state or city paid sick leave laws, but rather that you are basing it on reasons not protected by statute (e.g., traffic, oversleeping, etc.).

SCENARIO 35

Exempt Employees Who Choose to Come and Go as They Please

All this discussion about tardiness leaves one more target area needing redress: exempt employees who see nothing wrong with arriving two hours late or leaving two hours early. After all, exempt workers aren't paid for their time: They're paid for their work product and the result of their labors. Since they're not paid for their time, they may reason that time shouldn't be a boundary or a hindrance.

Funny enough, in a way this logic is right on the button. Nonexempt workers are protected by the provisions of the Fair Labor Standards Act (FLSA) and by similar state laws. They are paid for their time and will be docked if they come in late but receive overtime pay for hours worked in excess of forty in a week and (depending on the state) daily overtime as well. Exempt employees, in comparison, are "exempt" from the protections of the FLSA (which is where the term *exempt* comes from) and can work until midnight every night without receiving a dime extra in pay. The question is, does that give them carte blanche to come and go any time they want, and does that limit your discretion as their supervisor to insist that they adhere to normal business hours?

The Solution

Before you engage in a debate about the merits of differing interpretations of the FLSA's intent, just remember to keep it simple: Even though exempt employees are not paid for their time, you still have every right as a supervisor to expect all employees—exempt or nonexempt—to adhere to regular hours.

Here's how the situation played out at a research hospital where one particular scientist felt he had the discretion to come and go as he pleased. The laboratory head confirmed with human resources that, generally speaking, he had the right to insist that the researcher arrive at work at 8:00 a.m. and remain in the lab until 5:00 p.m. Furthermore, the laboratory head clarified for HR that there was a logical business rationale for his request: The employee in question needed to be available to meet with colleagues and clinicians who visited the lab on a regular basis. Armed with that information, the laboratory head held the following conversation with the researcher:

Doctor Johnson, I needed to meet with you in private because I see that you're keeping very erratic hours. This morning you came in at 10:30 a.m., and last night you left at 4:00 p.m. I'm not quite sure why that's happening since you haven't mentioned anything to me or gotten my advance approval to arrive late or leave early, so would you mind sharing with me what's going on?

[*Well, I had to come back at midnight the night before last to check on my petri dish experiments, and I thought it would be appropriate to sleep in this morning. Last night I left at 4:00 p.m. because I knew I'd have to be back in the lab at midnight, so is this a problem?*]

Well, yes, it is for two reasons. First, you didn't ask for permission or otherwise give me any heads-up that you'd need to come back at midnight. As a result, I didn't have all the information I needed to assess the situation accurately. If you told me, I wouldn't have had a problem granting you that flexibility. But because I didn't know, other employees felt that it was unfair that you could come and go at your own discretion, which creates a morale issue. Had I known about your midnight returns, I could have explained that your schedule has been approved for legitimate business reasons and is not a problem.

Second, though, I want to be clear that there is a legitimate business need for you to be present during normal hours so that you can meet with colleagues, clinicians, and others visiting the lab on a regular basis. Just because you're an exempt employee doesn't mean that you're not accountable for your time or that you can come and go as you please. It's true that we don't pay you according to the hours you log in, and we also don't track your comings and goings in that sense. However, I still expect you to be here at 8:00 a.m. and work until 5:00 p.m. unless you've received advance approval to leave early or arrive late.

Special Note

Treating exempt employees as nonexempt workers in any manner may risk destruction of their exempt status. Deductions for work-rule violations requiring exempt employees to punch a time clock or awarding hour-for-hour compensatory time off are examples of how an employer may destroy exempt status and be required to pay back overtime. Although that's not really at issue in the previous example, be sure and check with your human resources department or with qualified employment counsel to ensure that your approach poses no threat to the exempt status of your workers.

SCENARIO 36

FMLA Abuse: Failure to Provide Appropriate Medical Documentation

Administering FMLA leaves is a challenge in many organizations. Some employees may perceive time away from work as a guaranteed entitlement, not realizing that they have defined responsibilities throughout the leave period. Many companies do not strictly hold employees to the terms of their FMLA leave—whether they fail to provide appropriate documentation or follow their doctors' documented directives—due to a lack of proactive lead management or perhaps a fear of creating a claim of retaliation and disability discrimination. Making matters worse, FMLA abuse carries with it the possibility for liquidated damages, and some courts have held that supervisors may be deemed personally liable. As an operational leader in your organization, it becomes all the more important that you partner closely with human resources, your leave administrator, and legal counsel to address these matters.

> The Family Medical Leave Act, or FMLA, is a labor standard and leave law enforced by the US Department of Labor. Qualifications are worth discussing with legal counsel, but generally speaking, covered workers must be employed for at least twelve months, have worked at least 1,250 hours in the preceding calendar year, and work at a worksite where there are more than fifty employees within a seventy-five-mile radius.

FMLA leave comes in two varieties, block leave and intermittent leave. Employees with doctors' notes permitting intermittent leave sometimes believe they can come and go with impunity, assuming their employers have no say in the matter. Wrong! As an employer, you can require employees to justify their FMLA-protected leaves by complying with the terms established under company policy and their physicians' guidance. When faced with a scenario where an employee fails to provide appropriate medical documentation to continue with a leave of absence, the employer is a bit behind the eight ball because the leave is already underway. It's optimal, therefore, to meet with the individual before the leave is approved, to establish your expectations moving forward with the FMLA leave of absence—whether it's a block or intermittent leave.

The Solution

Before the leave commences, establish your expectations as follows:

Farid, Sandy from human resources met with me to let me know that you brought in a doctor's note authorizing one to four days off per month as an "intermittent leave" under the FMLA, which we're happy to grant. Further, we're here to support you in any way we can while this intermittent leave is in effect. So one of the reasons I wanted to meet with you was to let you know that I'm here for you and want to tell you that your getting better is my first priority, as it is yours. That being said, Farid, whenever anyone is about to initiate an FMLA leave, I like to meet with them to discuss our expectations moving forward. Does that sound reasonable? [*Sure.*]

Good. Then let me begin by saying that while your health comes first, this job-protected period isn't something to take for granted. You'll be expected to produce medical certifications from time to time that justify your continued intermittent leave of absence, and I expect you to stay on top of that key responsibility, to make things easier for the leave administrator in HR. Does that sound fair? [*Yes.*]

Next, there's a timeliness issue at hand in situations like this. I've seen employees misunderstand the leave rules in ways that cause problems for their coworkers. For example, in our call center when I first began ten years ago, employees would simply vanish for the afternoon and ask their coworkers to tell their supervisor that they had to leave because of "FMLA" (said with a wink). That's not how we do things around here any longer. . . . If possible, intermittent absences should be scheduled in advance. If you need to leave, then out of respect for your supervisor and coworkers, you have to speak with your supervisor directly before you walk out the door. And you need to inform your supervisor that the occurrence falls under your open intermittent FMLA claim, so the supervisor can alert human resources to document the time away from work.

If a supervisor isn't available, then I expect you to tell me, and if I'm unavailable, to inform another supervisor. In the off chance that no member of the management team is available, you can leave but you should email or otherwise notify your supervisor, explaining the emergency. I want this process to be honest, transparent, and thoughtful so that there's no drama down the line or assumptions of ill intent. Is that a fair approach, in your opinion? [*Yes.*]

Good. Then let's work together to get you well again, and let me know if you run into any unforeseen roadblocks along the way. Making sure that your medical documentation is submitted on time and remains current is your key responsibility, along with ensuring that company policies are followed and that your supervisor is in sync with your needs. No surprises, Farid, and honesty and openness all around. Do I have your commitment that you'll take that approach to this upcoming leave? [*Yes.*] Glad to hear it, and I'm here if you need me for anything.

Once the leave has begun and an employee fails to provide the necessary medical certification to extend the leave via a medical provider's note, continue as follows:

Farid, Sandy from HR, our leave administrator, reached out to me to share some concerns she has about your not providing appropriate medical documentation to justify your ongoing intermittent FMLA leave of absence. As you know, company policy states that we have the right to require medical certification for an employee's serious health condition. And employees are given fifteen calendar days to submit medical certification to justify or extend the leave. Are you familiar with that policy? [*Yes.*]

The certification of a serious health condition typically includes the date the condition began, the estimated duration, and that you are unable to perform one or more of the key functions of the job. Further, recertification may be requested after the time period that the healthcare provider estimated in the original certification. So I'm confused: Sandy said that HR has reached out to you on three separate occasions, and you haven't provided the appropriate medical documentation to continue your leave. What am I missing or not understanding about the facts that Sandy shared with me? [*Sorry, I haven't had time to see the doctor.*]

Okay, let's take care of this today then. Why don't you contact your medical provider and ask for an emergency appointment this afternoon? We'll arrange to cover your desk, and this way you can focus on complying with the FMLA requirements, so we're able to continue your leave without undue interruption. If your physician can't get you in today for any reason, let me know when they're next available, so we can ensure you get this taken care of. Remember, Farid, this leave isn't a guarantee—you've got to uphold your end of the bargain by providing medical certification at appropriate intervals. Are we clear on that going forward? [*Yes.*]

Farid, there's one other thing. . . . This can become a disciplinary event if you fail to provide the appropriate medical certification when required. I really don't want to go down that road and would appreciate our not having to discuss this again. Do I have your commitment that you'll comply with HR's requirements in all instances relating to your intermittent FMLA leave? [*Yes.*] Great. Why don't you call your healthcare provider now and see if you can get in later today and, if not, when they'll be available to meet with you next. At the end of the day, please follow up with Sandy with a status update from your physician.

Nothing replaces an open and honest conversation about medical leave expectations when trying to get employees to adhere to the program. As an operational leader, stepping in may make sense, but keep your discussion focused on your expectations of timeliness, ongoing communication, and compliance. Avoid straying in the direction of the underlying medical condition: You generally don't want or need to know what's causing the need for a leave. When you acquire knowledge of the underlying medical condition, you may become vulnerable to an accusation that you used that knowledge to behave in a discriminatory manner. Remember that under the FMLA, some courts have held that supervisors may be personally liable, and legal remedies include the potential for liquidated damages. Not something to take lightly.

Special Note

The law is changing rapidly in this area, and many states and cities are enacting paid sick leave laws protecting employees who need time off from work to care for themselves or a family member or for other protected reasons. It is critical that you check with qualified legal counsel to ensure that your attendance policy and FMLA leave program are compliant with these laws, especially before you terminate or discipline an employee for excessive absenteeism, tardiness, or failure to follow FMLA guidelines when a protected FMLA leave of absence is in place.

SCENARIO 37

FMLA Abuse: Failure to Follow the Terms of the Medical Certification

Unfortunately, employees sometimes abuse their protected FMLA leaves. For the scenario that follows, let's examine an employee who comes in late often, while the physician's note makes no mention of the need to accommodate tardiness for the individual's particular health condition.

The Solution

Sarah comes in late a lot, and her supervisor assumes that her tardiness is covered under the employee's intermittent FMLA certification. It all comes to a head when Sarah calls in and states that she won't be able to make it into work due to inclement weather; two hours later, the weather warning is lifted, and Sarah calls back and states she won't be coming in for the rest of the day because of her intermittent FMLA leave. The supervisor then meets with you, the department manager, and with human resources to discuss the ongoing issues with lateness—only to learn that Sarah's medical note makes no mention of a need to accommodate sporadic lateness.

The meeting then takes place with the department head taking the lead role and with the immediate supervisor and human resources leave administrator present, as follows:

Sarah, there are numerous issues we need to bring to your attention regarding your failure to abide by the terms of your medical certification. First, yesterday you called in at 8:00 a.m. and said you weren't coming in due to inclement weather. By 10:00 a.m., the weather warning had lifted, and you then called and stated that you wished to use intermittent FMLA time instead of an inclement weather day, to cover this particular absence.

You don't have the discretion to arbitrarily designate time off as FMLA time, unless it falls under the terms of your current medical certification. Out of frustration with your ongoing incidents of tardiness, and especially yesterday's events with the twists and turns relating to your excuses, your supervisor notified human resources of potential abuse of the FMLA system. I was called in as the department head, and we all reviewed your current medical certification together. Suffice it to say that we were surprised to learn that arriving late at work is not an FMLA-protected activity, according to the terms of your current medical certification.

Your supervisor didn't realize this, and it appears that you may have taken advantage of the situation. You have the right to have your medical certification updated and amended, but understand that going forward, we expect you to adhere to the terms of the FMLA medical certification that's on file with us. Use of FMLA outside the terms of your medical certification is not acceptable and may result in disciplinary action, up to and including dismissal of employment. Further, except if authorized (meaning if your medical certification is amended, or your supervisor approves the tardiness in advance), the tardiness clock starts again now. While we won't discipline you for the tardies you've taken up to now when your supervisor incorrectly assumed they were covered by FMLA, your supervisor now has clear instruction and my support to hold you accountable to departmental attendance and tardiness standards—the exception being for anything specifically outlined in your medical certification.

Again, you can have that document reviewed and amended by your physician at any time. Let me make myself clear, however: FMLA isn't a game; it's not a free pass to do as you please, and if you fail to abide by the terms outlined in the medical certification on file, then disciplinary action, up to and including dismissal, will likely result.

I'd like a commitment from you right now that you'll revise your assumptions about the FMLA benefit, that you'll appreciate it for the value it provides and not attempt to take advantage of its protections, and that we'll not have to have another conversation like this, because you're about to become a role model and example for others of how to work within the FMLA program. Do I have your commitment? [*Yes.*] Do you have any additional questions that we can answer as a group? [*No.*] Good. Thank you for meeting with us, and please see Sandy in human resources any time you have questions about how the leave program works or if you need to have your medical certification updated.

By focusing your expectations on good faith communication and holding the individual accountable to the terms of the medical certification, the problem should disappear. You called Sarah out on the assumptions she was making about the leave protection program, you presented a united front so that she couldn't later pit her department head or human resources against her supervisor, and you reminded her to appreciate the benefits this relatively new law provides. Congratulations on completing a multifaceted discussion for her betterment and the betterment of her team.

SCENARIO 38

FMLA Extension: Engaging in the ADA Interactive Process

The federal ADA defines a "disability" as a physical or mental impairment that limits one or more major life activities. (State interpretations may be more restrictive than the federal standard.) Interestingly, the ADA covers people who may be "regarded as" having an impairment, even if they don't. And unlike many other employment laws, the ADA applies to job applicants, not just to employees. Further, knowledge of a disability may be imputed to an employer, even if an employee doesn't request an accommodation. So the ADA can be exceptionally difficult to manage on a practical basis. This is compounded by the fact that it carries punitive damages for any employer that runs afoul of its requirements and guidelines.

Bottom line: Don't rush through anything that has to do with ADA reasonable accommodation obligations. Case law is still being actively tested and challenged, and you don't want to one day inadvertently end up as a footnote in some law book with a citation reading, "*John Doe vs. [YOUR COMPANY NAME HERE]*." Always consult with outside counsel to ensure that you're in compliance, your documentation is sound, and you've requested all the appropriate documentation without "overreaching" into the realm of privacy or HIPAA (Health Insurance Portability and Accountability Act) violations.

The Solution

You still have certain rights as an employer, and it's critical that you ask the right questions to ensure that employees uphold their end of the bargain. For one, employees must engage in the interactive process with you, which means they have to speak with you about reasonable accommodations that can return them to work faster. (For example, they can't just say, "Speak with my doctor," or "Refer to my doctor's note.") Further, you usually have the right to require recertification at certain intervals. Job restructuring or schedule reassignments may be considered reasonable accommodations that your employment attorney can argue should return the individual to work. And you have the right to challenge medical opinions with second and third (final and binding) opinions.

Without getting into the nitty-gritty of the ADA's scope and reach, here's what a standard discussion might sound like. Feel free to amend this questioning template to meet your needs, but vet it with your employment lawyer to ensure that it adheres to both state and federal guidelines.

Dina, I've reviewed your current medical provider's note, and let's discuss again the nature of your reported restrictions. I always focus first on limitations and areas you'll need to avoid, so tell me about your current state when it comes to some of the basics—walking, standing, sitting, lifting, climbing, or other tasks that you should avoid or restrict. I want to make sure the restrictions you're listing match my own understanding of the situation.

I see that your physician has directed you to stop working completely until Friday, May 10. Your physician is approximating that you should be able to return to work on or around Monday, May 13. How confident are you, and how confident is your physician, about that return date?

ALTERNATIVE

Dina, the information from your medical provider is insufficient because the doctor's explanation of your need for an accommodation didn't include a description of your relevant functional limitations. The request for an accommodation needs to be supported by appropriate medical documentation. We'll need supplemental information that addresses your functional limitations in more detail. Can you follow up with your physician and request that additional information? [*Yes.*]

Great. Remind me again of all the accommodations you'd like to request that will help you return to work or that will otherwise justify a continued leave of absence. Can I expect to hear back from you in a week, after you've connected with your doctor? [*Yes.*]

At this point, it makes sense to list the accommodations discussed, using a simple template like the following:

ACCOMMODATION CONSIDERED

☐ Offered by employer and accepted by employee:

_____

_____

☐ Details of accommodation:

_____

_____

☐ Considered by employer but rejected because employee unable to safely perform essential job functions, or employee did not possess occupational qualifications (details):

_____

_____

☐ Suggested by employee but rejected by employer because:

_____

_____

☐ Offered by employer but rejected by employee because:

_____

_____

☐ Other considerations and discussion points:

_____

_____

Employ this documentation format for each phone call and in-person visit you have with your employee while he is on leave to demonstrate your attempts at returning the individual to work and engaging in the ADA interactive process. Note that it's truly a "process," not a one-time event, and it's crucial that you document your efforts over time at proactively rehabilitating the employee.

During such ADA reasonable accommodation discussions, it's common to share a copy of the current job opening list with the individual. Likewise, the HR specialist or office manager who handles such dialogues with employees will recommend a preliminary list of positions the company believes may meet the employee's occupational qualifications and restrictions. When reassignment to a vacant position is possible, congratulations: This special form of accommodation will return your employee to work, which is always the best remedy for prolonged leaves of absence where workers sometimes prefer to remain at home. (*The longer they're out, the longer they're likely to stay out*, goes the common sense mantra of leave of absence professionals.)

However, there may be no reasonable accommodations available to return the employee to work or to accommodate a current work restriction: no adjustment to her current position or temporary transfer to an open position may be at hand. Under such circumstances, an extension of leave due to current medical restrictions may be the only option available. The question is how long must your company keep the position open? And the answer to that question is a book unto itself!

An indefinite leave beyond the FMLA twelve-week period is not required by the ADA and shouldn't necessarily be accommodated. But on a practical basis, it can be difficult to end the ADA interactive dialogue when the employee is trying new medications, new physical therapy regimes, switching doctors, and so forth. Just remember that there's no six-month "magic window," and most defense lawyers will advise you that even the one-year anniversary mark of a leave is no guarantee that you can separate employment without significant risk. Again, speak with qualified employment counsel on a case-by-case basis—consider it a cheap insurance policy that will help you sleep better at night. More significantly, the extension of time may protect your organization from unwanted liability and help your employee return to work in the healthiest and safest way possible.

Special Note

As an employer, you may have the right to confirm that the employee has a physical or mental disability under the ADA, when the disability isn't obvious. However, the inquiry should be limited to what is necessary for verifying the existence of the disability and for ascertaining a reasonable accommodation. Medical information must be kept confidential and should only be reviewed by authorized individuals in the human resources department or other designated members of management. Supervisors and managers may need to understand the offered accommodation (the "how"); on the other hand, they don't need to know anything about the employee's physical or mental restrictions (the "what" or "why"). If an employee accidentally discloses the nature of the underlying illness, a supervisor should simply state, "I don't need to know what the nature of the illness is, and it won't be used as a consideration in returning you to work or otherwise continuing to engage with you in our accommodation discussions."

7

Lack of Requisite Skills

Have you ever wondered what makes some people successful in the business world, while others never quite reach their desired level of achievement? Generally speaking, three ingredients are necessary to make someone successful: intelligence, motivation, and communication skills. If any of these three factors is missing, a career will typically fall short of its potential. For example, deep intelligence without motivation will typically not go very far. Intense motivation without the ability to bond with others makes it difficult for a career to take root because people skills make up the glue that bonds us together. And great communication and people skills without intelligence and motivation will make it equally difficult to launch a successful career in business.

All people have differing levels of intelligence, motivation, and communication abilities, and all three of these traits determine an individual's competence. However, although employers can't really impact these innate character traits in others, there are subgroups of characteristics that are indeed "influenceable" from the standpoint of human interaction and conditioning.

When employees excel in areas such as organization, time management, technical know-how, and logical problem solving, their careers will typically stand out, and your company will reap the benefit. However, when these same skills atrophy due to lack of application or motivation, then careers stall and company performance suffers.

When you're challenged by subordinates who suffer from mediocre performance, look first to create a work environment in which they can motivate themselves. Look second at providing the appropriate training and skills acquisition opportunities to ensure their success.

And look third at holding them accountable for their own growth and development. After all, no supervisor can force a subordinate to educate herself by reading a technical manual, annual report, or industry newsletter. However, every supervisor can set high expectations and raise the bar so that an entire team of individuals excels, feels supported, and works together to reinvent themselves in light of your company's changing needs.

This chapter focuses on topics where requisite skills will make or break a new hire or determine how far a tenured employee will go in his career at your company. Keep your requirements simple, keep your employees' eyes on the goal, and keep your expectations high. These issues may feel subtle to you and difficult to articulate at times, but they're very important both for your team's performance and for the good of the individuals involved.

SCENARIO 39

Inferior Job Knowledge

Where do workers acquire the skills, knowledge, and abilities necessary to perform in certain roles and excel in their careers? Well, it depends: If your company prides itself on hiring a lot of recent graduates and training them (while benefiting from their motivation, willingness to work hard and put in long hours, and low salary expectations), then industry and technical knowledge will typically come from your corporate training and development group. On the other hand, if you generally hire seasoned professionals with strong records of industry knowledge, longevity, and career progression, then you'll end up paying higher wages for the benefit of that level of experience and accomplishment.

The Solution

Let's assume your company falls in the latter category, and you've hired someone with the experience and competencies that make her well qualified to perform in her current role. You soon find out, however, that she just doesn't seem to be catching on or applying herself. As a result, you wonder about the investment she's made into her career and into your company since joining your organization. Your conversation might sound like this:

Marilyn, we need to talk. The videoconference that we just participated in exposed some issues that I've been questioning, and we should really address them at this point. There's a saying that you can tell a lot more about a person's gravitas by the caliber of the questions they ask than by the statements they make. On our videoconference call with Atlanta just now, you asked a few questions that lead me to believe that you're not as up to speed with certain things within our company as you should be.

For example, when you asked what the revenues were of the XYZ Company that we're planning on acquiring, I think you threw everyone back. The due diligence has already been completed, and we went through various discussions regarding revenue history and projections two calls ago. Your question was so out of the blue that I'm sure others were wondering if you had been on the calls—which you had—or if you were having a temporary brain freeze.

Then you asked a question about the pension funding liabilities and wage and hour claims exposure we had, which were both accounted for in the due diligence report, which you should have read prior to the call. Am I missing something here, or does what I'm saying have merit? [*No, you're right. I'm sorry.*]

Okay, but there's no need to apologize. Finish your sentence: "I'm sorry" and what? [*Well, I'll be more careful about asking questions about things that have already been discussed.*] I agree, Marilyn, but it's more than that: Your questions aren't only off relative to the conversation at hand, but they're out of sequence with the whole acquisition and due diligence processes, at least in terms of how our company handles them. Listen, I don't know what to say other than the fact that you've got to bring yourself up to speed very quickly. With all due respect, you're in damage-control mode at this point, and you've got to assume responsibility for fixing this perception problem. After three months with our company, you should know these things. You've already been trained, you've completed two due diligence assignments on potential acquisitions, and you've visited some of our portfolio companies to understand what those business models look like from the inside out.

I don't want to think that there was some misrepresentation on your résumé in terms of accurately describing your background and achievements, or that you've somehow either burned out early or lost interest in our company. But something is amiss.

I like you personally and enjoy working with you, but I have to let you know that you're at a critical juncture in your career with us at this point. Sleep on this, talk it over with family and friends, but when you come back to work tomorrow, I need to know if you're on board, and if so, what your action plan will be to reinvent yourself and sharpen your image in the eyes of the rest of acquisitions and the asset management teams.

Will you make that commitment to me? [*Yes.*] Good. Then set a time for us to meet tomorrow and let me know what you decide. Remember, I'll respect your decision to leave if that's what you ultimately come up with. But if you decide to stay, I'll expect a full plan of action demonstrating how you're going to excel and reinvent yourself now that you've spent three months at our company, and we've invested that much time in you. Thanks very much, and I'll wait to hear from you.

Phew! Not an easy conversation, but in light of the misdirected comments that Marilyn made, you'll certainly want to have this conversation with her first, before any of your peers who were on the conference call ask what's going on. If that happens, your simple response will have to be that you recognized the problem and addressed it with her right after the conference call. She'll let you know tomorrow if she's on board or if she'll resign. It's unfortunate that these types of conversations have to take place from time to time, but salary is typically the highest expense on a company's operating statement. If you show that you're not guarding and fostering resources correctly, it can reflect poorly on your own career.

SCENARIO 40

Lack of Technical Skills

Inferior job knowledge occurs when an employee demonstrates an overall lack of understanding of process flows, product knowledge, and generally how things get done. A lack of technical skills, in comparison, is a subset of inferior job knowledge where a worker doesn't know how to apply the tools of the trade.

Let's look at the case of an administrative assistant who doesn't know how to complete basic spreadsheet functions. As a result, she spends much of her time asking coworkers for help rather than communicating with her boss about her shortcomings. She's taken the company's Introduction to Spreadsheets class but still is very intimidated every time she has to open an Excel spreadsheet.

The Solution

Inviting employees to take classes that help strengthen their skills is a critical first step in improving performance. Indeed, plaintiff's attorneys have proffered a legal concept known as "failure to train," whereby they allege that companies were remiss in providing workers with the tools necessary to succeed and therefore committed wrongful termination in letting the substandard performer go.

Some people are just afraid of computers, and you can't seem to understand how they've gotten this far in their careers without them. When that is the case, proceed as follows:

Leah, we've got to talk about your Excel skills again. I know that we sent you to training for a full day last month to go over the basics of spreadsheets, and I recall your telling me how helpful that class was. [*Yes, it was.*] Okay, so let me ask you, how comfortable are you with spreadsheet basics at this point? [*Oh, I'm fairly comfortable.*]

Well, I'm glad to hear that, but when I walked by Sally's cubicle this morning, I saw you standing over her asking how to perform a simple sorting and filtering function. Do you recall that? [*Yes.*]

That concerns me. Filtering is as simple as spreadsheeting gets. I'm wondering how you spent eight hours of company time and company expense learning Excel basics, only to not understand how to sort data appropriately. [*Well, sometimes I forget and need to be reminded.*]

I'm sorry, but that's not an acceptable answer. When the company pays for you to attend a daytime workshop, we have an expectation that you'll assume responsibility for educating yourself, staying abreast of what you've learned, and filling in any holes by practicing on your own. Simply going to an eight-hour workshop and assuming that you've fulfilled your commitment isn't enough.

Here's what I'm thinking: You need to review all of your notes and all the materials that you received at last month's workshop. I'll then want you to prepare a report of all the various functions that you know how to do using Excel. Grade each of those functional areas on a scale of 1 to 5, with 5 meaning that you're an expert in that area, and 1 meaning that you really don't understand it or remember how to do it at all.

I'll keep a copy of your assessment with the understanding that I will assign you work in all areas where you graded yourself a 5. I'll then expect you to bring your skills up to par (which I'd say is a 3) by the end of the month. At that point, I want you to enroll in the Intermediate Excel course that we offer. When you're done with that course, I'll want you to do the same exercise.

I won't force you to take an Advanced Excel course because I probably don't need that level of support, but I would encourage you to do that on your own using the company's tuition reimbursement program. In any case, Leah, I want you to change how you think about company-sponsored training: It's not a free day away from work and a chance to have a break from routine. If we're investing in you, we expect you to master the material that you've learned or actively follow up with the instructor if you have questions.

You really can't keep leaning on your coworkers for help. That's inappropriate and an inefficient use of everyone's time. If you really feel that you can't master these technical basics, then this may not be the right job for you. If that's the case, let me know, and I'll be as supportive as possible. Maybe we could work out a transition plan where you give a longer notice than usual, maybe six to eight weeks, and we'll allow you to interview elsewhere during the business day.

I don't want you to feel like you have no options here. Truthfully, though, if you can't master basic and intermediate Excel within the next month or so, I'm afraid I'll have to initiate formal corrective action in the form of progressive discipline. And that could end up in a termination for cause.

Think about all this, Leah, and let me know how I can help. I know it's frustrating, but it's better to face these things together, openly and honestly, and agree on a plan of action, rather than work around the problem and allow frustration to build up inside. I'll wait to hear from you.

It's interesting how you can make a tough conversation like this very supportive, in essence placing yourself on the same side as your assistant. Remember that one of our golden rules is that it's not what you say, but how you say it. In this case, you were very supportive and presented your ideas objectively, empathetically, and on a problem-to-solution level. As an alternative, you could have simply given Leah a written warning, letting her know that failure to improve her technical skills immediately would result in her being fired. Ouch—talk about pressure!

Whenever possible, demonstrate empathy and understanding, give your subordinates choices and alternatives, and respect whatever decision they ultimately make. However, don't compromise your expectations because you have every right to insist that members of your team have the technical skills necessary to ensure a smooth workflow.

SCENARIO 41

Inadequate Problem-Solving Skills

Much like technical skills, which ensure that employees can use the tools of their trade adequately, problem-solving skills require a basic, logical understanding of your business and its operations so that subordinates can move the work forward. Unfortunately, some employees live more by fear than anything else, and freeze up when it becomes time to make a decision. They defer all issues back to you, which frustrates you and negates their value in the workplace.

Let's go back to Leah, the administrative assistant in the previous example. Let's assume that Leah acts like a deer in the headlights any time she's asked to do something on her own. Instead, she prefers to get step-by-step approval from you every time she needs to do the smallest of things, and she basically avoids any risk associated with making mistakes. Before too long, you realize that you're creating a monster by allowing her to go on this way, and you decide that you have to wean her off you so that she can become an independent member of the team.

The Solution

Once Leah comes in asking an unnecessary question about your approving something, it's time to outline your expectations as follows:

Leah, you shouldn't have to ask me that. We've been working together for a full year now, and I think I've allowed something to get out of hand: You're coming to me to verify things that you already know the answer to, and I'm afraid I'm responsible for that. I should have ended this way of doing things long ago.

Okay, let's review this one more time: If an employee comes into our benefits department asking if he can add his spouse to our company benefit program, what's your response? [*They can add a spouse only if there's been a change in circumstance. In other words, if they just got married or their spouse lost a job within the last thirty days, then the spouse can be added; otherwise, the employee has to wait until the open enrollment period in October to add a family member to our benefits program.*]

That's correct. Now why would you need to ask my permission to add Ted's spouse to our benefits program, knowing that they just got married and you have a copy of the marriage certificate in your hand? [*Well, I always like to check.*]

Okay, then that's what we'll change. You don't need to check with me on things that are that basic. Sure, you could let me know that you put in to add Ted's wife to our benefits program seeing that he just got married and presented you with a marriage license, but you don't need to ask me for permission. Do you see the difference? [*Yes.*]

Good. Then I've got one more rule for you to follow from now on: Whenever you have a question for me, come to me with two suggested solutions. Think through what those solutions are and ask me which one I prefer. In essence, I want to change your thought pattern about our daily working relationship: My job isn't to give you answers; it's to approve one of the choices you present to me. How's that sound? [*Well, okay, I guess.*]

I'm glad to hear it. Okay, then, how would you redo your question about adding Ted's wife to our benefits program using this new paradigm? [*Well, I'd ask you if you felt it was okay to add Ted's wife to our benefits or if you wanted him to wait until open enrollment.*]

That's right. And what would my answer be? [*Well, it's not really a valid question because we have no choice: We have to add Ted's wife to our benefits because it's a valid change in circumstance that's occurred within thirty days of the event.*] Bingo! That's exactly correct. And that's why this new method of asking questions and suggesting two answers for me to choose from makes so much sense. It will eliminate a lot of unnecessary questioning, and it will get you used to thinking things through more thoroughly and independently.

I'd say this was a very good conversation! How do you feel? [*Well, okay, I guess.*] Great. Then I'm looking forward to your next question and my two choices. Before you know it, you'll have all the answers to questions that come up day to day, and that's always a great feeling.

Problem-solving skills have to be taught—almost forced—when the opportunity arises. If you ask one of your subordinates, "Well, what do you think?" and the person automatically replies, "I don't know," then ask the magical follow-up question, "I know you don't know, but what would your answer be *if you did know*?" It may sound silly, and that question usually raises an eyebrow and a smirk, but getting subordinates to think things through and problem-solve on the spot is a gift. More than anything, it will help build their self-esteem and prepare them for their next promotion.

SCENARIO 42

Substandard Written Expression

Poor writing skills are the plague and scourge of the workplace. The inability to write clearly causes confusion and consternation on the company side, and limits careers on the employee side. For that reason, many companies add a section to their employment application asking job candidates why they want to work for the company and how a position there would help their overall career progression. Yes, the answer itself can be illuminating; but more often than not the employer is looking to see if the individual can write a paragraph.

In certain states, you can't simply terminate someone for poor writing skills. In California, for example, companies with more than twenty-five employees must reasonably accommodate and assist any worker who reveals a problem of illiteracy and who requests company assistance in enrolling in an adult literacy education program, unless that would cause an undue hardship on the employer. In short, you can't terminate an employee who is illiterate but who is otherwise satisfactorily performing his work.

Okay, now that I've got your attention, keep the following in mind as well: Many employees who demonstrate substandard written skills aren't illiterate, they're just sloppy and lack attention to detail. Let's assume that a member of your team has difficulty expressing himself via email. He's by no means illiterate, but he has difficulty with grammar and punctuation as well as composition and style. Between the grammatical errors and the skewed structure of his messages, reading his emails is painful.

The Solution

You'll want to go back to the basics. As an employer, you're under no obligation to turn this writer into Shakespeare, but a training and skills enhancement would go a long way in tightening up his written message.

> Michael, we need to talk. I wanted to spend some time with you reviewing that last email that you sent to the safety committee. It was about three paragraphs long and you sent it last night at 5:00 p.m. Do you recall the one I'm talking about? [*Yes.*]
>
> Good. Tell me about the message you were trying to convey. [*Well, I wanted to reconfirm our assumptions about the safety committee's role and the responsibilities of the floor wardens in case the fire alarms went off.*]
>
> Okay. Do you remember anything in particular about that email? Anything that made it stand out in your mind? [*No.*] Fair

enough, then. Here's a copy of it, so would you mind reading it aloud for me? [*Sure.*]

Now that you've read it out loud, what's your initial impression? [*Well, I see some grammar and spelling errors, and overall it's a bit confusing.*] Yeah, I'd agree, and that's why I wanted to meet with you. Truth be told, your writing skills here don't reflect your abilities in a positive light.

Looking just at that one email as an example, how would you describe the writing? [*It's a bit long-winded and doesn't seem to make a clear point. Now that I'm reading it out loud, I see that the last sentence is probably all everyone needed to know, and it feels like I added those first three paragraphs as a warm-up. I see what you're saying.*]

Good—that's half the problem. Now what advice would you give you if you were me? [*I'd advise me to use the spell checker before I click send, and I'd also advise me to read the memo out loud before distributing it.*] Bingo! That, in and of itself, would go a long way in tightening up your written message. There's another problem, though: Your grammar and punctuation are fairly far off the mark. Let me give you a few examples (showing him the paper): Here you wrote "between you and I" when it should be "between you and me." Here you used the term "irregardless" when the proper word is "regardless." And here you used the term "it's" when you should have written "its."

How do you feel we might be able to strengthen those basic grammar and punctuation skills? [*I could buy a book.*] I totally agree! Your written message will often precede you in the business world, and people's first impression of you will be found in your written word.

There's another issue as well: What was your overall message in your email? [*I wanted everyone to know that the floor wardens needed additional training from the safety committee before they'd be ready to certify.*] Okay, then: Where did you finalize that key thought? [*In my last sentence.*] Then how about we move that up to the top of the memo? In fact, you could make that the subject line of your email message. This way, everyone has the key point without even having to double-click on the message to open it up.

Remember, less is more when it comes to business writing, so whenever you can shorten or sharpen your message, readers will be more inclined to read the entire thing. I don't have a book on composition and style that I could recommend to you offhand, but I'd like you to consider purchasing a book on business writing basics that I think would really help you. Are you game? [*Yes— and thanks for the heads-up.*]

Proper writing skills can be self-taught, and there are a number of excellent works available at your local library or bookstore. Encourage your employees to educate themselves, and consider suggesting that they find a business writing workshop or two through providers like the American Management Association. They'll be giving themselves a critical advantage careerwise, and all you have to do is point them in the right direction.

Just be careful not to base a termination decision solely on a subordinate's literacy challenges. That may open doors that you'd prefer to keep closed in terms of legal vulnerability.

SCENARIO 43

Poor Time Management

There's been so much written about time management that this particular topic could easily fill its own book. Employees who demonstrate poor time management skills often lose things, forget things, and fail to meet deadlines. Supervisors who manage employees with poor time management skills suffer untold anxiety and frustration just because their subordinates didn't learn these critical life skills at an early age. That may seem unfair to you as a supervisor, especially if you're an excellent prioritizer and time manager yourself, but it's a common challenge in the workplace.

When faced with a subordinate who has difficulties keeping on schedule and keeping you up-to-date with everything going on around you, structure your talk around shifting the responsibility for improvement away from the company and back to the employee. Yes, you'll make suggestions and even sign the individual up for a workshop or two on mastering time management. But it's not your responsibility to force subordinates to learn these skills—mastery is up to them. What matters to you is that the work gets done efficiently and on time.

We're too socialized by the time we enter the workforce to change our basic personalities and assumptions about life. Time management is one of those founding principles in our lives that defines who we are. Your job isn't to retool the employee with basic life skills; your role is to point the individual in the right direction as far as acquiring the appropriate skills, while insisting that work productivity continues at an expected level. Your benchmark and your concern is productivity; the employee will have to figure out how to meet the goals of her department and company. That's where this talk might come in handy.

The Solution

Managing professionals should not require that you monitor their every move. If you've ever felt the urge to ask someone on your staff to jot down everything he does for an entire day because you're frustrated with the person's inconsistency in meeting deadlines, reconsider it: Although that may be a worthwhile exercise when someone claims to be underresourced and that additional staff support and head count are needed, it's generally not your responsibility to measure employees by the minute when it comes to their own productivity. Our jobs as managers are to assist our subordinates without holding their hands.

Let's assume that a staff recruiter is responsible for producing monthly metrics for the head of human resources: cost-per-hire, time-to-start, turnover and vacancy analysis, and the like. Your expectation is that the monthly stats should be completed by the first Friday of the first full week of the month. Lo and behold, your staff recruiter misses the deadline three months in a row. When you ask for specifics, you find that she just can't gather all the data to finalize the report. Your conversation might sound like this:

Nancy, I'm frustrated. I'm sure you are too, but the reality is that you haven't met this deadline three months in a row. If I felt it was unrealistic, I'd push it back. Truth be told, though, I feel that if I push it back, you'll simply miss that deadline too. How far off am I in my assumption? [*Probably not too far.*]

Okay then, let's try this again. I want you to conquer this particular challenge of ours because it's important for you to know you can. Are you open to hearing what it looks like from my point of view? [*Sure.*]

Well, first of all, I don't see you taking notes in one consistent place whenever a position is open or a hire is made. If you discipline yourself to note these things as soon as they occur, say in a notebook, on your dry-erase board, or in a spreadsheet, then gathering the data at the end of the month would be far easier.

Second, when you fill a position, you don't immediately close out the requisition folder by pulling all the new hire information that you need (background check results, references, and the like). Likewise, you don't log on to our applicant tracking system and close out the requisition electronically and take the posting down. As a result, candidates keep applying, and you end up chasing your tail at the end of the month trying to sweep all your filled positions into the filled category on the master staffing report. There's a much easier way, which we've discussed before. But I feel like now would be a good time for a reminder. Does that sound like a good idea? [Yes.]

Okay, first, you've got to follow what I call the Five Rules of Effective Time Management:

1. Prioritize. Focus on the 20 percent of your work that generates 80 percent of the results. Only you know what those priorities are, but I'm holding you accountable for meeting our department's needs at any given time.
2. Create a to-do list and track your progress by marking A, B, and C next to each item based on its significance and timeliness. And be sure to keep your A items on the front burner at all times.
3. Schedule your biggest project for your peak energy period. Remember, racehorses work in sprints. Pace and structure your day so that you're generating key activities when you're most focused and free of distraction.
4. Touch each piece of paper only once. If you find that you can't file or toss something, bring it in to me for review. We'll determine together what to do with it, and you'll soon get a feeling for how to prioritize your in-basket.
5. Do everything possible to a file or a piece of work before retiring it to your drawer. Along the same lines, keep a yellow flyer on top so that as soon as you open a folder, you know exactly what needs to be done next.

Second, I want you to let me know if you run into any stumbling blocks with the monthly metrics report. I'm not going to remind you or ask you anything about it in any way. As far as I'm concerned, no news will be good news, and unless I hear anything to the contrary *well in advance of the pending deadline*, I'm going to assume that you're on target to meet the first Friday deadline. Does that sound fair? [*Yes.*] Good. I'm a resource, but it's up to you to use me for help when you need it.

Finally, it's time for us to get serious about this. I want you to think about how you feel I should respond if you miss another deadline. I'd also like to know how you'd handle it if you were the department lead and a subordinate missed a deadline like this three months in a row. How would you respond, how would you feel, and what would be the consequences? [*Well, I guess there'd need to be some kind of disciplinary response on your part.*]

Correct. So do me a favor and commit to me right now that we'll never have to have a talk like this again. [*Okay, you've got my word.*] Good—thank you. That doesn't mean you can't come to see me if you have questions or to keep me abreast of your progress. Just no more blindsiding me with news that we're not going to have the report ready by the agreed upon deadline. Fair enough? [*Yes.*] Okay, we're done then. Thanks for your support with this.

And there you have it: a lesson shared, a lesson learned, and a goodwill effort to push your employee to raise her own expectations and standards. It's a bigger favor than she'll know because many managers wouldn't have the patience to explain this as thoroughly and cogently as you have. Consider it a gift you've given to her. Should she fail again after this verbal intervention, then a gentle reminder about this conversation or even a letter of clarification may be in order.

A letter of clarification is an alternative to a written warning. Unlike a formal warning, it doesn't contain consequence language stating that "failure to demonstrate immediate and sustained improvement may result in further disciplinary action up to and including dismissal." However, much like a written warning, it outlines the problem as well as your written expectations, and serves to escalate your emphasis on the need to improve in a particular area.

SCENARIO 44

Lack of Organization and Neatness

Much like time management skills, organizational skills are taught at a young age and mastered hopefully by the college years or thereabouts. Without them, life becomes one hectic paper chase after another, as individuals scurry in panic to locate important documents and emails that are critical to justify a business cause of action or decision.

You know what it's like to work with someone who is disorganized: "Oh, where did I put that file?" "Well, I don't have the information on hand, but I'll find it and get back to you." "I'm afraid I can't locate the hard copies, so I'll have to go back and print out all the emails and recreate the paper trail, although they won't have my handwritten notes on them." Excuse after excuse comes your way, which slows you down and frustrates you due to someone else's inefficiency and poor work habits.

The Solution

How do you handle a conversation when one too many files or documents goes missing? You'll want to be firm but fair, nonjudgmental yet insistent that this unacceptable habit change for the better immediately. As a supervisor, you have every right to insist that a subordinate's sloppy desk or unkempt office be reinvented to make documents and information easier to locate whenever you walk into the room. Here's how your conversation might sound with your banking credit manager subordinate who has a particularly challenging time closing deals because of sloppiness and disorganization.

Laura, I wanted to schedule some time with you in your office to discuss neatness and organization. After the Lehman file debacle earlier today when we couldn't close the loan because you couldn't locate the original loan documents, I felt it was time that we have a talk. Do you know what I'm about to say? [*Ah, yes, I'm afraid I do.*]

Okay then, my goal isn't to beat you over the head with a "What were you thinking?" diatribe. But you know that this has been a problem before, and to not be able to close a customer's deal on the spot because of misplaced paperwork is about as bad as it gets.

Let me open up by asking you, how would you propose we fix this problem? [*Well, I'll commit to keeping a much closer eye on all of my paperwork, whether it's loan documents, insurance applications, home equity line files, or whatever. And I'll ensure that this doesn't happen again.*]

That all sounds great, but it only addresses the *what*; I want to know the *how* of it all. What's your action plan for putting a system in place that will ensure that you're on top of all your work and, more important, that I can find information in your absence because your system becomes totally transparent? [*Uh, I don't know and will have to think about that.*]

Well, let's think about it now and put a plan in place. That's why I wanted to meet with you in your office rather than mine. There are a whole lot of messy desk people out there, or MDPs, as I like to call them. Sometimes it's a mild irritation; at other times, a person's whole career can hinge upon it.

If we know that coworkers and clients judge you based on the perception of organization and neatness that you create, then you've got to take certain steps to ensure a streamlined office operation. More important, it's wonderful to be known as someone who can come up with relevant information in a heartbeat because of your exceptional organizational skills. In short, Laura, in the field of banking and finance, you really want to become one of those people.

Looking at your desk right now, how could we get there? Remember again that you're not just doing this for yourself—you're doing it for me. That means that we need to create a short map of where you'll store things like pending files, closed files, files pending signatures, and files missing information. Do this for me thinking that your goal is to teach me how to find things in your absence. That will help discipline you and educate me, and that's what this meeting is all about. Now where do you want to start?

This "teach me" approach to organizational awareness makes the process somewhat fun and takes the sting out of the negative discussion that could potentially happen in its stead. There's no need to punish at this point: This is your first verbal counseling session. Granted, if the problem continues, then your response may appeal to guilt ("I'm really disappointed that this has become an issue again, especially after we sat together, and you made the commitment that we wouldn't have to worry about this again.") or formal progressive discipline in the form of a written warning.

For now, make it a shared learning exercise. Laura's walking you through her processes out loud. Showing you where she plans on strategically locating all of her work documents helps her learn about the process as well. After all, she's presenting a logical case for organizational skills that she's "teaching" you about, and that will help strengthen her understanding of a process that she may not have given enough thought to.

Besides, she'll always remember how painful it is to mishandle documents because of disorganization now that the Lehman incident is behind her. In essence, you'll have taken a moment of embarrassment and weakness and turned it into an opportunity for shared learning. That's a very enlightened way of handling an uncomfortable workplace situation and turning lemons into lemonade. Bravo—well done!

PART III

INAPPROPRIATE WORKPLACE BEHAVIOR AND CONDUCT

8

Sexually Offensive Behavior

Harassment refers to a wide spectrum of offensive behaviors. While subtleties and innuendos can be difficult to prove, one thing is clear: When sexually charged issues become pervasive in the workplace, a claim of sexual harassment is likely to be sustained.

Furthermore, claims of harassment and discrimination, unlike other workplace situations, require that a company conduct an internal investigation. The expectation is that employers will intervene and remedy the situation in a timely manner after completing a thorough investigation and reaching a reasonable conclusion. In fact, failure to take immediate corrective action after conducting a timely investigation, especially in cases of repeated harassment, can be viewed as evidence of a company's "malice" and be the basis for an award of punitive damages.

There are two types of sexual harassment claims: (a) quid pro quo and (b) hostile work environment charges. Quid pro quo cases make up about 20 percent of case law and occur when the proverbial Hollywood "casting couch" scenario is in play: "Sleep with me if you want a part in the movie."

Hostile work environment charges, by contrast, make up roughly 80 percent of the claims that find their way into courtrooms. In cases of hostile work environment charges, physical sex need not come into play. Instead, a workplace charged with ongoing unwelcome sexual innuendo or banter may make the work environment intolerable to the employee bringing charges against your company.

Two conditions have to occur for a sexual harassment claim to be substantiated: First, the harassment must be sexual or gender-based in nature. Second, the conduct must be unwelcome. Here's the catch, though: Employees can "consent" to behavior that they don't necessarily "welcome," and it's a fairly low threshold to argue that an employee put up with intolerable behavior for fear of retaliation or out of peer pressure not to say anything.

This section, therefore, is aimed at ridding your workplace of unnecessary exposure to these potentially lethal elements. Since harassing behavior can be physical, verbal, visual, or auditory in nature, we'll present tough conversations that ensure your employees get the message regarding anything that could be construed as offensive. The goal is not to rid the workplace of compliments and flatteries to the point where your managers are afraid of putting their socks on in the morning; it is to sensitize workers as to how their behaviors and comments may be perceived. Once again, we'll be using the term *perception management* as a tool to help get our point across.

Because potentially harassing behavior is among the most serious of conduct infractions, it is often in the company's best interests to respond formally to claims in writing. Remember that with conduct-related (as opposed to performance-related) infractions, the company has a tremendous amount of discretion to accelerate through the progressive discipline process. Even a first offense may result in immediate termination or in a final written warning stating that "if you ever again engage in behavior that could be construed as offensive, demeaning, hostile, or that in any way makes a coworker feel diminished or less of a person, you will be immediately discharged for cause."

This chapter focuses on offenses that do not rise to the level of immediate termination. For an example that does lead to summary dismissal, see Chapter 14. Otherwise, let's work through some common offenses that if left unchecked can lead to a hostile work environment claim.

SCENARIO 45

Foul Language in the Workplace

Foul language comes in many forms and, as the saying goes, it's sometimes not *what* you say but *how* you say it (and whom you say it to). For example, if an employee stubs his finger in the drawer and shouts, "Oh, f---!" that could be a disciplinary offense that results in a written warning but is very unlikely to be terminable.

On the other hand, if your subordinate looks at you and shouts, "F--- you!" then it's pretty safe to assume that you've got a summary dismissal on your hands. Egregious and insubordinate conduct aimed at the supervisor personally allows you little room as an employer to reason, "Well, I'll just give him a warning this time so that he doesn't do that again." If a company were to waive terminating an individual under such circumstances, it could be remiss in its responsibilities for two reasons: First, it would appear irresponsible for allowing such inappropriate conduct to potentially continue and for creating a record of its failure to act. Second, it could create a dangerous precedent for future occurrences of gross insubordination and potentially harassing behavior. After all, if the company didn't terminate under those circumstances, what would justify a termination for someone else in the future?

The Solution

When an individual takes pride in employing more colorful language than you'd like, and especially if a coworker puts you on notice that she's not comfortable hearing that type of language in the workplace, respond to the offending employee this way:

> Jim, I called this meeting with you in private in my office because we've got a situation that's come up that I'll need your help in solving. I know that up to now, you've been pretty loose with your language, and I know you tend to use colorful words to make others laugh. And while we all appreciate your sense of humor, we've been put on notice that some folks on the team feel like it's getting out of hand. Whenever we're put on notice as a company that language or behavior potentially offends anyone, we've got to notch things back a bit so that everyone feels comfortable again. I'll need your help in fixing this perception that a problem exists, and I'd like your commitment now that we won't be hearing any expletives or inappropriate sayings from this point forward. Will you support me in that?

Okay, that's a very reasonable opener and one that most people will be able to accommodate. What happens, however, if Jim tells you that he really can't help himself? In fact, he's not even aware of when he's using foul language because it's such an integral part of who he is. His family used that language from the time he was born, his friends used that kind of language when he was growing up, and, well, there's really not too much he can do about it. Besides, we're all friends in the group, aren't we? Can't we all agree to just keep things the same? What's all the fuss about anyway?

When the justifications and rationalizations come out, it becomes time to lay down the law a bit more sternly.

> Jim, you're not hearing me. This isn't about you any longer—it's about your coworkers and our company. When someone puts us on notice that they're not comfortable with the curses and loose banter and jokes that have arguably become pervasive in the workplace, there's a whole new paradigm in play. At this point, we no longer have the discretion to laugh it off and ignore it. If we do, we can have a hostile work environment claim levied at us, and as you know, hostile work environment claims are a subset of sexual harassment, which fall under our company's antidiscrimination policy.

> In short, we're putting you on notice that the language and behavior have to stop immediately. If you really feel you can't accommodate our request, then you may have to make an employment decision. If you honestly can't or won't stop at this point, you'll either have to resign or be terminated for cause should this occur again.

> I don't like having this conversation with you because you're an excellent worker and one of our most popular employees, but you've got to understand this and get it right: As much as we enjoy working with you, we can't allow you to expose our company to a hostile work environment claim.

> In that case, here's what the record would look like: Employees inform company that they're no longer comfortable with foul language and inappropriate jokes made by Jim Smith. Company does nothing to amend the employee's behavior and allows the foul language to continue. Employees who made the complaint sue the company for failing to take reasonable action to fix the problem. Do you see the challenge we're facing and why I need your help now?

Once you couch the legal concerns in such a straightforward manner, even the most steadfast offenders will take you seriously. If you need any additional fodder to convince Jim of the urgent need to change his behavior, you can include the following:

Oh, and Jim, there's one more thing: I'm not saying this to frighten you, but it's just that I want you to be fully educated. If the company were to be sued, you could also be named as an individual defendant in the lawsuit. In fact, in cases where the company warns the employee and the employee refuses to change his ways, he may be considered to be acting "outside the course and scope of his employment." And under those circumstances, the company's legal team wouldn't protect you. You'd have to find your own lawyer and pay the damages that arise from the claim.

We don't pay you enough money to risk your home and your bank account for work-related lawsuits, so any time you find yourself slipping back into your old ways, be sure and stop by my office so that I can remind you about the risks you're assuming when it comes to foul language in the workplace.

If he doesn't take you seriously after that discussion and persists in his argument that this is all silly, put your concerns and expectations in written form, either as a written warning or letter of clarification (which doesn't contain any consequence language stating that "failure to demonstrate immediate and sustained improvement may result in further action, up to and including dismissal"). Seeing things in writing often escalates the sense of urgency.

SCENARIO 46

Email Misuse

Employee misuse of email is a fairly common concern in corporate America. Many employees see email as a more casual rather than formal style of communication because it is so readily available and efficient. And it's this casual view of email that causes many problems in the workplace. Further complicating matters, many workers operate under the false assumption that personal email messages are somehow protected from the company's scrutiny.

This casual informality with email often lulls users over time into losing some of their inhibitions and reservations. As a result, what should be *formal corporate communications disseminated through the company's electronic distribution system* become expressions of uninhibited candor and thoughtlessness. Unthinking workers use company email to circulate off-color sexually explicit jokes or photos or to make bigoted remarks.

What they fail to realize is that electronic mail remains on the system and in archives, and is one of the key things that plaintiff's attorneys look for in the legal discovery process to prove animus or prejudice against their client. You'll want to frequently remind employees about the company's expectations regarding appropriate usage of the company's email system.

The Solution

Let's assume that one doctor at your hospital sends a fellow doctor an off-colored email called "The Long-Tongued Toad." Let's also assume that the attached animation of this toad was particularly offensive, especially to women. Finally, just for fun (not that this would ever happen!), let's assume that when Doctor A intended to forward it to Doctor B, the email "to" line prepopulated the name of some other doctor (we'll call her Doctor C) elsewhere on campus who didn't even know Doctors A or B. It's safe to say that Doctor C was fairly upset when she received the email, and she promptly called Doctor A's supervisor, the chair of the department, to voice her dissatisfaction.

The chair then calls a meeting with Doctor A to review the call he just received from Doctor C (much to Doctor A's chagrin), and the meeting sounds something like this:

Doctor A, I called this meeting with you to discuss your email. Your email account is working, correct? [*Yes.*] And what would you say the hospital's email is there for?

Doctor A astutely responds that the email system is to send work-related messages to others at the hospital and in the general community. (Doctor A is clearly very smart!) The department chair continues:

> I agree with you then. The hospital's email was designed to distribute business-related correspondence electronically. Have you used it that way consistently? [*Uh, I'm not sure what you're referring to.*] Okay then, let me be clearer: Does the "Long-Tongued Toad" mean anything to you?

At this point, the chair knows she's got him: That's why the chair is the chair. She continues to delicately probe to see if Doctor A will assume responsibility for the problem or continue to hang himself. Wisely, Doctor A cops to having sent an email of this well-endowed toad to his friend, Doctor B, but he wonders out loud how the chair would have known about it. The chair continues:

> I don't think that Doctor B ever received it. That's because I got an email today from a Doctor C who was not very amused and who expressed extreme dissatisfaction with your lack of discretion and misuse of the hospital's email system. [*Doctor A gulps and turns red.*] Why don't we review some of the basics about email and sexual harassment claims to see if I could make this clearer for you for future reference?
>
> First, let's consider this a CLAM: a career-limiting move. You've alienated and isolated a doctor clear across campus who was offended by your email and who felt it necessary to promptly notify me to ensure that she doesn't receive any other emails like this one from anyone on my staff again. I feel it's safe to say that she'll remember your name even years from now, so you might want to cut a wide swath around Doctor C if you ever run across her on campus.
>
> Second, I shouldn't have to tell you that nothing should be put in an email that you wouldn't be willing to write on stationary with company letterhead or make a headline of in the local newspaper. That's because emails never go away—they're always retrievable. As a matter of fact, they say that email has become to civil law what DNA has become to criminal law. In other words, it's always traceable back to its source. And even if you deleted it, or emptied out your computer's trash bin, or even slipped into

the server room and attempted to delete the information from the server itself, the metadata would still be traceable back to you. Computer forensics firms are always happy to help with that. Of course, in that case you would be obstructing justice, and that could carry punitive damages, so I know you'd never consider doing that.

Finally, even if this email didn't end up in the wrong in-box, think of the record you'll have created. If Doctor C or anyone else on campus wanted to later make a claim that they were being harassed, they could simply retrieve that electronic record that you created with your email and use it as evidence against the hospital.

Therefore, I'm going to assume that we'll never have to have a conversation like this again because you now know how serious an infraction email misuse can be. You also realize that the hospital has a well-defined policy regarding forwarding non–work-related emails to coworkers, especially if they have a sexual or otherwise offensive tone. Most important, you know that now that I'm aware of the matter and have placed you on notice of the hospital's expectations, any future violations will be met with, let's say, severe dissatisfaction and disappointment on my part. Are we clear, Doctor A? Good! Have a good day, and please clear out your in-box of any unrelated emails that might mistakenly be distributed.

Oh, one more thing before you leave. You might want to disable the "Auto Complete" function in your email setup. This way your system won't "predict" the target email address as you type it in, which could save a lot of future embarrassment, if you get my drift.

Yes, I've chosen to employ a bit of a condescending yet friendly tone to this example, but the points outlined here can be used in any situation and with any audience. This case probably didn't lend itself to a written warning because even though the email was off-color and a bit gross, it wasn't overly sexual. In addition, Doctor A didn't intend to forward it to Doctor C—that was done by oversight. Still, you made your point very clear, and there's a strong likelihood that Doctor A will *never* risk making that mistake again—at least while he's on your staff! And that's as good a verbal intervention as any.

SCENARIO 47

Finding Pornography on an Employee's Computer

Thanks to the internet, pornography in the workplace has become a growing problem for many companies, especially for employees who have private offices. Many companies conduct workshops on sexual harassment, code of conduct, and management 101 training to ensure that all employees understand that they have no reasonable expectations of privacy when it comes to their desks, lockers, and data stored on the computer. That's because company equipment belongs to the enterprise, not to the individual employee, and corporations know that it's in their best interests to remind employees of that fact from time to time.

The data security team within your company's IT department may very well be the best resource for solving these challenging issues when they surface. Turning on a data filter will be all that's necessary to track an employee's whereabouts on the internet whenever suspicion arises. Remember that this is an offense that may result in immediate discharge, especially if child pornography is involved (which is a far more serious issue than adult pornography and which requires immediately involving law enforcement).

The Solution

Let's assume that an administrative assistant notifies you that she suspects that her boss is looking at pornography in his office when behind closed doors. She suspects this because she walked in on him recently and saw him quickly and awkwardly trying to cover the screen and close the application, but she thought she briefly saw nudity of some sort.

Armed with this information, you meet with the data security team and ask them to turn on the filter that screens that individual's computer and traces all internet sites visited as well as the length of time spent on each. Within a few days you find that the individual is visiting websites that present infomercials on what would be considered light pornography products—not the heavy-hitting XXX material or anything related to child pornography—but the "college girls gone astray" types of video commercials that are tasteless and offensive but not necessarily hard core. You then meet with human resources regarding the problem and learn that watching these types of online video commercials is not necessarily a terminable offense, but it's certainly a "documentable" offense. In other words, according to your company policies and in line with past practices, a written warning is warranted to demonstrate that your company took the issue seriously and handled it in a timely manner. HR draws up the written warning, and your meeting with the employee may sound something like this:

Chester, I've called this meeting with you and asked Rose from human resources to be present because we've got a serious situation that we need to address with you immediately. As you know, your internet connection and computer are property of the company, and from time to time, data security will review websites visited by our employees as well as monitor the length of time spent on those websites.

In this case, data security notified me that you're visiting inappropriate sexual websites during the workday. Would you concede that that's true? [*Yes.*]

I'm disappointed by your choice, Chester, and I'm also questioning how you have extra time during the day to spend surfing porn sites, but that's a separate matter. For now, I want you to know that such behavior has to cease immediately. In addition, as is consistent with company policy and practice, we're giving you a written warning stating that if you *ever again* engage in this type of activity on company time and premises or using company equipment, you'll likely be terminated for cause.

There's not much else to say here. However, I do want your verbal commitment right now that this problem will end today and that we'll never have to have conversation like this again. Will you agree to that? [*Yes.*] Good, then here's the written warning that human resources has prepared, and you can sign it and return it to me by the end of the week. Of course, you're more than welcome to draft a rebuttal to the warning if you disagree with it. The warning and rebuttal, if you choose to write one, will be placed in your personnel file, and it will also become part of next year's annual performance evaluation and merit increase review. Is there anything else you'd like to add before we conclude this meeting? [*No. I'm sorry.*]

You'll notice that the tone of this meeting doesn't have the usual niceties of other meetings outlined in this book—"I'll need your help to fix this" or "You've got a perception problem on your hands." Instead, it's very factual and straightforward and said without a lot of emotion. That's because once Chester admitted that he was visiting porn sites, there was very little else to discuss. There's nothing to defend and there's no other side of the story to consider. Make your message short and firm, and be sure he understands the link to his performance and merit increase as well as the fact that the written warning will become part of his personnel record.

That should make him think twice before engaging in conduct like this again. Oh, and if he happens to forget and visits those websites again, the written warning will give you full discretion to terminate for a second offense. In essence, he'll be firing himself for violating the reasonable terms that he's agreed to, and that's the cleanest record you could have on file.

SCENARIO 48

Bullying

Schoolyard bullying—the torment of one child by another—has long been a challenge for students and teachers alike, and it is getting more attention in the workplace as well. Insecure adults may taunt and tease others to increase their own perceived power through humiliation; it's easy to see how this workplace issue may contribute to a toxic work environment.

Any incident where a worker is abused, threatened, intimidated, teased, or ridiculed can be grouped under the category of intrusive and harassing behaviors, and such emotional and psychological violence should be taken very seriously in your organization. The aggression may be verbal, physical (as in blocking someone's way), or visual (as in leering or "staring someone down"). Although prevalent in the workplace, bullying tends to be far less covered by legislation than, for example, sexual harassment or racial discrimination. And because it can be subtle and easily denied, bullying may be difficult to prove.

Research shows that a bully is just as likely to be a woman as a man. In the workplace, the bullying comes from bosses the majority of the time. Much like their schoolyard counterparts, adult bullies tend to be insecure people who are easily threatened by others. When they sense a nonconfrontational style in peers and subordinates or when they feel threatened, they may turn their insecurity outward and launch attacks aimed at diminishing the self-worth of their intended targets.

The Solution

When a staff member complains to you that he feels that he's being stripped of his dignity or publicly humiliated by his boss, you may have a bullying situation on your hands. Despite the sports folklore of coaches who humiliate and browbeat student athletes to supposedly get the most out of them and to help them "be their best," bullying in the workplace destroys morale for those who witness it and may expose your company to severe financial damages.

Employees often fear going directly to their department head or to human resources to complain about an immediate supervisor for fear of retaliation. It becomes all the more important that you proactively address any incidents as soon as they surface, even if no formal complaints are made by the bullied staff member:

> Butch, I called this meeting with you this afternoon because I witnessed a staff meeting that you had with your team this morning and was very concerned about how you apparently handled it. I saw you engage in something I would call a public humiliation session with Ron, and from what I could see, your attacks were intended to strip him of his dignity in front of the rest of the group. Can you picture the meeting and specifically what I'm talking about? [*Pause.*]

At this point, the supervisor may launch into an all-out defense to justify his actions: "Ron did the stupidest thing I've ever seen. He called a client on the phone and said. . . . " Your best response is stop him right there.

> Butch, this isn't about the merits of your argument, and I certainly don't need a justification of any sort for your behavior. Whatever Ron did or didn't do is not what we're here about. We're

here about you and the behavior that you demonstrated in that staff meeting earlier today.

Let me be clear. Bullying your subordinates for any reason and under any circumstance violates company policy. More significantly, it makes me lose faith in your ability to lead and your ultimate suitability for the position you're in.

Here's how I see it and how I feel you should see it from now on: Stripping people of their dignity or humiliating them publicly is no longer an option for you. Simply take that tool out of your management toolbox and throw it away.

If I had to describe your behavior today, I would say that you humiliated, overruled, ignored, and isolated your subordinate in front of his peers. That's bad for morale, bad for teamwork, and creates a culture based on fear. As a company, we pay for that over time in lost efficiency, turnover, absenteeism, and unnecessary separation packages and lawsuits. Your actions this morning created a tremendous liability for our company, both in terms of stress-related health and safety exposure as well as the costs associated with unnecessary turnover. I'm here to make sure that you don't do that again. Am I clear? [*Yes.*]

Good. I'm choosing not to put this in the form of a written warning at this point, Butch. Just know that if I ever again have to address this with you, my recommendation to human resources will be that they pursue the matter as aggressively as possible, including a consideration of immediate discharge. Thank you very much.

Okay, you threw the book at him, yet by not documenting your meeting in the form of a written warning, you let him off fairly easily. That's certainly your right. Just be sure and keep a close eye on Butch and his staff to make sure that no further flare-ups arise. In addition, jot down the highlights of this conversation as well as the date, place, and time so that you can refer back to it should you ever need to. And don't forget to give human resources a heads-up just so they're aware of the problem.

If you feel strongly that another such incident should result in immediate termination, you're best off documenting your findings now in a final written warning, rather than a simple discussion. Don't miss an opportunity to document egregious misconduct. It may be harder to terminate after the next offense if you neglected to document this infraction and establish a record of ongoing and repeated violations of company policy.

SCENARIO 49

Discriminatory Comments or Racial Epithets

Discriminatory comments in the workplace can take on many forms:

- ▶ Telling sexually explicit jokes
- ▶ Persistently asking a coworker to go on a date, when the coworker is clearly uninterested in the proposition
- ▶ Asking questions about a person's sexual practices
- ▶ Subjecting a male worker to taunts disparaging his masculinity
- ▶ Name-calling or belittling a coworker by using degrading terms to describe her race or religion

What becomes important is that companies publish and disseminate zero-tolerance policies regarding such workplace intrusions and enforce them via meaningful training programs and attentive follow-up when someone makes a complaint. Likewise, it's critical that you create the appropriate record when someone makes a complaint, including your efforts at conducting a thorough and reasonable investigation as well as a timely action plan. Finally, remember that you're responsible for following up with the individual who initiated the complaint to let that person know how your company handled the matter.

The Solution

Let's take the case of name-calling. Suppose an employee from India meets with you, his department head, to go on record that his coworkers refer to him as "camel jockey" and taunt him with phrases relating to "riding camels." The employee has tried to take their rude and condescending comments in stride up to now, choosing to interpret them as off-color jokes and hazing that he had to accept as a new employee. But it hasn't eased up (if anything it's getting worse) and he's no longer a new employee. So these taunting remarks have been going on for a long time by the time you heard about them.

In cases like this one, which smacks of discrimination and offensiveness, it is best to respond in writing in the form of an individual written warning. Let's assume, though, that this has become a group habit, where all employees engage in banter relating to each other's heritage: The Italian, Polish, Hispanic, and Chinese workers all call each other by offensive names, and you also learn that the Indian employee has actively engaged in such banter as well (i.e., dishing it out but no longer willing to take it). Yes, you could certainly write up the entire group of individuals, but you reason that it's best to rid the workplace of the problematic language by placing the entire team on verbal notice first. Your group discussion might sound like this:

> Everyone, I've called this staff meeting today for one reason: It's been brought to my attention that some of you regularly engage in potentially offensive banter, referring to each other by derogatory names and comments relating to race and ethnicity. I'm not here to name names, but I can tell you that as of right now, June 20, this behavior must come to an end. This isn't a "please be more considerate of your coworkers" type of speech. I've discussed this with human resources, and we seriously considered giving each of you a formal written warning to impress upon you the seriousness of the offense. In addition, we were going to add consequence language at the end of the warning that read: "If you ever again engage in behavior or conduct that can be construed or interpreted as discriminatory, harassing, prejudicial, or otherwise biased, you will be immediately terminated for cause."
>
> However, in fairness, it seems like you've all been engaging in this type of behavior to some degree, and I didn't feel it was appropriate to issue a written warning seeing that this is the first time that I'm addressing the matter with you. That being said, you need to understand that today's date and the time of this meeting are written down in a little black book in my office. Everyone in attendance is noted as well.
>
> Folks, understand what I'm telling you: If any of these comments continue, you could be placing this company at risk, and I have no intention of allowing that to happen. If any one of you

engages in this type of banter or these types of crude and dehumanizing remarks, I'll consider it the same as your tendering your resignation. I'll ask human resources for permission at that point to terminate your employment for cause.

From this point forward, this department has a zero-tolerance policy when it comes to inappropriate, derogatory, defamatory, insulting, offensive, disparaging, menacing, or threatening remarks relating to heritage, language, religion, or anything else along those lines. Do I make myself clear? [*Yes.*] Good. Now is there anyone in this room who can't meet these expectations or is unclear about the new rules or the consequences for breaking these rules? [*No.*]

Good. I believe this meeting has served its purpose, and I'll write in my notes that everyone present is on board and fully willing to comply with this new directive. Please be sure that we never have to have a group or, heaven forbid, one-on-one meeting about this again. Thank you very much.

Okay, you've thrown the proverbial book at them, but that's a far better alternative for them than issuing individual written warnings. In exchange for sparing them formal written warnings, which could impact their annual performance appraisal score and prevent a merit increase, you chose to administer a stern verbal warning instead. That's actually very benevolent of you, so be sure to let your team know that your goodwill and largesse regarding this issue are now spent.

SCENARIO 50

Leering

It's great to have a policy outlining your company's expectations and consequences regarding harassing behaviors such as discriminatory banter, email and internet misuse, and bullying. However, these are all concrete, visible phenomena that can be seen and heard in the workplace or can be proven via the presence of a witness.

However, certain behaviors are difficult to pin down because they fall below the radar screen; they are difficult to prove and can be easily denied. One such example is leering—staring at a coworker in a lewd, lustful, or sexually suggestive way. The person being accused of leering can easily deny that any sexually suggestive looks were made at the alleged victim. In addition, the perpetrator can easily say that the victim is being too touchy or is overly sensitive to something that's clearly being misinterpreted.

How do you address something so easily denied and not directly witnessed? As in many of our other confrontational conversations outlined in this book, the answer is in the use of the word *perception*.

The Solution

Let's look at a case that you'll probably face in your career at some point: Bill, one of your staff members, is a short male with squinty eyes who may have a bit of a visual problem. When Bill speaks with women in the company who are taller than him or wear lower-cut dresses and blouses, he appears to "speak to their breasts." Entire conversations can take place between Bill and "the girls," much to the chagrin of the women who are uncomfortable that he is staring at their breasts instead of looking at them eye to eye.

Here's what your discussion might sound like:

Bill, I've called you into this meeting with me because three of your female coworkers have complained about you. They met with me this morning around 9:30 to tell me that you "spoke to their breasts" rather than to them while riding up in the elevator this morning.

Here's what they told me: "Our eyes are up here, yet he stares at our chest while speaking with us. He's done this before to all three of us, and this morning's elevator ride was the straw that broke the camel's back because his actions were so flagrant."

Now understand something, Bill—you're not in trouble. I'm not even sure if you're aware that this is how you're coming across. However, you have to understand that when employees put me on notice that they're uncomfortable with a coworker's behavior, I have to address it immediately. Would you agree that that's the right thing to do? [*Yes.*]

Okay, let me ask you this, Bill. In all fairness, is it possible in your opinion that their complaints are accurate? I mean, even if you're not doing it on purpose, could there be some legitimacy to their claims? [*No. I'm sorry for all this, but I have no idea what they're talking about.*]

Fair enough. Bill, there's a difference between *perception* and *reality*: Reality is what you know to be true or what you do purposely; perception is what others see, regardless of your intentions. As they say, perception is in the eye of the beholder, and even if you don't realize it, you are creating a perception that's offending others.

From this point forward, I want you to think of it this way: You have to hold yourself accountable for your own perception management. In other words, you have to become sensitive to how you're coming across to others. When you speak with someone else, especially a woman, make sure you look at her eye to eye, even if she's much taller than you.

Likewise, don't stare at anyone's chest under any circumstances—men or women—so that no one can accuse you of inappropriate behavior. Does that make sense? [*Yes.*]

Finally, Bill, like I said, I have no reason to doubt your sincerity. However, I also have to take other people's complaints seriously. As a result, I need a commitment from you right now that you'll be very conscious of the perception you're creating at all times and, more important, that after today we'll never have to have a conversation like this again. Do I have your commitment, Bill? [*Yes.*] Great. Thank you for coming in and helping me solve this little challenge of ours.

Again, there's no need to accuse someone of something that's so difficult to prove in the first place. The key, instead, lies in making them aware that you're aware. Under most circumstances, that will be enough to do the trick. If they really weren't aware of how they were coming across, they are now. And if they thought they could get away with overtly offensive behavior by simply denying it, they now know that you're on to them. Any future complaints could be handled via a formal written warning, with consequence language that reads as follows:

Despite our specific discussion on [DATE] regarding complaints from female coworkers that you "leered" at their breasts when you spoke with them, and despite your commitment at the time to hold yourself accountable for your own perception management, new complaints have recently arisen complaining of the same inappropriate workplace behavior. Therefore, this written warning serves to establish that if you ever again engage in conduct that could be described as leering or if you otherwise demonstrate offensive conduct in the workplace, you will be immediately discharged for cause.

Oh, what if Bill asks if he should apologize to the three women involved who rode up on the elevator with him that morning? That's ultimately his call, but in cases like this, those who complain simply want the behavior to stop. They don't particularly want conversation and apologies. You might want to advise Bill not to worry about apologizing and to simply refocus his energies on mastering the perceptions he creates. You could then let the three female coworkers know of Bill's request to apologize along with your recommendation that he simply prove his regret via his actions rather than words. You might then want to apologize on his and the company's behalf. Of course, you'll want to remind them to see you immediately if any staring or leering problems occur again in the future.

SCENARIO 51

Sexual Harassment Findings (Reverse Harassment)

Sexual harassment training is important for many reasons, especially in terms of mitigating damages that your company may face if an individual supervisor acts outside the course and scope of his employment. Although companies are generally responsible for the acts of their employees through legal concepts known as "strict liability" and "vicarious liability," companies, as corporate citizens, can substantially mitigate damages if they can show that they acted reasonably and responsibly by training their managers and supervisors in this critical area of the law.

However, managers who attend sexual harassment workshops sometimes complain that such training depersonalizes the workplace and creates a sterile work environment where people aren't free to be themselves and should be afraid of complimenting each other for fear of a lawsuit. In reality, supervisors need to understand how sexual harassment charges may be levied against them as individuals, separate and apart from the company, if they are deemed to be acting outside the course and scope of their employment.

It's not enough, however, for managers to look at this potential landmine face forward (i.e., for straightforward claims that can be easily categorized and witnessed). Sexual harassment claims often find their way in through the back door, meaning that employees sometimes make sexual harassment claims *before* they sense they are about to be disciplined or terminated. In other cases, plaintiff's attorneys representing already terminated workers look to expand a wrongful termination claim into a "triple cocktail," including not only wrongful termination but also harassment or discrimination and retaliation.

It's at times like these when threatened staffers are looking to make a preemptive strike to save their jobs or when plaintiff's attorneys are looking for fodder to substantiate claims that include punitive damages that sexual harassment poses the greatest threat.

The Solution

Let's assume that a female supervisor (Charlotte) complains that she is being harassed by her male department head (Chuck). In conducting your investigation, however, you find that Charlotte is equally responsible for the sexually charged work environment. Specifically, although she complains that Chuck engaged in inappropriate discussions regarding her personal life, including bantering about favorite (sexual) positions and other exploits, she frequently initiated similar inappropriate banter.

In addition, you learn that most staff members believe that she was looking to pursue a more personal relationship with Chuck. Although Chuck did engage in the inappropriate discussions, most staffers feel that she was teasing him and showing him attention in an inappropriate manner. In addition, your staffers inform you that she's been hitting on Chuck for a long time, even though she knows he's married.

Your conversation with Charlotte might sound like this:

Charlotte, after hearing of your complaint against Chuck for inappropriate workplace discussions of a personal and sexual nature, we conducted our own investigation. Chuck admitted to engaging in appropriate discussions and one-off comments with you, and we are taking appropriate action with him in light of our findings.

You're not technically under any obligation to disclose the nature of the action that your company is taking with Chuck. For example, you're not obligated to state whether he's being given a written warning, a final written warning, or other such disciplinary measure. However, if you feel the situation warrants it, you can certainly share this level of detail with the complaining employee. Just check with human resources or qualified legal counsel first.

During the course of the investigation, however, we found two things: First, that as a supervisor, you initiated, encouraged, and participated in conversations of a sexually explicit nature with your own subordinates. Second, that a number of employees reported that it appeared to them that you initiated much of the inappropriate sexual banter with Chuck and that, more often than not, he responded to your initial promptings.

Along those lines, Charlotte, it appeared to those whom we spoke with that you initiated the behavior, showing him attention inappropriately and flirting with him, and are now turning it all around to blame him for the sexually charged environment that exists.

Therefore, I'm going on record with you to confirm two things: First, as a company, we're open to investigating and correcting any and all legitimate claims of harassment that you feel may exist in the workplace. Second, however, is that we can't overlook the evidence that you appear to be responsible for unacceptable conduct as well. As a result, you'll be receiving a written warning for inappropriate conduct in the workplace.

Since you're giving Charlotte a written warning, be sure and give Chuck either a written or final written warning for this same incident as well. You won't want a record that shows that you only disciplined the subordinate who originally lodged the complaint because that may smack of retaliation.

The warning will state that if you ever again engage in this type of banter with your staff members, your supervisor, or anyone else with whom you come into contact throughout your workday, including clients and vendors, you'll be immediately dismissed.

In this case, if the staff members point to Charlotte's role as the leader in the problematic behavior, you're on safe ground to discipline her as well as Chuck. This also protects your company should she again levy a complaint of sexual harassment in the future. Remember, without a crystal ball, you can't tell who's telling the whole truth. Simply let your investigation trail be your guide without judging the matter yourself. Chuck handled things inappropriately, and he's now on formal written notice. Charlotte also handled matters inappropriately, and she's now in the same predicament as Chuck.

Could she make a claim that this was handled unfairly and in a retaliatory fashion for having originally raised the complaint? Of course she could, but you, the objective third-party investigator of the event, simply relied on your staff members as witnesses and reasonably followed their lead. That's an excellent record to have down in writing, and it will provide your company with significant downside protection should Charlotte ever again make a preemptive strike in order to set the stage for a future claim of retaliation.

SCENARIO 52

Sexual Harassment and "the Talk"—Stopping Problematic Behaviors Dead in Their Tracks

We know that sexual harassment is alive and well and concerns employers of all sizes and in all industries. States have passed mandatory training requirements that have to last a certain amount of time or include subtopics like workplace bullying, yet there's little sense that the issue is on the wane. Recent headlines alleging sexual misconduct, abusive behavior, and even assault have led to the fall of entertainment moguls, on-air talent, and politicians in the highest offices of the land.

The underlying problem stems not from a lack of knowledge, however; most trained managers can instantly tell you the difference between quid pro quo harassment and a hostile work environment. Instead, toxic behaviors and corporate cultures sometimes inadvertently allow such behaviors to pepper the workplace. In other cases, it's the behavior of individual managers toward subordinates or peers that perpetuates ongoing problems, creating both corporate and individual liability that becomes difficult to defend in he-said-she-said situations.

Worse, even executives, managers, and supervisors with MBAs don't receive classroom instruction that individual liability can be imputed for what are known as "managerial bad acts" and for "acting outside the course and scope of your employment." Harassment, intimidation, bullying, and overtly sexual behavior often trigger such claims, and it's only when the leader finds himself on the sharp end of the investigative spear that he realizes he may have risked personal assets like homes and bank accounts for engaging in egregious misconduct that can somehow be linked to another person's sex, gender, or sexual orientation.

The Solution

While it's easier to throw more resources at the problem in the form of training in a box, articles, books, and whatnot, the key solution lies in tying employees' behaviors to personal liability. Let's look at a young male television producer in the Golden State of California, who has a hit show and feels justified in hitting on all the young female production assistants and interns. How can you turn around an aggressive personality and cocky arrogance when the individual feels he can't be touched? Very simply—hit him in the pocketbook. Watch how it works:

> [General Manager]: Ted, as the general manager of the studio, I invited Paul from human resources to join us for a discussion that may be difficult for you to hear but that's critically important to you at this stage of your professional development and career. I know you've got a top-rated show, and you're a hot commodity in town, but we've learned about something that could seriously hold you back or damage your reputation if you don't gain control of it quickly. Paul, can I ask you to provide Ted with more details?"
>
> [HR]: Sure. Ted, what I've heard is that you may be hitting on several of the younger female production assistants and interns. I haven't experienced anything myself, but I've heard through some people on set that this may be happening and making people feel

uncomfortable. No one on your team wants to come forward to speak with you directly, so they came to my office, and I informed our GM. That's why we're here today.

I'll make this short and to the point. Most executives in your line of work and at your level of success lose sight of some of the basics—namely, that as a high–net worth individual, you're a high-profile target, that our studio is also a high-profile target with deep pockets, and that any lawyer in town would love to get their hands on some type of sexual harassment claim coming out of here because there are two juicy targets—the studio and the production executive—and an incredible desire to avoid negative publicity and settle any claim as quickly as possible. That means we're ripe for a lawsuit, and so are you.

Most executives don't realize that in most states they can be sued for up to $50,000 of their own money for engaging in what are known as "managerial bad acts," which harassment clearly falls under. (For California employers: That's not the case in California, which has no cap on individual liability.) [*Pause*] So I want to be clear about this and make sure you're aware that we don't pay you enough to risk your home, your savings account, your car, and whatever else for unwittingly creating a perception that you're hitting on multiple young ladies on your team.

I'd be doing you a disservice as a client if I didn't inform you of this, and I'd never want you to learn about this unlimited personal liability for "acting outside the course and scope of your employment" only after being served with a sexual harassment lawsuit. Further, remember that under the code of conduct, you're not allowed to date anyone on your team who is a subordinate. As the executive producer, you're the top of the totem pole, so that means everyone on your team is a subordinate. If you sense that a romantic relationship is beginning, you have an affirmative obligation to disclose it to us immediately. Just so you know, our response will likely be to transfer that individual off your show, to prevent any future allegations of abuse down the road if you break up.

This advice isn't just for here and now, Ted. I want you to keep this in mind for the rest of your career, no matter where you're working. Your success is our success, and we certainly want it to continue, but we can't allow you to inadvertently set yourself up because you were unaware of how the system works. Do you have any questions about what I've shared with you just now? [*No—I wasn't aware of any of this.*] Okay, good then. It was an excellent investment of five minutes of your time because you now have a much clearer understanding of how quickly things can go wrong. My door's always open if I can help with anything, and please know that I'll always be here for you, if and when you need advice or guidance on these sorts of things.

Bravo! A five-minute story that this young, hotshot executive will take with him for the rest of his career. Nothing makes more sense to successful executives, salespeople, and yes—even Hollywood directors—than the potential of hitting them in their pocketbook. They'll remember you for this, and they'll likely see you in a different light—both as a professional mentor and a go-to resource. That's quite an accomplishment when dealing with the "highest of the high" at your organization.

SCENARIO 53

Sexual Harassment and Culture Change—Creating a Healthy and Respectful Work Environment (Beyond Training 101!)

Besides having a one-on-one conversation with an errant employee or manager *after the fact*, how do you get in front of the problem so that it never rears its ugly head in the first place? How can you, as a corporate leader, ensure that harassment never plagues your workplace to begin with? The answer lies in transparent communication and appropriately setting expectations. While there are no guarantees, approaching the topic openly with intermittent reminders can do a lot to make this a front-burner issue, either eliminating the problem or at least mitigating its negative effects, both in terms of culture and legal liability.

The Solution

Hint: It's not about additional training videos or knowledge-based solutions. It's all about respect in the workplace, inclusion, selfless leadership, and creating a sense of having each other's backs should the need arise. Scenario 52, which also addresses sexual harassment, focuses on raw, brutal force: Attach errant behavior to the dollars and cents associated with personal liability lawsuits—especially for high-net worth individuals—and you'll often get a visceral response that scares the individual or team into compliance. (There's nothing wrong with creating a healthy sense of paranoia, which works well for some.) In comparison, the proactive group solution we're proposing here falls squarely within the "emotional intelligence" quadrant, and while it's sometimes challenging to raise people's awareness of how they come across to others, it's a valuable exercise that proffers real-life lessons that will likely stand the test of time.

Here's what your team discussion might sound like:

Folks, I called this meeting to discuss a topic that's of concern to all of us: sexual harassment. Now, don't roll your eyes: I'm serious about this. Nothing defines us more as a team than the way we treat and respect one another. I'm holding this meeting not because I have to but because I want to. The scope and tone of our interpersonal relations is key to our getting along. I want you to know that I always have your backs, but certain behaviors and forms of conduct cross the line with me, and the consequences for doing so in my shop will be swift and severe.

First, sexual harassment falls under our company's antidiscrimination policy. Further, our code of conduct sets the standard for how we're expected to treat one another, in both the letter and the spirit of the law. There are real consequences for people accused of and found guilty of violating this particular policy, including disciplinary action or even termination for an egregious first offense. In other words, the policy has teeth, and the company is willing to enforce it and won't turn a blind eye.

Second, conduct is handled differently than performance. People sometimes mistakenly think that they're entitled to steps of progressive discipline for any workplace infractions—verbal, written, and final written warnings. That's true on the performance side of the equation, but not on the conduct side. For cases of egregious misconduct—think theft, fraud, forgery, and yes, extreme cases of sexual harassment—a final written warning or even outright termination may be the logical company responses, depending on the circumstances.

Third, with this defensive strategy in place, it's even more important that we discuss our offensive strategy. What do I expect that to look like?

Here are my rules for teambuilding: (1) What you want for yourself, give to another. (2) Perception is reality until proven otherwise. (3) We judge ourselves by our intentions, but others by their actions. I'm holding you all accountable for your own perception management going forward, meaning that you're responsible for how others receive your actions and statements. Yes, that means you'll have to raise your awareness about how you may be coming across to others, you'll have to periodically self-check how others are perceiving your communication style at any given time, and you'll have to feel self-confident enough to make yourself vulnerable on occasion. Vulnerability begets trust, and I need to make sure we have a high enough level of trust in one another that we can err on the side of compassion and assume good intentions when faced with challenges.

As for my expectations, you're obligated to be aware. You're not permitted to be the monkey that sees, hears, or speaks nothing. I'm not asking you to tattletale on one another. Rather, when it comes to the *potential* or *perception* of harassing workplace behavior, you have an affirmative obligation to disclose the matter to me; to human resources; to Jennifer Cho, our in-house chief legal officer; to Dennis Nguyen, our division head, or to the compliance hotline (which can be done anonymously). In short, you have numerous resources at your fingertips and a flexible reporting chain, so not disclosing the matter is unacceptable and can land you in hot water. Nondisclosure is synonymous with complicity, and we can't let that bad worm burrow its way into our apple.

Finally, remember that it's not what you say but how you say it. I know you learned that in the second grade, but it's as important now as ever. Respect begets respect, goodwill comes back to you thousandfold, and knowing that we're looking out for each other will make this the best job you've ever had. My goal is to raise your awareness of potential perception problems that can be misinterpreted. As the saying goes, make of your life a gift. You set the role model behavior for others to follow, and you be the first domino—the one willing to apologize when there's any doubt about intentions or actions. That's the team I want to work with and work for. That's the behavior that will be honored and rewarded in our department. My commitment is to assure all of you that I take this seriously and that I want you to as well.

Do any of you have questions or comments to any of the guidelines I've established just now? [*No.*] Great! Then we'll move forward with these expectations established firmly in your minds. Thank you all for a ten-minute meeting that will bear all sorts of goodwill for our team. Let's celebrate our victories, and remember that life is too short to get mired in webs of drama. We're about openness, transparency, and helping one another become the best that we can be. That's my expectation and my commitment, and I'm always here if you need to discuss this further when particular situations arise.

Clearly expressed, said with heart and selflessness, you've now moved the needle in your group in a new direction. What an important message from the top, what a critical admission of who you are, what you believe in, and how you expect them to act when challenged with this potentially devastating issue. Congratulations—you just walked the walk, established yourself as a role model, and made it safe for your employees to do their finest work every day, while simultaneously helping others reach their full potential.

9

Substandard Communication Skills

A rguably the most important skill that workers need to excel in their careers lies in their communication abilities. Survey after survey finds that employers look to staffers' communication skills above all else to ensure that business progresses without undue interruption. Still, communication is more than just how well someone speaks when spoken to. More often, it has to do with a level of awareness or sensitivity in terms of feeding information *up* to management and keeping senior leaders in the know, lest they find out about surprises from individuals outside the group.

There is even a further issue of concern regarding communication abilities: the record being set by employees who engage in activities in a particular order, without regard to the consequences of their actions. Let's look at an example that is fair game for managers who report to you at your company.

Let's say you're the vice president of sales in your company, and on a Tuesday night, John, your director of sales, comes in to complain about the performance of one of his account executives, Stephanie. John tells you that Stephanie isn't meeting her numbers consistently, has demonstrated a bit of an entitlement mentality lately, and seems to be isolating herself from the rest of the sales team. You and John agree that a written warning may be in order and that you will both look further into this issue soon. However, John wants to think about it and sleep on it a bit further before any formal action is initiated.

On Wednesday morning, Stephanie comes in to see you unannounced. She starts to tell you that she's very unhappy under John's leadership and feels that he treats women sales executives differently than males, has a bit of a machismo complex, and demonstrates behavior that is indicative of harassment.

Before she goes any further in her conversation, should you (a) tell her that John, her boss, was in to see you the night before complaining about her job performance or (b) say nothing about the performance issue at all and simply listen to her harassment complaint as the two issues have nothing to do with one another?

Interestingly enough, more people would say the correct answer is (b), but in reality, it's (a). That's because the record you create in meeting with complaining employees often has to do with timing and honestly setting the record straight. If you don't tell her that John was in the night before complaining about her *performance*, then you open up the company to the possibility of a retaliation charge should he (legitimately) want to give her a performance-based written warning after she's made the initial harassment complaint about his workplace *conduct*.

After all, the last thing you want to do is create a record that a female employee came to you (or human resources or your company's legal department) in good faith, only to be given a written warning a few days later for what could be considered a pretextual reason. That record could smack of retaliation even to the untrained eye, so you could only imagine how a plaintiff's attorney might see it.

In fact, it's not uncommon for subordinates to strike first when they sense they're about to get into trouble. How you, as a manager, field those complaints can have serious ramifications for your company. And you'd be surprised how *preemptive* employees with long memories can be. Sometimes the complaint will go back more than a year as employees try to insulate themselves from any harm by striking first and hoping the company will then grant them some kind of immunity from discipline or other consequences.

Communication has to do with the record that you set, as evidenced by the previous example. Every employee is responsible for communicating effectively. Just remember that communication has a lot more to it than how someone speaks or listens; it's equally about how one keeps the boss informed and not feeling like she's flying blind by failing to communicate changes in the game plan. This chapter will provide you with conversations to help you teach your subordinates about these critical issues.

SCENARIO 54

Gossips, Rumormongers, and Snitches

Gossips typically initiate unfounded rumors; rumormongers perpetuate them, even if they lack any foundation of truth or could potentially damage others' reputations or hurt their feelings. And snitches—well, snitches are just snitches, and most of us know intuitively that playing the tattletale role is just plain wrong.

These behaviors occur around us all the time to differing degrees, but few things in the workplace do more to damage employee morale and trust than corporate "grapevining" that is allowed to go unaddressed and unchecked. People who initiate unfounded rumors and who gossip about their coworkers' or bosses' personal problems, workstyles, or private challenges stir up drama for no good reason. They act like a worm in an apple, slowly coring away the goodwill and respect that creates camaraderie and trust.

The Solution

Asking the employee who was the brunt of a rumor (we'll call him Pete) whom he suspects originated the rumor about his personal life isn't really at issue—unless someone voluntarily admits it, there's very little blaming or finger-pointing necessary. What is important, however, is how you address the situation and reset expectations with your staff:

> Everyone, I've asked Pete to join me in this meeting because a rumor has developed about his personal life. We don't know who originated the rumor, and if any one of you would like to speak with me in private after this meeting about your involvement in starting or perpetuating the rumor, I'd be happy to hear what you have to say.
>
> For now, I want you all to know how hurtful this is. We're a team, and anyone who could raise issues like this against one member of the team raises them against us all. And I personally would be very offended and hurt if anyone started or continued a rumor about my personal life, which had nothing to do with my performance at work.

Whether there's any truth to this rumor is not the issue; it's simply none of our business. This is about respect—respect for each other as individuals and respect for our team.

Therefore, let me be very clear: I expect that no one will engage in this type of character assassination or public shaming exercise ever again. I also expect that everyone in our department will stop others from spreading rumors of a personal nature. In short, if you have nothing good to say, say nothing at all. Do I have your agreement and commitment on that on a go-forward basis? [*Yes.*]

Pete, on behalf of the entire team, I'm very sorry for anything that was said that hurt or offended you. We'll commit to stopping these types of behaviors in their tracks in the future. Again, my apologies.

In light of cloak-and-dagger rumors that attack someone's character, personal challenges, or other areas of vulnerability, the best course of action will always be to address the rumor openly with the group in front of the intended victim and to apologize for the perception problem that was created by someone's lack of discretion.

Now what if you've caught a gossip-monger *in flagrante delicto* (i.e., with his hands in the proverbial cookie jar)? Such instances require a firm and immediate response.

Justin, as a result of your actions, Joan has become the brunt of some mean-spirited office banter. And as you can imagine, she was embarrassed and humiliated for something that she had absolutely nothing to do with. And that leaves me feeling very disappointed at your lack of discretion and insensitivity.

Let me be clear. At this point, you've got a perception problem on your hands. The perception is that you've gossiped and fed the corporate grapevine, which has made our work environment that much more toxic. And I'm holding you fully responsible for your own perception management from this point forward.

I would think that an apology may be in order here, but I'll leave that up to you. For now, I really want you to think about your actions and how you may have inadvertently made someone look bad in the eyes of her peers, feel diminished, and feel like less of a person. That's very sad, Justin, and I want you to know that I'm counting this as a verbal warning. I want your commitment right now that we'll never have to have a discussion like this again and that should it occur again, further discipline up to and including immediate termination could result. Are we in agreement here? [*Yes—sorry.*]

Okay, it's true that you may have gone out of your way to "overcommunicate" your expectations in this scenario, but come on—selfless leadership may be about putting others' needs before your own, but it's certainly not about babysitting! Mean-spirited actions like this deserve a firm response on the company's part. And note the use of guilt (rather than anger) in your approach: "I really want you to think about your actions and how you may have inadvertently made someone look bad in the eyes of her peers, feel diminished, and feel like less of a person." Now that should get him thinking about the error of his ways and assuming responsibility for his wayward actions.

Finally, snitches need to be addressed as yet another subcategory of this universally human problem. Snitches often hit you with a "Psst. It may be none of my business, so please stop me if you feel I'm being inappropriate by sharing this with you, but . . . " And once they've opened up with that disclaimer, they unload all sorts of details on you that typically serve to get their coworkers in trouble. When faced with a snitch who believes she's "doing you the favor" of acting as your eyes and ears, stop her dead in her tracks:

Rachel, I understand that you believe that I need to know these things, especially since they occur when I'm not in the office or behind closed doors. And I appreciate your always trying to keep me in the loop as to what's going on. But there's a bigger issue that I want to sensitize you to, and it's a moral issue that has a lot to do with principle and doing the right thing.

Not to sound ungrateful or unappreciative, but I don't know that sharing that kind of information about Suzie with me is the right thing for you to do. Don't get me wrong: If you witnessed someone stealing or being harassed, I would want to know about that immediately. But those are serious *misconduct* infractions that could have dire consequences to the company. When it comes to *performance* issues that you become aware of, though, I don't think that you should necessarily feel compelled to volunteer that information.

First of all, I'll probably be able to find that out on my own before too long. Second, it places you into the role of mole or corporate snitch, and when that gets out (which it will sooner or later), you won't be trusted by your peers. And that will bring more long-term damage to the department than the current performance-related problem that you felt compelled to report. Do you see why sometimes withholding that kind of information may be better for both you and for the department in the long run?

Yes, these issues are sometimes a slippery slope. And yes, often these actions are done with little thought of the damage that could be done. Nevertheless, left unaddressed, they can damage team spirit and goodwill. Be direct, be open, and shy away from nothing when it comes to eradicating these insidious forces from the workplace. Your team will benefit, your subordinates will respect and appreciate you, and wrongdoers will learn the errors of their ways before those same types of mistakes wreak havoc on their careers.

SCENARIO 55

Whiners and Complainers

Whiners and complainers are unfortunately common in the workplace. Parents often struggle with whiny children, but to date, no recessive gene in a human's DNA can be found to account for negativists, whiners, complainers, and others who are just plain difficult to deal with. So if science doesn't have an answer, what's a poor manager to do?

Generally speaking, negativists tend to whine to people who will buy into what they're complaining about. Sometimes it's just idle conversation; other times the whining is meant to clearly express anger and resentment at how others are favorably treated while the whiner is somehow victimized by situation after situation. Whatever the cause, most managers simply want it to stop. No excuses or apologies are needed. Just stop it! Ah, if there were only a way to transmit that message clearly and skillfully to subordinates who find the glass half empty in so many different circumstances.

Well, fear not. This too is something you can address with alacrity and aplomb. After all, it's your department, and sometimes it's easy enough to institute the change in an employee's behavior because, well . . . it's your department. There are no magic bullets here, other than to sensitize an employee to his own perception management. But we're not looking to change personalities—only behavior and conduct in the workplace.

The Solution

With children, it's said that if you ignore the whining, it will diminish once the kids realize that they're not getting any response from you. Some actually mock their whiney children outright and put them down for their annoying behavior. Still other parents resort to whining right back at their kids to give them a taste of their own medicine. Some of these tactics may work with children, but none of them typically work with adults.

Try this approach the next time you're faced with a constant complainer:

> Marianne, we need to talk one on one. I've called this meeting in private in my office because I need to share something with you that borders on being personal and that, frankly, may upset you. I don't know if anyone's ever told you this before, but from my vantage point as your supervisor, your communication style can be somewhat caustic. You may not realize it, but you tend to complain a lot. Let me give you an example. When I told the staff that we were upgrading from Kronos Workforce Central Suite 7.0 to 8.0, you challenged my statement before I could even finish my explanation. You appeared to become frustrated, saying how much you liked Kronos 7 and didn't want to upgrade to a new version. You said that we were all proficient on 7 and that upgrading to any new system would set us all back considerably, and then you said in front of the whole team that you're going to be the last to convert.
>
> I'm not sure if you realize that your public displays of frustration and dissatisfaction are perceived negatively by the rest of the team, but I'm here to tell you that they are. If you had let me finish my sentence, I would have confirmed that the whole company would be going through the upgrade and everyone would be adequately trained. However, I wasn't asking for a vote or how

anyone felt about it—I was just announcing the new direction we were going in. By voicing your frustration before even hearing the full explanation, you made a lot of people in the room feel tense and uncomfortable, and undermined the chances of a smooth transition to the new suite.

Let me explain it to you this way, Marianne. Everyone is responsible for her own perception management. What I mean is that others may not know what's in your heart but the perception you give off creates the impression of who you are.

As they say, perception is reality until proven otherwise, and if people associate you with negativity or classify you as a complainer, your effectiveness in the workplace and your opportunity to grow and develop in your career will be severely limited.

Again, I don't mean to hurt your feelings, but I need you to really think about this. The big question for you to ponder is, who are you in light of the changes that affect us in the workplace from time to time, and how do you want others to think of you? You can be a positive, open, and constructive team member who's always willing to help when a new challenge arises, or you can be a negative, closed, limiting, and complaining individual who resists change and openly voices a negative attitude toward things that initially appear challenging or overwhelming.

It's up to you. For the rest of your career and the rest of your life, you have to define who you are. If you weren't aware of how you were coming across at work, then this conversation will help sensitize you to how others may be seeing you from time to time. On the other hand, if you *were* aware and felt that you had the right to express your dissatisfaction just as you have the right to voice your opinion, then with all due respect, Marianne, you're incorrect.

As the manager of the group, I need to let you know that negative comments really pull down morale, and I just can't let that happen anymore. I want you to think about all this overnight. Once you've slept on it, come and see me tomorrow and let me know what you've decided. I'm here to help and coach and mentor my staff members in their careers, but I'm not here to coddle anyone. I'm holding you to the same expectations as everyone else in the group, and when we meet tomorrow, I'm hoping that you'll agree with me and work with me to make this better for you in your career and for the rest of us in the department.

Do I have your commitment that you'll think this through seriously overnight and come back tomorrow to discuss some solutions that we can implement together? [*Yes.*] Good. Then I'll wait to hear from you tomorrow.

Bravo! Very well done. You treated this individual like an adult and helped guide her in a direction to raise her own expectations of herself. You were not accusatory and acknowledged that she might not even be aware of how she's coming across to others. But you certainly explained that you would hold her to the same standards as everyone else in the group, and that's about as much coaching and counseling as you should have to provide under the circumstances. She'll thank you one day. Any further incidents of outright whining or bellyaching can reasonably be met with a decisionmaking leave or formal written warning.

SCENARIO 56

Requests for Confidential Conversations from Other Supervisors' Subordinates

Be wary any time a staff member who reports to a supervisor other than yourself asks to speak with you confidentially. Again, communication has so much to do with the record being created, and many a well-intentioned supervisor has walked into the lion's den unknowingly while attempting to help the employee who initiated the meeting.

As a supervisor, you have to be aware of what I call the preemptive strike. When it comes to employee relations issues and lawsuits, the party that initiates the claim often has the upper hand because she makes the first record of a complaint. An assistant who senses that he's about to be disciplined or terminated, for example, may be the first to run to human resources and make a claim of discrimination or harassment against his supervisor. This way, reasons the employee, some sort of protective veil may be established that protects him from disciplinary action because he's now raised the possibility of a retaliation claim.

The supervisor who promises a member of someone else's staff confidentiality may unwittingly fall for this preemptive strike pitfall by allowing a record to be created that damages the company's credibility. For example, if the employee speaks to you, Supervisor B, about her direct supervisor's (Supervisor A) problematic conduct and you agree to maintain this information in confidence, then, in the eyes of the law, the entire company will have been officially placed on notice of the employee's complaint.

Your keeping the information confidential precludes the company from responding appropriately, and then you're left to bear the full brunt of the lawsuit. After all, in such circumstances, you could be deemed to be "acting outside the course and scope of your employment." That's because the company's attorney will argue that you knew (or should have known) that you had an affirmative obligation to disclose certain employee complaints. Arguing later that you were only trying to help by following the employee's request of maintaining the confidence is no excuse and, more significantly, no defense.

The Solution

How should you initially respond to such a request for confidentiality from another supervisor's subordinate? In most cases, you'll want to respond this way:

> José, whenever an employee who reports to another supervisor asks to meet with me off the record or confidentially, my antennae go up. I need you to understand that it wouldn't be appropriate for me to hold a meeting with another supervisor's staff member if that individual wants to complain about management in any way. In that case, my responsibility would be to refer that employee back to his supervisor or, if that's not comfortable, on to the supervisor's supervisor (i.e., the department or division head).
>
> So before you open up to me with your concerns, let me confirm that if what you're about to say involves your relationship with your current supervisor or is a problem with discrimination, harassment, or potential violence in the workplace, I'll have an obligation to disclose it to senior management or human resources.

Now, if it sounds cold to turn away an employee who is in need, remember that you could always offer the employee your help in other ways. For example, in the case of potential harassment, you should encourage the employee to go to human resources and can offer to go with him so that he feels like he has an ally on his side. That's a very caring way of extending yourself while adhering to company policy and practice.

Second, without knowing the nature of the problem, you can hand the employee an EAP brochure. If your company retains the services of an Employee Assistance Program provider, then that outside service provider can help handle an employee's concerns confidentially and avail the individual of the appropriate resources to help him through the situation. Mental help, assistance with drug addiction problems in the family, and financial counseling referrals often fall within the realm of the EAP's services.

Finally, if the employee states that his issue has nothing to do with his immediate supervisor or any type of conflict of interest, then you can certainly take a "listen only" approach to see what he wants to talk about. For example, if the individual confirms that he simply wants your career advice, then you might feel inclined to talk away. Still, even in that apparently benign case, you should beware: Simply creating a perception that you're in a closed-door meeting with another supervisor's employee may make you vulnerable to the "Paul Falcone told me so" attack.

Here's how it works: If you're about to meet with an employee from another department who has ongoing disciplinary problems or is about to be terminated, then be sensitive to the possibility that something subjective could be attributed to you simply by your holding a private meeting with that individual. In such circumstances, it's best to avoid the meeting altogether. After all, you can't really defend yourself if someone says, "I was in Paul's office—just the two of us in private—when he told me that my job was safe and that my boss was going to be terminated."

How do you think that's going to sound when they invite the individual in to inform him that he's being terminated for cause for failing to meet the terms outlined in prior written warnings? Not too good, as a mad rush will ensue to see what Paul Falcone actually said in that closed-door meeting: How did Paul know that the employee's boss was going to be fired? Why would Paul guarantee anyone job security—he can't do that! What else did Paul tell him in that meeting?

And so goes the panicked questioning pattern right at the time that a neat, clean termination was supposed to take place. Keep in mind that as an employer, you always want a clean record of consistent verbal conversations, clear written warnings with documented consequences, and a termination meeting that upholds the individual's dignity and respect. What you don't want is drama, he said–she said accusations, and all sorts of mud to cloud the waters.

That's not fair to you or healthy for your company. In fact, it's what plaintiff's attorneys prey on. The bottom line under such circumstances: Don't be so nice! Protect yourself and your company by avoiding a perception where privacy, in and of itself, could permit the employee to attribute to you things that you never said. Remember that when it comes to communicating, sometimes what's not said is louder than what's said. Be sensitive to those times when your genuine concern and caring may be manipulated and used against you and your company.

SCENARIO 57

Poor Listening Skills

Yes, from time to time, we're all guilty of wandering off in our minds and not paying close enough attention to the business matters at hand. But when lapses in understanding or clarity occur frequently or people interrupt others without allowing them to finish their thoughts, poor listening skills may be the cause.

Communication is a two-way street: It's not just about giving information, but it's also about receiving and digesting new information that propels the next step in the business process. Someone who suffers from poor listening skills on a regular basis may lack the attention to detail necessary to get the job done or simply may lack the self-discipline to allowing others to finish their thoughts before interrupting. Here's how to handle both cases.

The Solution

If someone appears to drift off at meetings or asks questions about something that was said within the last two minutes, it might be a good idea to rein him back in and focus his attention on the matter:

Joe, I called this meeting in private with you because I'm concerned about a critical part of your communication skills—namely, your ability to listen actively. I bring it up because you sometimes appear to be elsewhere in our staff meetings. I don't know how to describe it other than to say that I can tell by your stare that your mind seems to be elsewhere.

You're not in trouble or anything. It's just something that I need you to focus on because it can clearly get in the way of your career development no matter where you work. It's more than just a perception, though. I could also tell by the questions that you asked that you either didn't hear or didn't understand parts of the conversation. Let me give you an example: In our staff meeting this morning, you asked when the departmental quarterly report would be due and who would be responsible for it. That caught everyone in the room off guard because we had just confirmed that the report would be due this Friday and that Tina was going to take the lead role in putting it all together.

Have you found this to be a problem from time to time as well, or am I totally shocking you with this news? [*Yes, it's been a problem but not to this degree.*] Okay then, let's discuss how we can make it better.

Do you consider yourself an audio, visual, or tactile learner? [*Mostly visual, I guess.*] Good. Then let's start there. I'm going to ask you to take the official minutes at our next meeting. I know we haven't drafted minutes before, but I've been thinking that it would be a good idea in general, and I think it will help you hone in on the details. Will you agree to do that and do you feel it's a good idea? [*Yes.*]

Okay, I'm also going to place you into the role of meeting leader more often than we've done in the past. I'd like you to guide our meetings and take the lead in moving things in the appropriate direction.

Finally, I'm going to ask you, Joe, to think about other things we can do to strengthen your listening skills. Let me know if you have any suggestions, and I'll be happy to help in any way I can.

That's a nice and respectable way of getting your point across without embarrassing the employee or questioning his overall intellectual capabilities. But what if poor listening habits stem from interrupting others and not allowing them to finish their thoughts? In such cases, your verbal coaching session may sound like this:

> Joe, I called this meeting in private with you because I'm concerned about a critical part of your communication skills—namely, your ability to listen actively. I bring it up because I'm not sure whether you're aware of it or not, but you tend to interrupt others before they finish their thoughts. As a result, it appears that you're not engaging in active listening or allowing yourself the benefit of the full complement of information before sharing your point of view.
>
> They say that you can tell more about a person's gravity or competence by the questions he asks rather than by the statements he makes. And I believe that's true. Well-honed questions display wit, thoughtfulness, insight, and objectivity. However, when someone jumps to conclusions too quickly or finishes others' thoughts for them, it displays what some would call a lack of business maturity. The person fails to demonstrate the self-restraint and discipline necessary to ensure an open and even playing field where everyone's thoughts have merit. It can also appear as conceit or condescension sometimes.
>
> Have you found this to be a problem from time to time as well, or am I totally shocking you with this news? [*Yes, I realize that I do that sometimes, but I never thought it was a noticeable problem.*] Okay then, let's discuss how we can make it better.
>
> Tell me, what's the first thing that comes to your mind when it comes to bettering this potential perception problem? [*I know that I could wait two seconds before responding to someone else's comment.*] Bingo! That's exactly what I was thinking, too.
>
> Joe, you'll need to heighten your level of sensitivity in terms of allowing others to finish their statements before responding, and counting to two afterward is a great way to do it. If you'll commit to increasing your awareness and level of sensitivity, then you've got my support. Do we have a deal? [*Yes.*] Good. Then I'm glad we had this discussion, and let me know any time you need my help with anything along these lines, okay? [*Okay.*]

Again, we've displayed respect and a sense of partnership in a situation that is subtle in its delivery, yet very significant in terms of the impact on the employee.

SCENARIO 58

Failure to Communicate Upward

Subordinates take cues on how to communicate from those above them. However, there will be times when people forget to share critical information with their supervisors. Sure, sometimes that's by careless oversight, but not always. Failure to communicate upward may be the result of a power play between a subordinate and her boss: By retaining information that could blindside the boss upon discovery, the subordinate may set the supervisor up for failure (or at least a lack of credibility). At other times, subordinates are afraid to be the bearer of bad news.

Adult-to-adult communication is not always a function of who's on top of the corporate totem pole. Younger managers sometimes supervise resentful older workers; subordinates who are the offspring of powerful executives in the company may feel they have no obligation to keep their bosses informed of anything. And subordinates having affairs with senior executives may feel they hold all the power in the department, even if they're not the department head. In short, it can sometimes be difficult to determine whether failure to communicate upward is an intentional strategy on the subordinate's part or simply a temporary lapse in judgment.

While you may not know what the underlying cause for the behavior is, you nevertheless have every right as a supervisor to insist that your staff members communicate upward effectively. Here's how you might address the matter with a subordinate who's forgotten that aspect of her job on one too many occasions.

The Solution

When it comes to working with your own subordinates, creating a culture of trust is an amalgam of formal guidelines that you establish as well as informal, unspoken cues that you give. The best way to establish your expectations about feeding information up the line to you is to set your expectations with your staff members up front:

> Listen, everyone: I have a very important rule that I'll ask you all
> to follow about communication while on my team. I don't mind

that bad news occasionally hits the fan; I simply need to know which way to duck when it does. You're responsible for communicating any problems with me before I learn about them from anyone else. There can be no exceptions while I'm at the helm. Is everyone clear on that? [*Yes.*]

If a feeling of flying blind plagues your relationship with a particular staff member, clarify your expectations clearly and unequivocally, using guilt (rather than anger) if at all possible.

Debra, I wanted to call this private meeting with you because I ran into a serious problem while you were out on vacation last week. Apparently, before you left, you realized that our Estimate 3 financial projections would not be ready by the quarterly deadline, but you failed to inform me. Instead, your coworker Raymond let me know about the problem.

The first issue with that, obviously, is that we were on course to miss a deadline, and you failed to tell me. As a result, Raymond and I had to work until 10:00 p.m. for two nights in a row to ensure that our information was properly integrated into the divisional report.

It's one thing to miss a deadline; it's another thing to feel like you're flying blind because a subordinate isn't keeping you abreast of important issues in your group.

Had you told me about your inability to meet the project deadline before you left, I could have assigned additional staff or resources to help you. Instead, you somehow felt that by telling your peer rather than me, he would somehow keep the secret and get the work done, and I'd never be the wiser.

First, I'm very disappointed by your lack of discretion. I thought we had a very open relationship in terms of communication, but that's not evident by your actions here. Second, your failure to inform me of such a serious potential problem could have really embarrassed me in front of the senior management team.

I guess the only thing I can say to you at this point is that I would do everything in my power to avoid setting you up for failure or embarrassing you in any way. I can't say I feel that you would do the same for me right now.

Oh, and Raymond didn't come to me and volunteer any information about this. I happened to ask him about the status of the report, at which point he showed me the report itself. When I saw all the holes in the information, I told him there'd be no way for us to make the quarterly deadline, at which point he told me that you had asked him to finalize the report in your absence. I just wanted you to know that you put him in a very precarious position, and I think you also need to think about your coworkers' best interests in situations like this in the future.

I'm choosing not to issue you a formal written warning or anything that will go on record in your personnel file, especially since you're just back from a week in Hawaii. I have to assume this was just a massive failure to communicate on your part because you were preparing to leave on your vacation. However, I need to let you know that if you fail to communicate appropriately with me in the future, I'll have the date and time of this meeting in my drawer and will refer to it as needed. Please think about this overnight and let me know if you have any suggestions or recommendations about how you'll handle such situations in the future.

Okay, this is clearly a tougher, more confrontational discussion than normal, but you had every right to issue a written warning for such a significant lapse in judgment. Whenever you opt not to move all the way to a written warning and to leave things at the verbal level, feel free to strengthen the tone of your message.

10

Personal Style Issues

ersonal style issues come in all shapes and sizes. In fact, you can categorize almost any attitude problem or work ethic shortcoming into a topic this broad. We'll focus on the most common and the most serious topics that are likely to come your way as a supervisor—everything from suspected alcohol abuse to oversensitivity to anger management to plain old laziness, while keeping an eye on predictable objections that may come your way.

Remember that when touching on topics that are close to an employee's heart and sense of self, your best bet is to proceed in a sensitive but firm manner. In scenarios like these, it becomes critical that you minimize any potential misinterpretations. Finally, you'll want to know when to get help from your corporate support team as well as from external vendors who may provide services to subordinates outside the workplace.

SCENARIO 59

Suspected Alcoholism or Substance Abuse

Let's start this chapter right on the money, so to speak. One of the most critical concerns that you may face in your career will occur when dealing with staff members who may be affected by alcohol or drugs in the workplace. Of course, you may not know for certain as your perception will likely be influenced by observable behaviors that you reasonably conclude may stem from some form of substance abuse.

And you can't tread too carefully here: If you're wrong in your assessment or if you march all over someone who is indeed engaging in such undesirable (or even unlawful) activities, there may be legal considerations that affect your ability to intervene. Therefore, here's the best advice right off the bat: Get legal help in advance of addressing these types of matters with your staff members. Don't look at the cost of the attorney's billable hours; consider it a cheap insurance policy to keep your company out of legal hot water.

Scenarios vary but usually sound something like this: You begin noticing certain oddities in an individual's behavior or comments. Then you perceive physical changes in the way the employee speaks (slur), looks (glassy eyes), or walks (uneven gait). You may even smell alcohol on the employee's breath or when standing nearby. At that point, you have a reasonable concern that even if performance problems aren't visible yet, they may become so in the near future, especially if the substance abuse problem continues to escalate. How do you open that conversation, and what can or can't you say under the circumstances?

The Solution

It's always best to come from a place of true concern for the individual when initiating such dialogues. It's critical in a business (versus personal) environment, however, that you justify your intervention based not only on the individual's good but on the company's business needs. In other words, you'll want to follow a paradigm like this:

- ▶ Describe the perception problem, based on your physical observations, without reaching a definitive conclusion.
- ▶ Describe the business reasons that justify your concern.
- ▶ Describe the consequences in an objective, matter-of-fact tone.
- ▶ Offer alternatives and resources to help the individual handle the matter privately.

Here's how that might sound in a talk you're having with one of your insurance adjusters whom you suspect may be drinking at lunchtime to get through the day:

Audrey, I wanted to have a meeting with you this afternoon here in my office, and I wanted it to be right after lunch. I've invited

Travis from our HR department to join me because I believe he might be able to help us a lot in terms of resources and support. What I want to talk to you about may be an uncomfortable subject, as it may potentially affect your personal life and job performance, but I will do my best to handle this respectfully and tactfully. I just want you to know that we're here to help in any way we can.

I told Travis in advance of this meeting that I have reason to suspect that you may be drinking at lunch and returning to the office under some influence of alcohol. If that's true, you're not in trouble and we're going to initially try to help you, but it could affect your job if the problem isn't fixed.

Of course, the caveat that Audrey won't be in trouble even if she admits to drinking during the workday depends on your company's policy. In this example, the company is willing to help the employee turn the problem around and employ its external Employee Assistant Program (EAP) provider to help her. But if your company's policy allows zero tolerance for such behavior, you'll have to amend the opening statement above.

So let me ask you, is it possible that you're drinking at lunch? [*No, I'm not, and I resent your even questioning me about this.*]

I don't mean to offend you. Let me share with you why I'm under this impression, and please listen objectively, Audrey, so that you can understand why I initiated this conversation with you. First, two of your coworkers told me that you carry a bottle of vodka in your purse when you go out to lunch. They've seen it on more than one occasion and reported it to me out of concern for you. Second, when you've returned from lunch over the past week or so, I noticed that your walk was sometimes unsteady. In fact, you tripped over yourself on Monday when you got up from your desk to go to Steve's office. In addition, when I spoke with you yesterday around 2:00 p.m., I smelled what seemed to be alcohol on your breath. And you slurred words twice in your conversation with me.

I realize that this doesn't mean that I'm right and that you're under the influence of alcohol. But based on these observations, I believe it's a reasonable and justifiable concern. Does that make sense? [*Yes, but I'm not under the influence.*]

Okay, I hear you. The observations I've made, though, relate to the legitimate business concerns our company has. After all, we can't allow our employees to be working if their performance is impaired by use of alcohol or other substances. And there's another reason: I'm concerned about your well-being from a personal perspective, but for the sake of this discussion, I'll focus my issues on the legitimate business reasons at hand. [*Okay, it's true that I carry a bottle of vodka in my purse, but it just makes me more comfortable knowing that it's there. I don't drink it.*]

You may have the right to send the employee for a reasonable suspicion test for alcohol or illegal drugs. Reasonable suspicion testing is a touchy subject, however, and may depend on the laws of your state or industry. You should clarify this issue with your attorney before initiating the conversation with the employee.

Audrey, the purpose of this meeting wasn't to offend you. However, if what you're saying is correct and you're not engaging in any improper use of alcohol or anything else, then remember our company policy: Being under *any* influence of alcohol or drugs during the workday may subject you to immediate dismissal. This isn't something the company takes lightly, and we have the right to test you at any time if we have a reasonable suspicion based on concrete observations that you may be violating our company's substance abuse policy.

Note that if you are tested, the standards aren't the same as when the police pull you over, and you have to be above a certain limit. If you test positive, this would be a clear infraction of company conduct rules, and it's not subject to progressive discipline. You will very likely be immediately discharged for violation of company policy.

One other reminder is that this may not have to do with *illegal* drugs or alcohol: It may simply be about misusing prescription drugs, or failing to disclose the use of a prescription drug that may impair your functioning at work, in violation of company policy. If that were the case and it were demonstrated through a drug test, you'd also be terminated immediately. Now again, these issues may not be at play here based on everything you're telling me, but I still have an obligation to remind you of the consequences if that were to be the case. Do you have any questions about any-thing I've said so far: the perception that your behavior appears at times to be altered, the fact that I've smelled what I believe to be alcohol on your breath, the fact that we have the right to test you or any employee if we have a reasonable suspicion of usage, and also that company policy allows us to terminate immediately for any violations, whether alcohol, illegal drugs, or prescription drugs used beyond their recommended dosage limits, are in-volved? [*No.*]

Okay, then, thanks for coming in to speak with us.

There's one more thing I'd like you to be aware of: We've come to you in good faith today to offer our help and provide you with this booklet on our company's Employee Assistance Program, or EAP.

An EAP is a confidential workplace service provider that the company pays for so that its employees can speak privately and confidentially with professionals who can help them through chal-lenges in their personal lives, whether that involves marital or fi-nancial problems, substance and alcohol abuse, or family issues. In theory at least, if employees have an external resource to help them with work-life stressors, then those issues won't find their way into the workplace, which is why the company pays for the service.

It's a free benefit to you, and as I said, we'll never know if you reach out to them. If you call, you'll speak with an intake coun-selor who will help you find a qualified professional in your neigh-borhood to help you and your family with whatever challenges you may be facing, and it would certainly justify our company's investment in that particular benefit. If you later decide to come to us or to reach out to the EAP confidentially, that's absolutely fine—you're always welcome to do so. And, of course, please let us know if there's ever anything we can help with.

Employee Assistance Programs are employee benefit programs of-fered by many companies, typically in conjunction with a health in-surance plan. EAPs are intended to help employees deal with personal problems that might adversely impact their work performance. EAPs generally include assessment, short-term counseling, and referral ser-vices for employees and their household members. Typical issues they deal with include substance abuse, emotional distress, trauma from life-changing events like an unexpected death in the family, and even financial and legal support.

Also remember that offering the employee an opportunity to come forward and voluntarily enter an alcohol and drug rehabilitation program and go on a protected leave of absence may be an employee-friendly alternative to help those suffering from alcohol or drug abuse.

Special Note

This issue can get tricky for a number of reasons. First, when you speak with outside counsel about your right to mandate drug testing for cause or to terminate someone under the influence at work, know that there will be legitimate concerns when it comes to interpreting an issue that borders on privacy rights, disability law, and the degree of potential impact to your business.

Second, when it comes to potential substance abuse charges at work, the Americans with Disabilities Act (ADA) and certain state disability laws come into play and generally preclude you, as an employer, from discharging a worker for their status as an alcoholic or a drug addict, or for perceiving the worker to be an alcoholic or drug addict, or for the worker's attendance at an alcohol treatment or drug rehabilitation program.

Third, if an employee is deemed to be under the influence of alcohol and the company decides to retain rather than terminate the individual, the company may have the right to establish a practice of random testing with the individual concerned under a "last chance" agreement. These issues go well beyond the scope of this book, however, and require qualified legal counsel to review the specific facts involved.

SCENARIO 60

Inability to Accept Constructive Criticism

One of the most irritating aspects of supervision has to do with providing constructive criticism to subordinates who freak out any time you tell them there's a hair out of place. Here's how to address this particularly sticky issue when it comes your way.

The Solution

Assuming your executive assistant seems to have disproportionate reactions to your criticisms and suggestions, no matter how benign or well-meaning, try addressing the situation this way:

> Gina, we need to talk about something that's been on my mind a lot lately, and I mean to do this respectfully and with the best intentions. However, I'll need you to listen objectively by giving me the benefit of the doubt in terms of how I'm feeling. Does that sound reasonable? [*Yes.*]
>
> I feel that it's very difficult to provide you with constructive criticism at times. From my vantage point, if I share something with you that in any way appears to you to be critical, your defenses automatically kick in. I need to hear from you because maybe I need to deliver the information differently, but I don't feel my feedback is biting or sarcastic in any way—at least, it's not meant to be. Yet when I ask you how something occurred or why something is the way it is, you become very defensive—at least in my perception—and seem to need to "convince" me that you're right a lot of the time. As a result, I feel there's a lot of unnecessary drama and histrionics in our day-to-day relationship, and I find myself constantly trying to avoid confrontation, which means neither of us is functioning as efficiently as we could be.
>
> Let me give you some examples. This morning I asked you why the Penske file had been transferred to New York City without the credit confirmation attached. I asked you that because our standard practice is to attach credit reports before forwarding them to the New York corporate office.
>
> Rather than answering me objectively and telling me that Josh Jones, the vice president of credit, had asked you to forward the file as is, you responded sharply, "That's not my fault! Josh Jones called and instructed me to send it to him immediately, and you found out about it before I had a chance to tell you." I don't understand why your response was so sharp and caustic. I was only

asking for objective information, which you could have shared with me in a whole different tone of voice.

A similar thing happened on Monday when I gave you feedback about how to close out all your email messages. I simply said that you should end each email with a "Thanks so much" or "All the best" type of closer. Up until then, you simply signed everything "Gina." That was a reasonable request that was both for your own good as well as the good of our department, yet you responded instinctively, "Well, other people don't always do that, so why should I have to?"

As your supervisor, this relationship isn't going to work if I don't feel comfortable bringing issues like these to your attention. Sometimes, we'll have to change the way we do things in light of changes within the company, and at other times there will need to be exceptions to the rule. I just can't have you react negatively each time there's some exception or change in plans. And it's certainly within my rights as your supervisor to recommend how to end your emails, isn't it? [*Yes.*]

Now tell me your side of the story. What am I missing from my vantage point, and what do I need to do differently to elicit a different response from you in the future? [*Employee explanation follows.*]

Good, then let's agree on the following terms:

First, I'll agree to . . . [*fill in whatever you glean from hearing Gina's feedback*].

In addition, you'll agree to remain cognizant of your behavior when it comes to receiving and accepting constructive feedback from me.

You won't assume ill intentions or any need to defend yourself or your actions when I ask you a simple question about why something was done a certain way.

You'll promise to avoid any reaction that could appear to be dramatic or overly sensitive so that we can work more comfortably together.

And you'll let me know any time if I'm not living up to my end of the bargain, just as I'll let you know any time you're not living up to yours.

Remember, Gina, I'm more than willing to meet you halfway now that we've both heard each other's sides of the story. Sound fair? [*Yes.*] Good. Thanks very much for meeting with me to discuss this.

Yes, it probably seems like a lot of work to have such an in-depth discussion about something so basic. However, you'll have created a record of active engagement with your employee about a problem that's fundamental to your working relationship. If any further examples arise, then your next logical step will be to formally document Gina's substandard conduct in the form of a written warning.

SCENARIO 61

Lack of Sensitivity and Protocol (Email Censuring)

Does it ever feel like you're working with troglodytes and bringing fire to the cavemen? Work isn't supposed to be so hard. Yes, there's always a tremendous amount of work to be done, but the people factor sometimes makes it unbearable. There's a reason why many people choose to exit from the corporate world and become sole proprietors—fewer people, fewer problems, right?

Well, before you jump ship too quickly, remember the other side of the equation: The main reason people work is for the *psychic* income— the feeling that they belong, make a difference, and receive recognition for a job well done. And that psychic income comes from a sense of community and the social aspects of work. Let's discuss how to make life in the business world a little bit easier for all us, especially when dealing with the Neanderthals (with all due respect!) who may be one or two steps higher than you on the corporate ladder.

The Solution

Let's assume you're sitting at your desk minding your own business one day when an issue surfaces in your email requiring attention. You're a loan officer being questioned about a client's loan approval status, and you're looking through the client's file to see if a missing form was ever sent out.

You decide very logically to send an email to your coworker regarding the status of a missing tax identification form. You then receive a nasty and scathing email from your coworker's boss who proclaims that it's your responsibility to send out tax identification forms on your own accounts and that she doesn't like the tone of your condescending email to her staff member. Oh, even more important, this executive copies your boss, your boss's boss, and the head of human resources in her response.

As far as you're concerned, you asked a legitimate and objective question in a neutral tone only to be hollered at electronically by someone you barely know. Wow, isn't work fun?

Your first reaction may be to lash back electronically, copying everyone on that email, letting them all know that you were asking a simple status question to a peer. But before you do that, you take a deep breath and realize that someone's either having a bad day or misreading your intentions.

So you meet with your boss about this inappropriate public flogging, and your boss agrees that both the tone of your note and the nature of the request were appropriate under the circumstances. Your boss may then agree to accompany you to meet with this hotheaded executive or may encourage you to handle that meeting with her on your own. Here's what your conversation "upward" with this more senior level executive might sound like:

Michelle, I'd like to talk with you about that email response that you sent out about an hour ago. I have a feeling that you may have either misread my email or misunderstood my intentions. As far as I could see, I asked a legitimate and simple question about a pending form in a customer's file, which is not only my right but my responsibility to do. You responded by "shouting" at me in your email while copying my boss and my boss's boss in your response. Would you share with me why you felt that you needed to respond that way under those circumstances? [*I'm tired of people blaming my staff for things that aren't in their control. You're responsible for sending out tax identification forms on your own clients. Period.*]

I hear you there, but I wasn't blaming anyone or asking anyone on your staff to do that work for me. I was simply questioning whether that particular form somehow made its way into Sandra's office. Does that sound like something inappropriate to you? [*No, but I've got to watch out for my people.*]

Michelle, with all due respect, you demonstrated an inappropriate response to something that, at face value, was very basic. To be honest, I'm very *hurt* by all this. You made me feel as if I was under attack for no good reason, and that's simply not fair or deserved. In fact, your attacks bordered on a public shaming session, leaving me to feel *humiliated* and *embarrassed* in front of my supervisors. I hope that if something ever occurs again where you don't agree with how I'm handling or even questioning something, then you'd have as much respect for me as I have for you and come to speak with me privately about it. Can you understand how I feel under the circumstances?

Well done! That was a very *guilt-driven* response to an unwarranted and unjustified personal attack. Yes, we all jump to conclusions without having all the facts sometimes, and you're not judging Michelle as a person—you're simply commenting on her behavior under these particular circumstances. However, learning how to do *corporate battle* the right way—by employing verbiage that invokes guilt rather than anger—will always help you win the day, even when you're the proverbial lower person on the corporate totem pole.

By the way, if you were the senior director in the group censuring Michelle for her inappropriate email attack on an underling, these same exact points could be made, only from your more senior perspective. For example, you might state, "I'm disappointed for your having made Lisa feel like she was under attack and for potentially embarrassing her in front of her peers and supervisors. I expect you to read your emails thoroughly before jumping to conclusions. Besides, email is not the way we resolve conflict around here—that's always done face to face." You could then add the magic lines: "If you engage in that kind of aggressive and unjustifiable behavior again, be clear that it could result *at least* in a written warning for antisocial and antagonistic behavior toward another staff member."

SCENARIO 62

Badgering and Challenging One's Supervisor

If you read the trades about corporate America's performance over the past ten years, one trend is clear: productivity per employee is way up. The digital revolution, artificial intelligence, and robotics may be very healthy for the economy, but wages generally have remained stagnant while companies have downsized, right-sized, outsourced, and offshored workers, all the while retaining consistent if not heightened productivity. That may sell well on a corporate balance sheet as far as Wall Street is concerned, but it leaves many workers feeling overleveraged and underresourced.

A natural way to offset that historical trend has been to "overhire." In other words, if a company hires a candidate who has much more experience and skills than a particular job calls for, then it stands to reason that more work will get done. And sometimes that formula does indeed work. More often than not, however, it causes problems because the overqualified hire ends up challenging his boss.

Let's look at an example: A biotech research company hires a very qualified bench scientist to support the laboratory head (we'll call him Doctor A). There's a tremendous amount of work to be done, and the bench scientist (we'll call him Doctor B) has actually held the title of laboratory head in his prior two companies. However, due to a lack of similar positions at local competitor organizations and close family ties to the area, the candidate has accepted this role at a lesser salary and with far fewer responsibilities. The company thinks it's getting a bargain for its money.

The first rule of thumb in hiring says that you should generally hire candidates with an 80 percent qualification factor. Less than that and it may take too long for the new hire to become a productive member of the team because the learning curve will be too steep; more than that and you'll end up with someone who's in a "been there, done that" kind of situation. More important, understand that candidates who take a cut in pay are often settling for a cut in responsibilities. If they accept a position one or two tiers below the level they held at a prior company, it may only be a matter of time before challenges to their supervisor and other problems arise.

The Solution

Doctor A, the supervisor, feels like the subordinate new hire, Doctor B, challenges him in front of others and questions everything from his management and communication style to his research and scientific abilities. Doctor A soon realizes that he's got to straighten out this problem before it goes any further.

Doctor B, I called you into this meeting because we've got a problem on our hands. I don't believe it would come as a surprise to you if I told you that I feel like you're challenging me at every twist and turn that comes our way. I know you're new to the team, and I realize that you were the lab head in your last position, but we had a clear agreement during the interview process that you understood this would be a different role than what you had before. You also told me that you "knew your place" and would be very supportive, especially in terms of allowing us to benefit from the greater level of knowledge and experience that you had to share in this role in our lab.

Instead, I feel like just the opposite is happening: You question my directions, you challenge my recommendations, you openly state that I'm not thinking things through thoroughly, and you do it all fairly openly in front of other staff members. It makes me feel like you believe you could do my job better than I could, which makes me question whether you're looking to take my job from me. [*No, that's not my intention at all.*]

Well, I hear you saying the words, but I don't see that in your actions. Let me give you an example: Last week in our staff meeting, I explained that we'll be changing course in one of our experiments and I reminded everyone that I'd need the lab books to be especially accurate in terms of reflecting these changes because the results hinge on them. Your first reaction in front of the rest of the team was to say, "Why are we now finding out about this? Why hasn't this been communicated before? And whose decision was it to change course so suddenly? That would jeopardize the premise of the entire experiment."

Not only that, but your tone of voice was condescending and indignant. That left some of my staff members confused as to who was running things and, as one person shared with me afterward, sounded like an outright challenge to my authority.

Let's be clear. The conversation we're having right now is something you could consider a once-in-a-career benefit. As much as I'd like to see you assume a senior role in the group so that everyone can benefit from your experience and expertise, I can't allow it to upset the balance in the lab. You've got to give some thought to our original agreement during the interview: Either you're comfortable in a number two role in this lab, or you're not. I'll respect your decision either way; however, I won't have any more open challenges or disrespectful questioning from you.

I'd like you to rethink your commitment to this company, our lab, and your role in it. Let's pick up this conversation again tomorrow so you can sleep on it and then you can share your thoughts with me. Understand however, Doctor B, that you're still in a probation period and that I'll have no hesitation to undo a hire that's not a good fit. There's simply too much at stake. It's up to you to determine your role in this group and the relationship you want to have with me. Make no mistake: challenging me or attempting to make me look like less of a doctor than you in this laboratory will result in our parting ways. Do you have any questions?

Yes, this is a fairly severe discussion, but whenever a subordinate questions your capabilities, decisions, or style of doing business in front of other subordinates, it may be time to draw a line in the sand. One thing's for sure: Either (preferably) right before or right after this meeting, be sure and meet with human resources and let them know what's going on. The smart management strategy when you're experiencing a challenge from a subordinate like this is to get human resources on your side from the beginning. This way, if Doctor B suddenly decides to complain to human resources about your management or communication style, you won't be placed in the position of having to defend yourself. Your arguments will already be lodged with HR.

SCENARIO 63

Lack of Teamwork and Relationship-Building Skills

Coworkers often work together with a sense of camaraderie and friendliness. Yes, work can be challenging at times and differences in opinion may flare up, but most people can take that in stride and are fairly forgiving, even if things don't go exactly their way. Besides, you can't help but get to know your coworkers on a personal level when you meet their kids or break bread together over lunch. We're all in this together, we treat each other respectfully, and we rely on each other for cover when we occasionally make a mistake or forget to do something.

However, it's not uncommon that one member of the staff purposely remains an outsider. That individual may keep to herself, share little, hold back from participating in group events, and want little to do with anyone else on the team. Loners often resent the fact that they're not popular or included, when in reality they are often responsible for pushing other people away. These are the same people who often complain that they do all the work, hold themselves to a higher standard than everyone else, and despite their heroic efforts are often victims to their managers' and coworkers' thoughtlessness and neglect.

The Solution

Turning around someone who may suffer from an entitlement mentality or "victim syndrome" may be one of the most challenging interventions that you'll have to face in your career. Still, when one employee provokes coworkers, assigns blame to others, or otherwise refuses to support peers, then intervention becomes critical. As we've demonstrated before in this book, addressing the matter in an empathetic yet firm fashion will probably be your best bet. Your goal will be to keep your eye on business reasons and rationale in explaining your position.

> Terry, I wanted to call a private meeting to speak with you about teamwork and relationship-building skills. I sense that you feel separate and apart from your coworkers, and my guess is that they feel that same way toward you. I'm not here to siphon through history or justify why you feel the way you do or why they

may not feel as comfortable approaching you, but I'm concerned about the way this affects the productivity of our department. It's obvious that if people are avoiding one another, then the work will suffer because communication stops. I'm also obviously concerned about your own feelings of belonging and involvement because that's such an important part of work.

First, let me ask you: Do you agree with my perceptions at least to some degree? [*Yes.*]

Okay, I'd like to hear you describe things from your point of view and perspective. Tell me how you see your relationship with your coworkers. [*I just want to be left alone to do my job. I don't bother them and they don't bother me; that's the way I like it.*]

I understand that may be the way you like it, but is that good for the department and fair to them? [*I don't know. You'll have to ask them.*]

Well, I can't mandate how you feel about other people on our team or in our company. I just want you to know that if you'd like to extend an olive branch to your coworkers, I'd be very happy to make sure it's accepted with good faith. Life is too short for squabbling, but I find that you sometimes take offense quickly when someone makes a comment that you don't agree with. It seems to me like you're keeping all your feelings inside when it doesn't have to be that way.

We hold weekly staff meetings where everyone gets a chance to share what they're working on, you and everyone else has total access to me because I rarely close my door, and I try and inject humor into the workplace whenever possible. Sometimes you're "into it," while at other times you seem bothered by the camaraderie and by my attempts at humor. As a result, it's probably not too far of a stretch for me to say that others in the department consider you moody and unpredictable, and that's not fair to them.

Listen, I can't make you like anyone or make you want to work here. But I can tell you that simply "doing your chores" isn't enough. I expect open and honest communication at all times, and if you don't feel like you can provide that on a consistent basis, then you need to find another team in another league to play on. I won't take it personally if you don't like working with or for me. Please understand, though, that I can't have everyone on the team walking on eggshells around you all the time for fear of upsetting you or otherwise setting you off.

I want you to think about this tonight. If you feel that you have every right to set yourself off from the group, do your nine-to-five job, and then go home, you're wrong. In that case, I expect you to come in tomorrow and tell me honestly that you'd prefer to look for work elsewhere, and I promise to be very supportive. On the other hand, if you come in to see me tomorrow and assume responsibility for the perception problem that you've got on your hands, coupled with a sincere desire to mend fences with your coworkers, then you'll have my full support.

Is there anything else you'd like to say or have I missed anything? [*No.*] Okay then, set some time with me tomorrow so we can pick up this conversation again.

Yes, these types of discussions can be challenging because they're fairly difficult to describe. However, all employees are responsible for both their performance *and* conduct. It's not enough for someone to act as if they're untouchable because they perform their job adequately. Contributing to a healthy work environment is equally, if not more important, and all employees are responsible for creating and sustaining a friendly and inclusive work environment. In short, permitting someone who is acting "on principle" to destroy relationships acts like a worm in the apple, and you have every right to address and potentially terminate anyone who refuses to support the broader team because of their own anger, bitterness, or personal agenda.

SCENARIO 64

On the Brink of Failure—Turning Around Teams That Are About to Implode

Newly created departments or newly minted supervisors sometimes find themselves in dire straits because of interpersonal conflict, misaligned talent, or organizational structures that lack efficiency and fail to mesh with their customers' needs. When such a situation rises to the level of an urgent distress call, it's time to take a candid look at either reinventing the group's structure or replacing certain individuals within it. As a new supervisor possibly faced with a department that's about to implode, you'll want to conduct small group meetings to learn firsthand what the specific problems are. You'll need to tally the issues you learn of, share them with the team as a whole, and then define everyone's commitments and priorities in eliminating these roadblocks.

If this process sounds like a lot of work, that's because it is. Still, there's no better investment of your time than turning a flagging team into a functional, highly accomplished group. It's the stuff legends are made of. Make yourself known as a turnaround expert for even the most dysfunctional teams, and you'll find yourself on the path to career growth and higher levels of compensation.

The Solution

Let's assume that you're responsible for the surgical unit at your hospital, and the team is constantly at odds: RNs blame LVNs, LVNs blame CNAs, and CNAs blame everyone else. All three groups complain that the management team doesn't hold people equally accountable, there's favoritism shown at every turn, and sides won't cooperate (for example, by not responding to patients' call lights when the primary nurse isn't available). Patient care is compromised, documentation is falling through the cracks, and no one wants to assume even partial responsibility for the core breakdown in team operations.

When faced with a scenario where no one seems to want to listen to the other sides, and apathy, anger, and distrust pepper the workplace, it's time to step in by meeting with each team separately—RNs, LVNs, and CNAs. Here's what your opening discussion might sound like:

> RNs, I'm calling you together as a group to learn what's going wrong in our team. No LVNs or CNAs are here because I want to hear your side of the story as honestly as possible. This meeting is about you, and here's where it will go next: I'll hold a similar, separate meeting with the LVNs as well as with the CNAs. My job now is to listen to all three groups and then afterward call us all together as a full team to discuss my findings.
>
> Once we map out the key issues with each of the three groups, I'm going to ask for commitments to solutions that we can all agree on and support. Does that sound like a fair approach? [Yes.] Good. Then let's start with this: What are the top three issues that

are bothering you and getting in our way as a team? And please tie your responses to how the problems affect patient care. After all, that's why we're all here and have jobs. Who wants to go first?

Repeat this intervention with the other two groups to gather commonalities, discrepancies, and frustrations. Once you finish with the first round of information-gathering meetings, call the entire team together to discuss matters openly and to gain commitment as follows:

Gang, as I explained earlier, this is the large group follow-up meeting where I get to debrief you on what I've learned through my interviews with the three subgroups in our unit. Interestingly enough, you all seem to agree on what the three biggest problems are: (1) Lack of holding others accountable, (2) perceptions of favoritism by certain managers toward certain medical staff members, and (3) a lack of respect, demonstrated by outbursts of anger, a condescending tone in daily communications, and an immediate inclination to blame others.

Does this surprise you? Also, am I missing anything? Speak now or forever hold your peace, because I'm only planning on doing this group-level intervention once, so I want to make sure I've captured everything correctly. Do you all agree that these three problems are your biggest concerns? [*Yes.*] Are there any other matters that need to be shared in this meeting, as we launch our turnaround strategy? [*Yes—patients complain that the CNAs aren't paying enough attention to them or addressing their requests fast enough. Also, the CNAs and LVNs aren't properly completing documentation, which puts pressure on us RNs.*]

Fair enough. Is there anything else I'm missing in what's now our top five list of concerns? [*No.*] I'm glad to hear that. This meeting can now move in another direction: During the small-group meetings, I asked you all for suggestions on how to fix the problems, including what you're willing to do differently to remedy the problems and build a greater sense of teamwork. Here's what I heard throughout the three sessions:

I'm willing to answer other patients' call lights, but only if the other nurses do the same.

I can commit to more accurate charting, but only if there are consequences for those who fail to chart accurately or thoroughly.

I won't challenge anyone with a higher license or rank than me, as long as they don't keep reminding me that they're higher than me on the corporate totem pole and always disregarding the fact that we CNAs have been here in the unit the longest and have valuable suggestions to contribute.

I think those are pretty fair commitments. Do you all agree? [*Yes.*] Would anyone like to add anything else? [*Yes: There has to be greater respect all around. How we treat people shouldn't be a function of our role in the "nursing caste." We all deserve to be respected equally, regardless of our title.*] I think that's a fair request—Do we all agree? [*Yes.*] Then let's map these commitments on the board and discuss what our unit might look like if they're being adhered to. I also want to discuss what you all feel the consequences should be if someone doesn't keep their end of the bargain.

[Conclusion] Okay, I've heard you all, both as individual groups and as a team. We've all agreed on the top problems plaguing our unit, as well as our go-forward individual and group commitments to turn this problem around. I appreciate your willingness to share this with me because I know you all want this to get better. There's enough work around here to sink a battleship, and when you add the indignities, the disrespect, and the drama to the mix, it makes it impossible to do your best work every day. Don't you agree? [*Yes.*]

Thank you. So here's my go-forward plan for all you individually and for us as a team. . . . I commit to demonstrating respect for all you, regardless of your title or role within the unit. I pledge to be the first domino, the person to assume good intentions, to serve as a role model, and to ask you all to follow my lead. I'm welcoming you all back to the company as of now—July 7—by drawing a circle on the calendar on this date and letting you all know it's safe to come out of your foxholes and reestablish our unit as "normal"—fun, supportive, inclusive, a place where your ideas and suggestions are welcome and sought after, and eventually a place where we all have each other's backs.

Understand, however, that if I'm holding myself accountable to these new standards that you've established for yourselves and for the rest of the team, I'm going to be holding you all equally accountable going forward. No more walking on eggshells, no more shouting matches in front of patients, and no more internal sabotage. Those things existed prior to July 7, but after July 7 they have no place in this unit. Please don't put me in a position to have to discipline anyone for failure to abide by these commitments you've just established. I'm assuming good intentions and placing my faith in all of you.

We are more than we've become, and we've allowed petty resentments to impede our path forward. Today you're free of those indignities, and you're now a key part to the turnaround solution. Is everyone on board, and do I have your commitment going forward to assume good intentions when dealing with one another? [*Yes.*] Then allow me to paint a picture of where we'll be six months from now: Our unit will be recognized as one of the highest-performing teams in the hospital. The physicians will be scratching their heads over how you've all been able to reinvent your relationships with one another and with them. The patients will be singing your praises because we'll become known for outstanding patient care, customer service, and operational excellence (including documentation).

And we'll become compliance wizards, ready for any surprise inspection that the Department of Health or the Joint Commission can throw our way. Are we all in agreement? [*Yes.*] Great! Then let this be your success story, and tell it proudly in the future. I've got your backs here, everyone. I only ask that you have each other's. Let the turnaround begin!

The strategy of listening openly by separating the subteams is critical, so they understand that you're on their side. They need a safe place to vent their frustrations when one team pits itself against another. The strategy of gaining their commitment to go forward with the action steps is the glue that binds the future: If they violate their own commitments, progressive discipline is a logical next step.

Finally, don't be surprised if there's some fallout over the next three to six months. Some people thrive on chaos and drama; if you remove those elements from the workplace, they'll resign and find a new opportunity where they can ply their trade. That's healthy turnover, not regrettable turnover. Just understand that large-group interventions like this usually result in casualties, so don't be overly concerned about terminating rulebreakers or watching others resign because the "new normal" doesn't fit their style.

SCENARIO 65

Laziness and Lack of Commitment

Laziness is always *special*, isn't it? Everyone on the team is working exceptionally hard and not complaining, while one member of the staff seems to be a holdout and appears to resist being assigned new work. Oh, don't get me wrong—he'll do it if he has to—but there's always a murmur under his breath or a slight rolling of the eyeball any time new assignments are distributed.

How do we turn these workplace laggards into superheroes willing to leap tall buildings in a single bound and outdo even the most industrious members of the team? Well, it won't be easy because work ethic and commitment are values established early in a person's life. If anyone (unfortunately) missed their dosage by having overindulgent and doting parents who gave them everything they wanted without having to work for it, it may be too late for you to change that life philosophy.

While it's true that we're all too socialized by the time we're of working age to change our basic selves, many people have experienced significant turnarounds because of wonderful bosses and mentors who helped them along the way. Now's your chance to offer that "gift of giving" to someone else. So be selfless, assume good intentions, and know you're making a difference in someone's life. Oh, and by the way, if your motivational conversation doesn't work, know that you've created an outstanding verbal record that will allow you to proceed along in the progressive disciplinary process and ultimately remove the laggard employee.

The Solution

Okay, so your new "first job out of college" new hire doesn't appear to be catching on that they call it *work* for a reason. He's looking for fun, a good time, and a way to keep occupied during the day so that he has enough cash on hand to party on Friday night (not to mention the weekend). Although he seemed enthusiastic and talented when he interviewed, he's not exhibiting enthusiasm, energy, or drive when it comes to his work.

You fret because everyone else on your team seems to be expending double the level of energy to get things done, while Junior seems to have idle hands and a mild disconnect with the rest of the team. So, you call Junior into your office in private and open your dialogue as follows:

Junior, I know this is your first full-time job after graduating from college, and I'm wondering how you like it so far. [*Oh, it's okay, I guess.*]

Tell me what you're seeing from your vantage point—the type of work we do, the amount of work per person, the pace we keep on the shop floor—you know, that kind of thing. [*Well, everyone seems to be busy and there's a lot of work, I guess.*]

And how would you compare how you're performing with the other members of the team? [*Uh, okay, I guess.*]

Yeah, that's where we have a disconnect. You're not performing at an acceptable level. Does it surprise you to hear me say that? [*I, um, I don't, um, I guess.*]

Well, it should surprise you—in fact, it should shock you. Here's what postgraduation reality looks like in our factory and every other company in America: Work isn't meant just to entertain you. Your focus needs to be on how to get the job done, not on how to help the time go by. And we're not paying you to be an idle set of hands while everyone else works right past you every day.

This isn't college—there's no more hand-holding. It's your responsibility to find the work, do it quickly and accurately, and keep coming back for more. I expect you to reach numbers that make others on the team jealous. I expect you to smile while you work, offer to help everyone else around you, and report back the minute you're done with one project, so you can get more. And you'll know you're doing things the right way when you're so exhausted at the end of the day that going out that night will be the last thing on your mind.

I know that I'm making this sound very serious, and that's because it really is. It's not my responsibility to ensure that you keep this job. That's your responsibility, and I hope you take it seriously. Every successful adult I know has a story to tell about how they loaded hay bales or watermelons onto trucks for a penny each in order to make ends meet and earn a living. That's what gives people character and self-respect.

On the other hand, you've got a perception problem on your hands: It appears to me that you see this work as beneath you and that you're not going out of your way to excel. I expect you to excel in every way, and I'm only giving you this one notice. If you don't demonstrate the appropriate work ethic, commitment, and sense of urgency on a consistent basis, then you won't be welcome to return here. Do I make myself clear? [*Yes.*]

There is always a question about younger workers integrating into the workforce until they prove to be hard workers. And, of course, this doesn't apply only to younger workers. The same structural outline will work for seasoned but "work intolerant" employees! Just remember that this conversation shouldn't happen more than once. Any further demonstrations of a lack of work ethic should be met with termination (for a probationary employee) or with a formal written warning (for a more tenured worker).

SCENARIO 66

Blamers and Excuse Makers

The best and most successful managers give praise to others in times of success and assume responsibility when things go wrong. Mediocre managers do just the opposite: They accept praise when things go well and are quick to blame others and point fingers when things go wrong. Anyone willing to throw others under the bus when problems arise will likely do the same to you, their boss. These folks either need an attitude adjustment or they need to move on in their careers. In short, they represent the managerial worm in the apple: Not only do they pose a risk to you personally but they'll wreak havoc on your staff retention plans because no one trusts them. Your best staffers will leave because they have no trust or respect for their supervisor, and you may not find out about it for a long time. After all, no one wants to speak poorly of a supervisor during an exit interview—that leaves a bad taste in the company's mouth, and who knows, the exiting employee may want to return to your company someday.

The Solution

When you suspect that blamers and excuse makers may be causing unnecessary havoc and turnover in their groups, it's time to step in wisely. You may want to initiate the following conversation with the target supervisor:

John, I wanted to call this private meeting with you because I'm concerned with what I'm seeing and hearing. Let me tell you what it looks like from my vantage point. Yesterday, I saw you blame Sarah for something that clearly wasn't her responsibility. When we were in our weekly staff meeting, I asked you why the systems switch wasn't completed, and you immediately answered that Sarah misunderstood her responsibilities and the overall time-line of the transition. You didn't even blink. It was like you were waiting for me to say something so that you could offer up Sarah. [*Well, it was her fault. She didn't—*]

Let me stop you right there. First, that project falls under your team, so it's *your* responsibility. Period. You get work done through your people, but if it doesn't get done, then you're responsible, and I expect you to assume responsibility for the problem, especially in front of others. Poor Sarah wasn't even there to defend herself. [*Then I should discipline her.*] Maybe. But this meeting is about you, not her. I don't expect everything to go perfectly smoothly all the time. More important, though, I don't expect you to take all the credit when things go well and assign blame when they don't. In short, *you need to rethink this whole paradigm you've created in your head.*

Here's how the new paradigm needs to work from now on: When things go right, share the kudos with the rest of your staff. When things go wrong, assume responsibility for the problem and shield your staff as much as possible. That's enlightened leadership, and that's what I expect from all my managers.

Understand how this works to your advantage: When you give the glory to your subordinates, your peers will jump in right away and say, "Stop being so modest." We know that you led the team to this level of success, but it's very nice of you to give them all the credit. And when things go wrong and you assume full responsibility for the problem, others will say, "Don't blame this all on yourself. I know you've got a few players on your team who are a bit green and need to learn these things, so no worries. I'm sure they'll get it together before too long."

That's the management paradigm I want you to follow, both for the sake of your own career and for the good of the company. If you remember nothing else, remember this: Your reputation as an ethical and inspiring employee and leader is the coin of the realm, the equity that you build up in your career over time. Everyone makes mistakes, and when you do, admit them openly, apologize, and commit to avoiding those same errors in the future. That's fine—we're all human, and no one's going to hold that against you.

But if you put your needs above everyone else's, hog the glory, and deflect the blame, then you'll have no goodwill in your career whatsoever, and people like that often come crashing down at some point with no life vest to keep them afloat. Do you see where I'm coming from? [*Yes.*]

Good, then reengage that way. From this point forward. No exceptions. Do you hear what I'm telling you? [*Yes.*] Okay, then this meeting is complete. Consider this an important career coaching and mentoring session.

Well done! Managers who readily blame others and grab all the glory aren't doing themselves or your company any favors. Help them see the error of their ways and restructure one of their basic thoughts about themselves. They'll thank you later (or else leave the company quietly).

SCENARIO 67

Coworker Jealousy and Employees Who Can't Let Go of Their Anger

Sometimes people just have it out for coworkers and can't seem to get over their anger or jealousy. Their inability to work together smoothly often reveals itself in subtle behaviors meant to undermine the co-worker's credibility in your eyes.

"Psst. I just need to let you know that Suzie is not at her desk enough. She's way too social and doesn't do her fair share of the work. It doesn't really bother me personally, but it may make it hard on the others." Well, so much for coworker camaraderie and trust! Soon enough, you'll realize the employee is almost always complaining about one particular person (or complaining about things that sabotage that person indirectly). The complaining employee is oblivious to the shortcomings of anyone else on the staff; it's just the one targeted coworker who gets the brunt of the complaints.

Your subordinates may find many such minor issues to bring to your attention theoretically for your own good, but much like a parent with squabbling kids, you have to teach them that turning each other in may not be a healthy way to conduct themselves. Of course, you want to know certain things as a manager because you can't be everywhere all the time, but the workplace isn't perfect and it never will be, so you've got to distinguish real problems from when one person is trying to get another in trouble.

The Solution

When faced with setups that appear to target a coworker, firmly take the complaining subordinate aside and explain the following:

Shannon, there's something that I've got to bring to your attention. I don't know if you realize it or not, but the only person you ever seem to complain about is Suzie. You typically open your conversation by saying, "Would you mind if I told you something that's none of my business?" and then you launch into some form of criticism about Suzie—how she's not completing her work on time, is wandering away from her desk, is being too social, or is otherwise performing at an unacceptable level.

From now on, if you ask me that question, the answer will be "no." I won't want to hear your tips about her problematic performance. Frankly, I don't need you telling me how to manage my relationships with other staff members, and you and Suzie do separate jobs and hold different responsibilities in the group, so I see no need for your censure of her work or work habits.

And I have another piece of advice for you, Shannon: You need to come to terms with and get over the anger and resentment that you harbor toward her. I don't know if you feel threatened by her for some reason or why she seems to get under your skin, but it's obvious to me as an outsider, even if you aren't aware of it. Why else would you only find fault with one person over and over again when I, as her supervisor, don't find those faults?

I'm serious here: If you don't find a way to get over your resentment, it will eat you up inside, and it may result in undoing your career here at our company. Please don't put me in a position to have to have this type of discussion with you a second time, Shannon, because if we do, my response will be in a written rather than a verbal format. Am I clear? [*Yes.*] Good. Thank you very much.

Once you lay these perception issues down verbally, it becomes much easier to move to a formal written warning because you can always say, "Don't you remember when we spoke on May 30 that you agreed not to say anything negative about Suzie or to try to get her in trouble? Well, you've done it again, and I'm afraid it looks like the only way I'm going to be able to break this habit is to formalize my findings in the form of a written warning. You'll have it by the end of the day, and you're more than welcome to write a rebuttal to it. The consequence language will be clear, though: It will say that if you engage in that particular type of behavior again, further disciplinary action may occur, up to and including dismissal." Enough said.

SCENARIO 68

Supremacists—Arrogance and Superior Attitudes

What can you say about employees who demonstrate a holier-than-thou mentality? Sometimes referred to as snobs, sometimes as highbrows, these folks come across as condescending, arrogant, and pompous. They're often characterized as having an unwarranted sense of pride and self-importance. They may fail to listen to others and persevere at expressing their opinions, even when uninvited. They sometimes persist at arguing their points until the other party is worn down and worn out—claiming victory but only via a war of attrition. In short, there's not much that's helpful about workers who demonstrate these traits.

The Solution

Quiet arrogance reveals itself in raised noses and eyebrows along with condescending smirks and utterances. *Loud arrogance* talks over others and insists on getting its own way. Whichever type you're dealing with will probably leave you feeling cold, so when you've got a subordinate who demonstrates either type of behavior, it's best to sit down and use the perception problem approach to sensitize him to how he's coming across. Here's what it might sound like:

> Peter, we need to talk. I scheduled this private meeting with you because I've got a concern that we need to discuss. This isn't about your job performance, so no worries on that end, but I would categorize it as a workplace conduct issue. Specifically, I wouldn't be doing you a service as your supervisor if I didn't tell you that you sometimes come across as arrogant and condescending. Does it shock you to hear that? [*Yes.*]
>
> Here's how it looks from my vantage point. When we were in our staff meeting this morning, Alison raised a point about the upcoming conference. She suggested that we man the conference booth with six people rather than four so that the two additional people could serve as extra sets of hands while we were passing out tickets for our raffle giveaways. I didn't think it was a good idea initially, but before I could say anything, you jumped in and interrupted her, saying, "Uh, no. That's not something we're going to do. That won't work." There was no explanation as to why, and you simply allowed the dead silence to waft there for a minute before you continued on in a totally different direction.
>
> I'm not questioning your answer because I happen to agree with it. My concern, though, has to do with *how* you put her down so easily. You totally dismissed her suggestion in front of the whole team and didn't show her enough respect to explain why you felt it was a bad idea. Let me ask you this: How do you think that left her feeling? [*Well, it was a silly idea. We can't fit four people, never mind six—*]

Ah, let me stop you right there. Remember we're not debating the merits of your argument—just how you communicated it. It almost seemed to me as if you waved your invisible hand to discount Alison's idea, making it seem unimportant and out of line with the conversation. Could you see why she might feel diminished or embarrassed by that?

[*Um, I guess, but I really don't have time to coddle these people. I'm not their parent. If they need hand-holding, work isn't the appropriate venue.*] Oh, it's too bad you feel that way. I happen to totally disagree with you. Here's how it works in my shop: Everyone has an important role to play, and everyone is valued as an individual. That means when people make suggestions to improve situations, their suggestions are taken seriously. More important, all staff members are made to feel welcome and encouraged to participate.

I don't feel like this conversation is getting very far in terms of my being able to sensitize you as to how you're coming across, so let me be more direct: You've got a serious perception problem on your hands. People regard you as aloof, distant, condescending, and arrogant. As a result, people tend to avoid you rather than deal with you directly. And that's a big problem for our group because your behavior impedes collaboration and open communication.

Here's how to look at it: Sleep on it tonight and determine whether you feel like you can amend your behavior to create a more inclusive work environment. Do you feel you can be more sensitive to other people's feelings and reinvent yourself in light of the feedback that I'm giving you right now? If so, that would be great, and I'll be fully supportive of the "new you" that you'll introduce to the rest of us tomorrow.

On the other hand, Peter, in fairness to the department and to the company, if you really feel like that's just not you, then I'll respect that as well. Not every individual's personality fits into any particular department's corporate culture, and I respect that. If pursuing other opportunities right now is the direction you want to head in, then just let me know. I'll be open to that idea as well and will support you in any way I can. Set some time to meet with me tomorrow and let me know how you're feeling about the whole thing, okay? Thanks very much for meeting with me.

Yes, this may be a "my way or the highway" approach to managing this individual, but you can't let one person kill the camaraderie of the entire team. You may be able to put up with it for a while, but at some point it's going to get old, so address your perception issue openly, honestly, and up front. That's always a better alternative than simply ignoring the person and forcing Peter to divine by your actions that he's not liked or appreciated. Is it tough talk? Yes. Is it necessary talk? Absolutely! (But if you have any concerns about legal issues due to the individual's tenure, age, or ethnicity, for example, be sure and speak with human resources or qualified legal counsel first for a conversational dry run.)

SCENARIO 69

Stubborn Employee Challenges—Entitlement, Resistance to Change, and Overt Defensiveness and Hostility

No doubt about it—the twenty-first century has brought incredible change at what sometimes feels like an unsustainable pace. If you've heard the term "evolutionary change at revolutionary speed," you know it speaks to what we've been experiencing since the new millennium began. Metrics and analytics, artificial intelligence, drones, and online algorithms seem to be redefining how we shop and what we view online, as well as how we communicate with one another and even who we are.

Still, many of us work with employees who balk at change. Resistance to new software systems is the culprit that comes to mind first , but it's more than that. What about employees who demonstrate an ongoing sense of entitlement and stubborn resistance to anything that appears to disrupt the status quo? For many individuals, software illiteracy isn't the core of the problem—the problem is rooted in abject fear of change or plain old stubbornheadedness. This tends to become more of a problem with longer-tenured employees, who possess a greater awareness of organizational history. But whether tenured or fairly new, some people don't want to get with the times, and you can end up in a difficult position if you don't proactively address the problem.

The Solution

There's an expression in leadership circles that people don't fear change—they just fear *being* changed. Maybe that piece of workplace wisdom is true at some deeper level, but it sure doesn't feel that way in the office. For many of us, it feels like certain employees fear change for change's sake, plain and simple. Getting ahead of change is best handled by putting everyone in the same room and allowing them to speak freely about their concerns, while you also reframe change as an asset instead of an impediment. Your group discussion might sound like this:

> Everyone, I'm calling this meeting to discuss something that may be uncomfortable for some of you: dealing with change and addressing the resistance to change that comes from what could be perceived as an "entitlement mentality." I don't mean to offend anyone by saying that. And I want this to be a group discussion and a safe place for us to discuss our ideas, concerns, and suggestions. However, the best way to address any type of inhibitor or drag on a team's performance is for us all to sit around the campfire and discuss the matter openly and honestly. You may not agree with everything I have to say, and that's okay. But I need to put something out on the table that I believe is holding back our team.
>
> First, there's no judgment in what I'm about to say—this is only my observation. I'm not about the "so what" as much as I am about that "what's so." In other words, there's no judgment about you or us in terms of dealing with the pace of change we see all around us. However, I can tell you that I sense stiff resistance at times when we're asked to change direction on a dime or adapt to a new program, policy, or system, like when management asked our group to take the lead in transitioning to the new CMS. And at times I feel there's overt defensiveness and even hostility when we're asked to pivot or move to a Plan B.
>
> As I see it, the pace of change isn't slowing down any time soon. That's true in both our personal lives and our business lives. Our ability as a team to adapt, regroup, change direction, and pivot all speaks to our group's agility. Agility is a key talent and competency in today's economy, and while they don't teach that

in school, it's a philosophy and mindset that I want you all to focus on and to hone—right here, right now—as an important part of your career development.

This isn't about change for change's sake. And I'm certainly not trying to frustrate you—that would never be my intention. Even so, I have to share something with you that I want you to think about and reflect on: our longevity as a team may be holding us back. Longevity is a wonderful thing, and it looks great on a résumé. I get that. But interviewers sometimes fear that too much longevity may indicate a fear of change on a candidate's part, and there's a reason for that.

Some workers—not necessarily us—dig themselves in, resist change at all costs, and hang on to the status quo, to their own and to a company's detriment. From a career-development standpoint, you want to be the exception: the one with excellent tenure who's not only open to change but also a driver of it, a "change champion," so to speak. That's what your resume and your LinkedIn profile should highlight.

My expectation going forward is that we become known as change experts, change ninjas, and a group open and willing to drive our organization (and our careers) in a new direction. I don't want us to become known as a tired group that resists change and fights fiercely to maintain the status quo. We can't afford to make ourselves a layoff target.

All of us need to recognize that organizational and system changes aren't the enemy. And I want to make the concept of "change leadership" a staple in every weekly staff meeting that we hold from this point forward.

I'm giving you all a homework assignment. First, being as honest with yourself as you can be, grade yourself on a scale of 1 to 10 for your strength as a change leader and a driver of innovation. Share your answer with no one. In three months, I'll ask you to regrade yourself in that area. Then, I'd like you to meet with me privately to discuss your two grades. Finally, I'll ask you why you changed your grade and how.

To do that, you need to think about what you want to focus on. For example, if you feel you're a seven out of ten right now in your willingness to adapt and flex from preestablished plans or expectations, and your goal is to become an eight or a nine, you'll have to choose something to master. And I'm here to discuss what that might be, if you'd like my help with this exercise. We have plenty of opportunities to choose from, and I'm happy to meet with you one-on-one to discuss what this might look like for you.

I must emphasize that this is for your own good, for both your career and professional development. There will be a by-product that's great for our company—our team, as a whole, will strengthen its ability to adapt, flex, and innovate. But that can only happen if each of you does your part in moving us forward. We can only go as fast as our slowest team member, so I'm hoping that in three months, we're all grading ourselves at a higher level compared to today and have concrete examples to demonstrate our improvement.

To make sure you're all as committed to this as I am, the process of becoming change leaders will be an important part of your annual performance review.

Now, tell me what questions, suggestions, or concerns you have about this new directive that I'm sharing with you. . . .

Effective leaders make challenges fun, and when they present a challenge, the narrative is interwoven with both the employees' individual benefit and the greater benefit to the team and company. These types of challenges are rarely easy, and you'll likely have naysayers that quietly roll their eyes at your new direction. But peer pressure will turn them around, if the majority of the team is on board; if peer pressure doesn't get them on board, they'll likely transfer to another unit or even tender their notice rather than abandon their self-imposed principles. However, when transfers and resignations don't happen, progressive discipline or failed performance reviews can provide the due process necessary to move stubborn resisters off the team and potentially out of the organization, no matter how long their tenure.

11

Leadership Style Challenges and Career Management Obstacles

Surprisingly little has been written about effectively dealing with managerial style challenges at work because it's too difficult a topic to pin down. But it's a topic that more than anything ties into an individual's ability to manage her career successfully. How do you tell someone something as subjective and subtle as the following?

► You appear to avoid confrontation at all costs.
► You've developed a reputation as someone who has an argumentative and intimidating disposition.
► You openly challenge and confront others who express contrary opinions.
► You tend to overdelegate and not do enough of the work yourself.
► You appear to instill fear in your subordinates.

These are strong accusations that more often than not will be met with stiff resistance: "No, I don't." "Who told you that?" "Name me one person who would say that about me." Of course, this creates yet another hurdle for you: fear of retaliation. Why? Because once you make someone aware that others may indeed think this way about them, they may become paranoid and initiate a witch hunt of an internal investigation to determine who indeed made those comments to you, their boss.

Telling a supervisor that her management style is confrontational, bullying, overly optimistic, wishy-washy, or anything in between creates lots of dialogue that—let's face it—you'd rather avoid if at all possible. That's why so many of us practice the path of least resistance and avoid dealing with these subtle and subjective perceptions and indignities that occur day in and day out.

How do you get someone to listen objectively to you when your message can be cutting? Well, don't expect it to be too easy, seeing that people are reflexively emotional toward anything that sounds like subjective criticism. Still, if you don't tell them about this perception problem that plagues them, they may never realize it's a detriment to their career until it's too late. Or worse, they may continue to bug you until you want to jump out a window, and let's face it—that's not good for any of us now, is it?

This chapter is dedicated to those under-the-radar leadership challenges that plague many managers and get in the way of their careers. Let's see if we can develop some scripted strategies to help subordinates improve their performance, make your life and their coworkers' lives easier, and hopefully propel them forward in their careers.

SCENARIO 70

Unwillingness to Confront Problems Head-On

Supervisors who avoid confrontation cause lots of angst and drama in the workplace. Small problems tend to become bigger ones if not addressed quickly, and turnover and lawsuits tend to result when perceptions of unfairness permeate the office or shop floor.

Some people are born natural leaders, while others need to develop and strengthen that ability. Whatever the case, it's in your and your company's best interests to ensure that problem issues are addressed head-on whenever possible. Sure, there will be times when a wait-and-see approach will make the most sense, but more often than not, bad habits need to be broken early so that inappropriate behaviors don't perpetuate themselves in the workplace.

Let's look at an example. Your company prides itself on its inclusive culture. Employees are generally treated with respect, your line managers create an environment where workers have input and say into the day-to-day operations of the plant, and yelling and screaming are just not what you're all about. In steps a new hire in your sales management group who was obviously raised by wolves and who comes from the General Patton school of "motivating" subordinates.

Before too long, the first incident gets reported about her publicly humiliating a subordinate at a staff meeting. You hear all the details about this incident from salespeople who were present at the meeting, but you hear nothing from your vice president of sales who oversees the group and ran the meeting. Patiently you wait, hoping to hear from your vice president, but nothing. You decide to wait and keep a close eye on the situation, only to hear about another incident of public shaming during the following week's meeting. Still, no word from your VP.

The Solution

Let's assume you've done your homework and received consistent feedback about both incidents from witnesses on site. You're ready to discuss the issue with the vice president who, in fairness, may have addressed this with the new hire. Still, it's funny that the vice president didn't mention anything to you up to this point.

Cindy, how are things going with your staff these days? [*Fine.*] Are there any issues that you want me to be aware of or that you need to bring to my attention? [*No.*] Oh, I see. How's your new hire doing: Charlotte, the sales manager? Has her on-boarding process been smooth or does she need anything at this point? [*No. She's fine.*]

Well, it surprises me to hear that, seeing that I've heard there were "shout-outs" at her first two weekly staff meetings. People who were present came to see me to provide me with blow-by-blow details of her attacks on Bill and Ryan for not making their outbound call numbers. Why don't you tell me how things look from your vantage point?

[*Well sure, there have been two incidents of calling to everyone's attention the fact that two members of the team weren't reaching their outbound call numbers, but I have to defer to Charlotte. This is her new role, and I need her to establish accountability and establish appropriate expectations for everyone.*]

Let me ask you this: I understand what she's doing; my question is, *how* is she doing it? Has she spoken to you about her intended approach before the staff meetings, or did you simply learn of her tactics during the meetings themselves?

[*A little bit of both, I guess. She told me she planned on "drawing a little blood" at first to make sure everyone was paying attention. From that point forward, though, she said she'd take a calmer approach to managing the day-to-day operations of the sales function.*]

And once you saw how Charlotte handled those meetings, Cindy, were you in agreement with her methodology? [*Again, I probably wouldn't have handled it that way myself, but I'll defer to her in terms of how she wants to manage the sales team underneath her.*]

Okay, at this point, you've calmly approached the issue to fact-find your way to the truth, and you feel disappointed that Cindy would allow new hire Charlotte to trample over the staff that way. First, that's not your management style. Second, Cindy knows that it's not your company's culture to strip people of their dignity in front of others. Third, you're now questioning Cindy's role in all of this: Is she afraid to address Charlotte or somehow intimidated by her? If not, why would she allow such inappropriate managerial behavior to go unaddressed? Your response is clear and unequivocal in its intent:

Cindy, I'm shocked and disappointed to hear your reaction to all this. First, you know that that's not how this company operates. When we have a problem, we address it professionally and appropriately. If Charlotte wasn't satisfied with Bill and Ryan's sales results, she needed to address that with them in private one-on-one meetings. We've never been known as a company to embarrass or humiliate coworkers for any reason. If Bill and Ryan are having bad months, then Charlotte should have taken the time to find out what was going on privately and behind closed doors. That's how I'd expect you to advise her as her supervisor.

Next, I'm wondering if she's going to be a fit within the organization. If her way of dealing with people is by stripping them of their dignity in front of their peers, then you've got to know that she doesn't have the style or temperament that would make for a long-term, viable employee.

Third, and most important, I'm now questioning *you*. How can it be that you didn't address Charlotte's managerial conduct as soon as it happened? Why didn't you call her aside and let her know that although that behavior may be accepted and condoned at other companies, it has no place here? More important, why haven't you kept me in the loop as to why this has been going on? Why would I need to hear about it from your staff members instead of you? [*I'm sorry—I can see your point about addressing her and keeping you in the loop.*]

Here are the rules regarding my expectations: First, any newly hired managers with a "my way or the highway" approach to leadership should be considered mis-hires, unless they can demonstrate very quickly that they're willing to switch over to our style of leadership. Second, any time there's a controversial new hire for any reason, I want to hear about it from you before I hear about it from your staff members or people from other departments.

Finally, I won't tolerate this sense of flying blind or having a vice president on my staff who doesn't proactively address both performance and conduct expectations of our employees, especially of those employees who supervise others. Am I clear? [*Yes.*] Good. Then you're sure that you understand that I won't tolerate a leader on my team who avoids confrontation? [*Yes, I understand.*] And you're doubly clear that I expect you to address these types of problems head-on as soon as they occur, while keeping me abreast of the situation? [*Yes, I do now.*]

I'm happy to hear that. Now tell me how you plan on addressing Charlotte's behavior in this particular case.

Phew! A tougher conversation, no doubt, but you have every right to question any subordinate who fails to keep you abreast of problems in your area or who otherwise appears to avoid confrontation at all costs. Avoiding confrontation is one of the cardinal sins of management: Be sure to break any bad habits or proclivities in your subordinates who seem to shy away from this necessary leadership discipline.

SCENARIO 71

Staff Motivation Conversations

Motivation is internal. Managers can't motivate their subordinates per se, even if they bring the biggest pompoms to the office every day.

However, supervisors are expected to create a work environment in which staff members can motivate themselves.

Some managers get this idea fairly easily: They find ways of making work fun, they welcome everyone's ideas on the team and share the glory whenever possible, they communicate openly while holding everyone to a high standard of expectations. Unfortunately, not all managers know how to motivate this way, and your job will be to help them understand how to get their troops into top shape by ensuring an optimal work environment.

The Solution

The next time you find one of your managers "leading through the mud," help her see the benefit of enlightened leadership as follows:

Denise, if you don't mind my saying, I don't sense that your subordinates are fully engaged, totally motivated, and 100 percent behind you. Is that a fair and objective assessment, and if so, would you allow me to help you help them plug in and reinvent themselves in light of your department's changing needs? [Yes.]

Great! I've always felt that no matter where you are in your career, there's no better time than now to begin recognizing, appreciating, and motivating your staff. Here are a few relatively simple ways that can help you do that:

First, I'd recommend that you consider implementing what's known as *open book management*. The concept is fairly simple: From time to time, assign someone on your team with the task of researching our organization and our competitors on Google or Glassdoor. Of course, you'll also want to do a group read of our company's 10(k) annual report to look for the SWOT analysis of strengths, weaknesses, opportunities, and threats. Help them see the bigger picture of where the company stands relative to its peers, and you just might have them thinking outside of the box in terms of finding new ways of adding value to your processes and systems.

Second, consider starting a Book of the Quarter Club. You've heard of the Book of the Month Club. Well, that schedule may be a little too aggressive for your team, but if you're looking to stimulate your staff and challenge them to think outside the box, then this best practice may win some big fans for you. Simply decide on one book that you'd all like to complete within, say, sixty or ninety days. Assign each member of your staff a chapter, and have that individual discuss the merits of the chapter in your weekly staff meetings. The real challenge will lie in getting your staffers to apply the theoretical knowledge from the book to the day-to-day workplace. That may just rejuvenate some of your folks who've become a bit staid and overly comfortable in their roles. Does that make sense? [*Yes.*]

Third is what I call *staff meeting leadership*. One thing that most employees often look for in an ideal manager is leadership capability. If you want to place them into roles of leadership and help them strengthen their own skills, allow each of your employees to run a weekly staff meeting—its structure, delineation of responsibilities to others, and follow-up. Placing future leaders into management development roles is probably the most important benefit that you have to offer your people. Besides, it's much easier to complain than it is to fix the problem. People responsible for attempting to fix problems are less likely to blindly blame others because they're more sensitive to the challenges involved in rendering a solution.

The final suggestion that I have focuses on external learning opportunities. Assume that many of your best employees are résumé-builders: They'll stay long enough to prove their worth so long as they're on the fast track. Once they feel blocked from upward mobility, however, they'll look elsewhere rather than forego their personal agendas. The key is to allow all your employees a chance to make a difference. People are much more inclined to feel like they're making a positive contribution to your organization if they're in a learning curve. So even if you can't promote them because of hiring freezes, you can challenge them to challenge themselves.

Two or three one-day seminars per employee per year may add very little to your overhead budget and can allow employees intermittent sabbaticals to reflect on their careers as well as on the application of the newly learned material to your work environment. It's a win-win situation for everyone, and all you have to do is set up the structure of the program along with your expectations. At that point, let their creativity and hard work forge the way.

I believe that if you implement some or all of these points, you'll have a much more motivated staff, and energy begets energy, so you'll all be feeling invigorated and renewed. Give this some thought and come see me later this week with ideas for implementation or alternatives. I think you'll like these creative exercises, and your employees will really appreciate it, too. After all, how many managers outside these walls go out of their way to help their employees gear up for promotions in their careers? I'm looking forward to working with you on this.

And speaking of fun, this is where the management rubber meets the road. Little is as rewarding as teaching future leaders how to lead effectively and efficiently. The beauty of these scenarios is that they cost the supervisor very little in terms of her own time and the company very little in terms of added expense. There's no better way to bond with your subordinates than finding low-cost means of making work fun and enjoyable, while educating your staffers and arming them with skills that will help them in their overall careers.

SCENARIO 72

Protecting Your Company from Legal Liability (Documentation)

You can't totally insulate your company from employment liability. However, you *can* place your organization in a highly defensible position by ensuring that you have the proper written record in place before taking adverse actions against a worker.

Stated differently, it's not so much an issue of getting sued because that's simply the cost of doing business from time to time. Instead, it's a matter of getting sued on *your* terms rather than theirs. When it comes to formal documentation—which is your company's primary defense mechanism against employment litigation claims—managers must learn to rely on your company's human resources department to be the "master of the story" and to make the appropriate written records. There's no easier way to ensure that your documentation doesn't make matters worse or somehow come back to bite you.

Document, document, document is a common piece of advice you'll get from employment pundits and labor attorneys who conduct performance management workshops and legal updates. The part of that message that often gets short shrift is that if something is worth documenting, it's most likely worth sharing with the employee at that particular point in time. Otherwise, as a manager, you'll end up creating a diary of substandard performance issues that serves neither as a training tool nor as documentation that could later be used to justify a dismissal and protect your company from a wrongful termination charge.

If communicating and sharing performance-related documentation is a problem for any managers on your team, you've got to sit them down and demonstrate how documentation (or the lack of it) can be used against them in the litigation arena. This is a critical area in terms of management development that has much to do with confronting problem situations head-on.

The Solution

The next time a manager fails to address substandard job performance or inappropriate workplace conduct *in writing* (and we all know that certain issues lend themselves to written warnings and not just to verbal admonishments), conduct your meeting as follows:

> Annie, a situation occurred with one of your employees that probably should have been documented. I found out about it after the fact, and I don't feel that it would be appropriate to go back now and write the person up. After all, it's not really fair to try someone twice for the same offense, and I'd rather take this as a learning opportunity for you than to readdress the issue with the employee in question. Does that make sense to you, and are you open to my helping you learn more about this? [*Yes, of course.*]
>
> Okay, as I understand it, one of your help desk employees, Bob Johnson, has had a number of performance problems relating to sloppy work, failure to follow up with his internal customers, leaving work unfinished without reporting status, and the like. I recently heard that he made a major snafu with the software conversion project in terms of messing up one of the executive vice

president's systems. I assume you've heard about this particular incident as well? [*Yes.*]

Okay, so as the vice president of information technology, I took the liberty of reviewing Bob's personnel file and found two things curiously lacking: First, there were no performance warnings on file, despite his reputation as a poor and inconsistent performer, and second, I saw that all of his performance reviews showed that he met expectations. Would that sound about right to you? [*Yes.*]

Fair enough. Then let's talk about each of these items separately. Performance reviews represent a lurking danger for unsuspecting managers. The path of least resistance is avoidance, and rather than addressing performance problems honestly and directly, many managers have been known to avoid confrontation by overinflating grades. Could that be the case here in Bob's case? [*Yes. I thought he'd become upset if I gave him a substandard score and a lower-than-expected merit increase.*]

Fair enough. So here's a simple litmus test to follow when doling out overall scores in the performance review process: If you have any remote hesitations about an individual's ability to make it in your department or in the company in the upcoming year because of subpar job performance or inappropriate conduct, then you should grade the individual as "not meeting expectations" in the overall score section at the end of the performance appraisal form. Otherwise, the positive record that you create today will make it harder to terminate the individual tomorrow. Is that fairly logical? [*Yes.*]

Okay then, the next part of our discussion has to focus on written warnings. Written warnings happen intermittently whenever an employee engages in inappropriate workplace conduct or substandard job performance. Sometimes you address an employee verbally, while at other times it should really be in writing. How do you know when your engagement should be verbal or in writing? [*Check with human resources?*] Correct! They're the keepers of such information and know both the rules and practices of our company.

Think of it this way: The annual review covers an entire year of performance, while a written warning may reflect one problematic point in time. In fact, the written warning often serves to break the chain of positive evaluations that are in an employee's file. Do you see now how annual performance reviews and written warnings fit together in terms of notifying an employee in writing about unacceptable performance or conduct? [*Yes.*]

Good. If you coordinate these two "tools," then you'll accord the employee with workplace due process, meaning that he's made aware of the problem, is told what he needs to do to fix that problem, and is informed of the consequences if he doesn't improve immediately. When that's in writing and the employee violates the terms outlined in the documents, then he in essence terminates himself. And that protects the company from a wrongful termination charge. Any questions, then? [*No. This is interesting and new to me. Thanks!*]

I'm glad this incident came up. We're now prepared to handle it differently in the future, and I was happy to share a little background so that you could see how the whole puzzle comes together in terms of workplace due process. That's an important backdrop for everyone to be reminded about from time to time.

There's nothing like having a heart-to-heart to educate your subordinates on the company's expectations, while providing them with information that makes sense and answers many of the questions they may have had in terms of wondering, "Why do we have to do all this documentation anyway?" A ten-minute conversation sets the record straight, fixes the immediate problem, and improves your employee's understanding of the larger legal process that governs employees in the workplace.

SCENARIO 73

Inability to Provide Constructive Criticism

One of the most critical skills any manager can have has to do with commenting on a subordinate's performance. Some managers are thoughtful, kind, and patient, while others are yellers, screamers, and humiliation hounds. Of course, it's up to you to determine what style works best in your company at any given time; when it comes to optimal management styles, a lot depends on your company's history and past practices.

Remember that writing a book on how to manage people is like writing a book on how to raise kids: All parents have a different answer based on their kids' personalities, their family histories, and any number of other considerations. It's up to you to determine what is appropriate and what will work under the circumstances you face from time to time in your company. For the sake of this scenario, however, we'll assume that we've got a manager on our hands who has difficulty providing constructive feedback and support on a consistent basis.

The Solution

If you've got a manager who runs roughshod over his staff members and delivers criticism with as much tact and diplomacy as a buzz saw, here's how to sensitize that individual to turn down the drama just a bit:

Dave, I wanted to speak with you privately about your management style. Specifically, I've noticed that when you give feedback to your staff members, it often has an accusatory and condescending tone. For example, you use phrases like "You should know that," "Why aren't you doing it that way?" and "I don't even understand why we're having this discussion."

Don't get me wrong: I respect your ability to lead the crew that you oversee. To your credit, you know their individual jobs better than they do, and that's a hard-earned accomplishment. However, you've got to temper your impatience at times and understand that your primary responsibility now is in leading others to get the work done. Once you understand that you'll primarily get work done *through* others rather than despite them, you'll come a long way in understanding how to get the most out of them.

Okay, first a quick exercise: Describe your favorite boss (besides me!) in your career, and tell me why he or she gets that special recognition. [*My favorite boss, Harry Johnson at XYZ Company, gave me lots of responsibility and lots of freedom to build my job from scratch. He trusted me and was a wonderful mentor.*]

Sounds good. So on a scale of one to ten, with ten being the highest, what score would you give Harry? [*I'd give him a ten.*]

That sounds reasonable. Now in all fairness, being as objective as you can, what grade would you give yourself? [*I'd probably give myself a seven or an eight.*] Okay, why would you grade yourself a seven or an eight? [*Well, I can't say my people feel as strongly about me as I felt about Harry, and I probably don't give them the same sense of trust that he gave me.*]

Good. Now we're getting somewhere! Here's an even tougher question: In all fairness, what grade would Harry give you right now in terms of his expectations of your leadership and management style? [*Ouch! That's a tougher question. I'd say he'd give me a five or a six.*]

Okay, why would that be? [*Well, he always expected me to do my best, and he wasn't really judgmental, always believing that smart mistakes were a part of learning and growing in a job. I can't say that I've instilled that same expectation in my subordinates.*]

And there you have it: A fairly easy way to structure a conversation with a subordinate to help him see the error of his ways. There's no need to escalate emotional feelings when it comes to stopping someone from running roughshod over his or her own staff members. Simply ask them to hold themselves up to their own role model supervisors. Chances are that once they have an opportunity to perform an objective diagnostic analysis of their respective management styles, your subordinates will figure this all out for themselves. They'll also be able to share with you their own recommendations for becoming stronger leaders and communicators.

Remember, telling people *what* to do doesn't always work that well, especially when they're under pressure and feel they made it up through the ranks on their own, so everyone else should as well. Instead, ask them to conduct a simple analysis of what's worked for them in the past versus what they've come to resent in other supervisors throughout their careers. Sometimes people learn more from poor leaders than they do from good ones, especially in terms of what *not* to do. No one wants to be someone else's nightmare supervisor, and leading the individual in question to the correct answer will always be much better received when the employee figures it all out on his own—thanks to your excellent and patient questioning strategies and guidance.

SCENARIO 74

Handling Group Complaints Wisely

Let's say that one day you're asked by your janitorial staff to meet with you in your office without the group's supervisor, only to find out that the whole department of six janitors is about ready to quit. You ask why, although you already suspect what the problem is: The janitorial supervisor is very hard on his people and difficult to deal with. However, he runs a clean shop, so there's never been too much of an argument that what he's doing is working.

This time it's different, however: You learn a few specifics in your meeting that alert you to the extent of this individual's behavior and that make you uncomfortable. Although you're not looking to terminate this individual, it becomes necessary to intercede and address these managerial conduct issues immediately.

The Solution

In this particular scenario, although you're not all that happy with the feedback you received from the group, you realize that much of what you heard is subject to interpretation. Here's what your conversation might sound like:

> Bob, I called this private meeting to discuss some areas I've been concerned about in terms of your conduct that have recently come to a head. Specifically, your staff asked to meet with me in private yesterday afternoon while you were out of the office, and I'll share with you that they're all about ready to jump ship. Do you have any idea why that is or why they might have asked to meet with me so suddenly? [*No.*]
>
> Well, here's the general feedback I received. Oh, here's a pad and pen in case you want to take notes.
>
> 1. They said that you can be verbally abusive at times. Specifically, they said that you yell at them, regardless of who else is around, and embarrass them publicly. I can't say I've ever seen that, but that doesn't negate their feelings.

2. The general feedback from the group is that everyone's afraid of formally complaining about you for fear that you will retaliate against them. They seemed to all agree that that's why they haven't formalized their feelings up to now by saying anything to me or to human resources. And that's what's made me wonder, why now? I assumed that something triggered all of this, but whatever it is isn't on your radar screen, so you might want to give that some additional thought.

3. Finally, some of them shared that you're very moody and temperamental, turning from normal to angry in a split second and for no apparent reason. They said that leaves them feeling like they always have to walk on eggshells around you.

So, now that I've shared with you all the issues they reported to me, I need to hear your side of the story. How do these issues match up to your version of reality? [*I know I can be hard on them, and I'm not saying I'm perfect, but they need a lot of structure and direction. The reason why the department works so well is because I keep an eye on everything they do. And I'm not here to be their friend. It's all about the work.*]

To a degree, that's true, I'm sure. But from a workplace standpoint, it's the *how* of what you're doing and the degree to which you're doing it that have me concerned. Bob, I think the janitorial function works very well in our company, don't get me wrong. And I always knew you were a demanding supervisor, which I can respect as a legitimate business style. But what I heard yesterday really concerns me for two reasons: First, we're not the kind of company that treats people disrespectfully, and any manager who rules by fear and intimidation doesn't belong here. Second, you also could expose yourself and the company to a hostile work environment or "bullying" charge, and I wouldn't want to see you get wrapped up in something like that. You've got a mighty big perception problem on your hands, and it's now time for you to fix it. I guess the question is, how would you plan to do that? [*I don't know—my style has always worked well for me.*]

Well, maybe not as well as you thought in light of the issues raised. Would you agree that it's something that could be improved on? [*Of course, especially in light of this feedback you're giving me. Tell me what suggestions you have.*]

I'm glad you asked. First of all, seeing that you're listening to this feedback objectively without feeling the need to defend yourself or put them down, I feel confident that we can solve this together with a little sensitivity training.

Second, I want you to research specific training workshops that are available from external vendors on topics like legal aspects of supervision and dealing with interpersonal conflict in the workplace. It will be up to you to develop a short list of programs and their costs to see which ones would make sense for you to attend.

Finally, an important word about *retaliation*: You can't do anything to the six janitors involved for coming to me with a good faith complaint about your managerial style. Retaliation is a separate infraction under our policy and far worse than anything we're talking about right now. I'm not saying you can't continue to manage and supervise them on a day-to-day basis: I expect you to do that as always. Just don't do anything that could be considered retaliatory for their coming forth to me with a good faith complaint about their working conditions. Do I have your word on that? [*Yes.*]

Okay then, I'll leave it to you to research training workshops that you'd be interested in. I also want you to check in with me from time to time over the next few months to let me know how all this is going. My only other question is, how do we want to address this with your staff so that they know it's safe for them to "come out of hiding" and that we've had a good discussion about this?

In a straightforward and direct manner, you've shared your concerns in a very clear format along with your specific expectations. Yes, this may have seemed a bit like *Mutiny on the Bounty* to him, but it's hard *not* to accept responsibility for a problem when the entire staff comes forward with such serious concerns.

Special Note

In cases where you want to mentor the employee one-on-one or avail him of external training opportunities that might help him to better manage his problems, be sure and put the burden on him to schedule time with you and to research appropriate workshops and seminars.

Of course, you could opt to do that for him, but there are two hidden traps in attempting to do that work yourself. First, if it's important enough to him, he'll put in the sweat and time to make sure he's getting the help he needs. That initial investment in his own research is part of the education and sensitivity process that's in turn part of his rehabilitation. After all, once he sees how many programs are available, he'll realize he is not alone in having this problem. He'll also be aware of the cost and therefore will be less likely to take the program for granted or as a waste of time.

Second, and more important, you always want to shift the responsibility for improvement away from the company and toward the employee. In this case, if Bob doesn't follow through with the research to identify appropriate workshops that will help him, then that will be his own fault. That's a far better record than if you, the well-intending supervisor, state that you'll find the appropriate workshops for him and then fail to do so because of time constraints or other pressing matters.

Just think of the record you'll be creating: If it ever came to a termination decision and Bob was fired for substandard conduct, the judge or arbitrator would specifically ask if any training was offered to help the terminated worker to improve. Your answer as the defendant/employer will be one of the following responses:

- ▶ Yes, we discussed it, your Honor, but I had other pressing needs, so I didn't get to it.
- ▶ Yes, we discussed it, your Honor, and I let Bob know that it was his responsibility to identify outside workshops and programs that could help him through the problems he was having. I also pledged that the company would send him to those workshops at our expense and on company time. However, he never followed through and didn't mention it again.

The astute judge will then look at Bob and ask, "Now why is that? Why didn't you pursue those avenues that were offered to you?" And Bob would sheepishly answer, "Well, I guess I didn't have the time." Now who is the responsible employer and who is the irresponsible employee? You could easily see why making the employee accountable for following up with you for occasional follow-up meetings and locating his own workshops makes more sense than doing that leg-work for him.

SCENARIO 75

Lack of Diversity Awareness

Diversity is such a big word in the business world today that it's difficult to pin down its meaning. It is often a misunderstood and misconstrued term, so how your company defines its diversity policy and practice is subjective and left to your own organization's interpretation. That being said, many companies today engage in active diversity outreach efforts, and for good reason: Diversity makes good business sense because it's a profitable business practice.

When companies view diversity as a strategic business imperative, then all sorts of good things follow: Your workforce reflects your increasingly diverse customer base, so company solutions more closely reflect customers' needs. Employees sense management's commitment to new ideas and collaboration, where people can feel free to express themselves without censure or judgment. And when that's the case, ideas flow more freely, differing points of view are encouraged, and people's differences are respected. Employees' careers can thrive in an environment where respect, dignity, and a sense of inclusion define your culture.

In fact, although diversity can be defined narrowly in terms of race, age, gender, or other protected characteristics, many companies wisely choose to recognize diversity in its broadest sense, encompassing personal differences like lifestyles, education, personality characteristics, and tenure with the company. Nevertheless, not all managers focus on this business imperative to the same degree. If you sense that a particular manager simply isn't sensitive to this issue based on the behaviors that you witness in terms of hiring, promotions, and even turnover in that particular group, it may be time to sit down and discuss these perception matters openly.

The Solution

Be conscious of the fact that this is a politically sensitive topic. If part of diversity awareness lies in recognizing others' individuality and personal differences, then you can't really force the issue on anyone because that would defeat its purpose. However, you can make a case for the benefits of becoming more sensitive to this particular issue, while stressing its benefits and advantages. Here's one way you might want to approach the topic:

Walter, I want to have a talk with you about a topic that we hold near and dear to our hearts at the corporate level and try to impart on our management team as a whole—diversity. Before we jump into it, though, I need to ask what that word means to you. [*I don't know. Hiring and promoting more minorities, I guess.*]

Well, that's an effect of diversity, that's true. But I'd rather stay on the cause side of the argument. Why would a company like ours want to encourage a diverse workforce, and what do you think it would look like? [*Well, I'm sure it would look a lot more diverse, with fewer white people and more people of color, and companies have to do it because it's the law, I guess.*]

Okay, I see where you're coming from. Let me define diversity first, at least in terms of how our company sees it, and then I'll make a business case for it. Does that sound fair? [*Sure.*]

First then, a definition: Diversity is a heightened level of awareness or a sensitivity that has to do with an acceptance of people's differences. It's not so much a law or a mandate as it is a corporate belief based on mutual respect and inclusion. Also, it's not about diverse people feeling the need to fit into the mainstream; instead, it's about accepting other people's differences as a kind of strength and an asset that benefits the company overall. Does that make sense? [*I guess.*]

Okay, let me give you an example. If people feel that they're respected by the company, then they'll respond in kind: respect begets respect, and everyone wins there. Do you agree? [*Yes.*] And if people feel that their ideas and differences are welcome, then they're more likely to share their suggestions and recommendations, correct? [*Yes.*] Then that benefits the company as well because we want the company's ideas to reflect the needs of the diverse customer base that it serves. Are you with me? [*Yes.*]

Good. Let's keep going then. If we then hire and promote people based on merit—on the results of their performance, ability, and achievement—then stereotypes that lessen people's worth will fall by the wayside. In short, it's a win-win-win scenario: The employees win because they feel respected and included, the management wins because we have a fully engaged workforce competing on merit, and the company wins because we're better meeting the needs of our customers. Do you see my logic? [*Yes.*]

Okay, then let's get back to the reason I'm meeting with you. Based on what I'm seeing in your group in terms of the hires and promotions made as well as the turnover in the past year, I'm not sure that sensitivity to diversity is on your radar screen as much as it should be. I need your help to make it a front-burner issue. As a company, we want to see diversity in our hiring and promotional practices. And we become concerned if we see a disproportionate number of diverse candidates leaving a particular department via resignation.

That appears to be the case in your group over the last twelve months. Let's talk about why you feel that may be the case and what we could do to help you with that.

Clearly, this is a huge topic that may lead in a million different directions. In addition, it may not be welcomed by supervisors who fear that you're forcing them to hire females and people of color. However, many companies review their diversity statistics and find "outliers" in certain departments where young white males tend to be the only individuals hired and promoted. No, diversity isn't about mandating hiring quotas for females and minorities; however, if left unaddressed, the perception problem can have real legal ramifications for your company in the case of an Equal Employment Opportunity Commission (EEOC) audit.

Three months from now might be a good time to schedule a follow-up meeting to ensure that the hiring, promotional, and turnover patterns you're seeing in Walter's group have improved. If that's not the case, then in light of the reasons you're given at that time, determine whether a more formal company response in the form of progressive discipline may be warranted. However, be sure and review that with human resources or with qualified legal counsel before formalizing anything in writing.

SCENARIO 76

Lack of Leadership—Risk Avoidance Gone Wild

Lack of leadership and the appropriate interpersonal skills to motivate others is what this chapter is all about. The topic is so broad, however, that it's challenging to limit it to one chapter or even one book. Management by fear, intimidation, and heavyhandedness, the inclination to overdelegate and pass off undesired work, rulebreakers who don't follow policy, and bureaucrats who reveal little creativity, assume little risk, or avoid confrontation by ignoring things are all manifestations of the lack of leadership problem that plagues many supervisors. Indeed, addressing every shortcoming in a leader is tantamount to addressing every shortcoming in a human being; what's important is that you choose your battles wisely and address these issues objectively and fairly so that the situation can improve. No, we're not shrinks or career coaches, but part of our jobs as managers and leaders is to grow the next generation of leaders for their own good and ours. After all, if we don't develop greater people management skills in those who report to us, then we'll always work as hard in the future as we're working today. If you're playing this management game correctly, then your life should get easier over time: You'll work less hard, make more money, and develop satisfaction in seeing others thrive while assuming new responsibilities that you can now delegate.

So how do you deal with managers and supervisors who exhibit some of the previously discussed traits? Once again, we'll rely on our perception management tool to help them come to terms with their shortcomings and then point them in the right direction to get appropriate help.

The Solution

Regardless of the particular management problems noted earlier or the variations of others not even mentioned, simply follow the suggested format that follows. As long as you follow the suggested structure, you can swap any of the previous problems and simply fill in the blank with a different issue. For the sake of our example, we'll use the "Bureaucrat: Lack of Creativity and Risk" category since that's a fairly common concern in today's workplace.

In our example, we'll assume that you supervise a vice president of finance (we'll call him Matt) who finds numerous and creative ways to avoid making decisions. No matter what the topic—head-count approval, accountability for budget variances, or supervisory and managerial leadership—Matt finds ways of avoiding making any calls. Instead, he defers to human resources, operations, strategic planning, and any other department under the sun to make decisions and bear the consequences. Matt has become averse to risk and accountability, and as a result takes a strict interpretation of his duties, rarely veering off the path of compliance and black-and-white answers to questions.

Now you're thinking, why am I paying this individual so much money? A machine can follow policies and rules. At the vice president level, I need someone who will not only interpret policies but create them! Yet Matt just won't play that game. He comes from the school of thought that those who stick their heads out will get them cut off; life in a corporate foxhole has much more appeal to him.

Yes, Matt has the right to determine for himself what the best course to travel is in the murky and somewhat turbulent waters of corporate finance. However, his interpretation leaves you feeling like you've got a clerk in VP stripes, and that's simply not working for you or for your company. Your strategy at sensitive times like this should rely on questioning Matt to the point where he sees the logic to your beliefs as well as the error of his ways. Here's how you might start:

Matt, I wanted to meet with you one-on-one to discuss your job performance in general. How do you feel you're doing in light of my management style and expectations for the division? [*Pretty well, I guess.*]

Okay. Would you consider yourself more of a creative force and risk taker or someone who plays it safe, generally speaking? [*I play it safe.*] And why is that? [*I've seen more damage to people's careers who took too many risks. I want to retire in seven years, and honestly, I'm not looking for the kudos and attaboys anymore. I just want to do my job adequately and accurately.*]

Well, do you feel that constantly flying under the radar grants you immunity from risk? Would it not be as plausible to argue that your strategy should focus on standing out among your peers and keeping yourself a valuable resource to the company in an effort to reach your seven-year retirement goal? [*I guess, but that wouldn't be my first choice based on my experience.*]

Well, thanks for being so truthful, Matt. That sounds like an honest answer, and I can't ask for more during this conversation. However, I've got to be honest too. Let me share with you what it looks like from my vantage point and where I'd like to go with this conversation.

On the one hand, you've pretty much developed a reputation as someone who avoids risk. I really can't say I see anything creative coming out of your group. As my head of finance, you provide me with compliance reports and answer black-and-white questions that I ask you. Yet I don't see anyone on your team "stretching the rubber band" to look at industry best practices and attempting to reinvent how we do business.

Think of it this way: I'm not paying you for compliance; I'm paying you for strategic leadership. I'm paying you to recreate how this company does business based on our financial results and forecasts. Those financial blueprints paint a picture of how we should amend our strategy. A staff accountant won't necessarily do that, but a vice president of finance certainly should. Can you see where I'm coming from? [*Yes.*]

Okay, then we've got to think about how we change the culture and the expectations in your group to think more strategically, meaning not just compliance but calculated recommendations. Of course, we can't change the group until you're in agreement with me as well, and I'm not convinced that you're there yet, but if my expectation of finance is different from your expectation of finance and I'm the supervisor in this scenario, how do we move in a closer direction? [*Well, it's a big question because that's never been expected of us before.*]

And again, Matt, I'll clue you in—that's no excuse. I'm asking you to stay abreast of trends in your field, apply those lessons here, and take the risk that you might be wrong. Anything shy of that doesn't make sense in my world, and I'm having this conversation with you because you have a perception problem on your hands. People don't see you as creative or as a risk-taker, and you've got to prove them wrong. That is, if you want to. I can't force you to go down this route, and I'm not saying what you're currently doing is *wrong* and what I'm asking you is *right*.

However, I am telling you that what you're currently doing may not serve you under my leadership, that is if what you say you want—job security—is really that important to you. Being as frank and honest as I can, if you can't demonstrate that you're capable of and willing to adapt and innovate, then you might want to give some thought to an exit strategy.

I'm not a particularly judgmental person, Matt: I just tell it like it is. Someone's done you a disservice over the years by allowing you to cocoon yourself and mistakenly think that there's no risk there. Let me assure you, there is! The risk is in failing to try and in not being willing to make mistakes for the company's good. Once you give up on that basic premise, you live life in retreat mode, as the effect of your actions rather than as the cause of them. And that leads to a state of unconscious living—clearly a place that's no fun because there's little excitement, achievement, or fulfilled curiosity.

I'd like you to think about all these things that we've discussed. There's no need to comment on anything right now because this is simply too much information coming at you very quickly. What I'll ask, though, is that you give it some thought, sleep on it, talk it over with friends or family members, and follow up with me by the end of the week.

We'll have to get this right, you and I, otherwise this persistent compliance culture will slowly erode our business. I'm open to hearing about your ideas and suggestions and the "how" of it all. I want you to know that I'll be supportive of your ideas, and I'll even respect your decision if you choose not to expend the energy necessary to pursue this change in course. Under that circumstance, though, I would hope that you'll respect me and the company enough to commit to an exit strategy so that we can find someone whose leadership style and work-related goals will be more in line with the expectations I've laid out.

Wow, can you really say that? Absolutely! When it comes to major shifts in business philosophy or the way an individual sees himself, you have every right to lay out your expectations, including the admonition that "I hope you'll respect me and the company enough to commit to an exit strategy." Those are certainly heavy words, but certainly worth their weight in gold when dealing with issues relating to weighty matters like this.

However, you do have to be careful here. A long-term employee like Matt may be age protected, and you'll want to ensure that you don't inadvertently create a "constructive discharge" claim where he, using the "reasonable person standard," felt that he was forced to resign. As always, keep your immediate supervisor as well as human resources in the loop prior to initiating a conversation this heavy, and consider having a witness in the room to validate your side of the story.

SCENARIO 77

Lack of Leadership—Resetting Expectations When Turnover Becomes a Problem

Whether in tight or loose labor markets, most managers remain concerned about unwanted turnover. Everyone knows that losing one key player can wreak havoc on any operation's performance. Retention of key employees comes from both offensive and defensive leadership principles. More importantly, retention stems from exercising leadership wisdom that allows team members to motivate themselves and find new and creative ways of solving problems—and when necessary removing roadblocks that may impede team growth. Minimizing the effects of unwanted turnover and building a team with solid tenure comes from each leader's ability to foster motivation in teams and instill a strong sense of accountability. All leaders in your organization should assess their own strengths and shortcomings regarding their ability to lead effectively and minimize unwanted turnover.

The Solution

When addressing leadership performance, try using something like a sports analogy to help your management employees place your advice more easily into a structural context:

LEADERSHIP OFFENSE

Louis, I want to take this opportunity to gauge how you feel your team is performing, in light of the recent turnover your area has experienced. I want to get all frontline leaders on the same page about motivation, employee satisfaction and engagement, and accountability. While that's no easy feat, it all begins with discussions like this.

Before we begin, I ask you to keep something important in mind: Your job as a leader isn't to motivate your employees; motivation is internal, and you can't motivate them any more than they can motivate you. Instead, your job as a successful leader is to create an environment where your workers can motivate themselves. It may sound like a subtle difference, but it's an important factor when discussing leadership offense strategies. When turnover becomes an issue, it's likely that you're missing some key signs of employee dissatisfaction that are holding back your team.

So, let me ask you a series of questions that I'd like you to respond to:

Have you had a chance to review exit interview trends with our HR department? What seem to be employees' primary and secondary reasons for leaving? Are you noticing any patterns in demographics—for example, are employees leaving at particular points in their tenure, are these changes occurring with males more than females, and are you seeing higher turnover among whites or diversified workers?

Do you have any thoughts as to what may be causing this higher turnover level on your team, or do you believe it may just be coincidental? How do you feel the turnover rate in your department differs from other groups? Are you concerned about losing anyone in the next six to twelve months that you might label as "critical talent"?

Have you identified your "on-deck" employees who will likely be ready for promotion within the next calendar year? Who are they, and what have you done to indicate to them that they're on your radar when any openings become available? Have you created development plans for them, so they have a greater understanding of our investment in them and our commitment to their future growth?

Have you conducted any "stay interviews" with your top performers? In other words, have you scheduled one-on-one time with them to discuss their career ambitions, shorter-term goals, or areas where they might need stronger career development support?

What percentage of your time are you dedicating to building on your top performers' strengths, rather than managing your lowest-performing employees' weaknesses?

If you had to rank your team members from highest to lowest in performance and potential, who would be at the top, and who would be at the bottom of the list?

As me move forward into the new quarter, what's your primary focus area for setting your own goals for team leadership and development?

This is your chance to recognize and acknowledge your team members' contributions, Louis, and employees will always feel engaged and excited when they're making a positive difference at work, while also building their resumes. After all, top performers will always be résumé builders, and learning is the glue that binds an individual to a company, despite offers from headhunters or competitor organizations. What, if any, opportunities have you taken advantage of to expose your team to new learning opportunities?

Are you clear on these "offense" areas I want you to invest your time and energy in? [*Yes.*]

LEADERSHIP DEFENSE

All right then, Louis—on the leadership defense side, I've found that one key reason for employee dissatisfaction that drives top performers to pursue greener pastures is a perception of unfairness or a leader's inability to hold everyone accountable to the same performance standards. On a scale of one to ten, with ten being highest, how would you grade your ability to hold everyone equally accountable and to the highest standards? [*An eight.*]

Why do you consider yourself an eight on that scale?

What would make you a ten?

Okay, taking this a bit further, how is your relationship with Sarah from human resources? Would you say you have a strong partnership with her, or is it more distanced and formal?

I ask because I expect you to partner with her appropriately and know when to run, not walk, to HR when you sense that someone may be hinting about leaving. She's your corporate partner in all things related to staffing and employment, and I want to make sure you're not shying away from her or otherwise failing to take advantage of HR as an internal resource to help you lead more effectively. With that said, do you have any ideas or suggestions about how you can strengthen your relationship with Sarah?

Louis, my observation is that you'll need to develop some critical muscle around stemming the turnover on your team and accounting for the reasons why people may be leaving. In a spirit of full transparency, I recommend that you announce to your team that you're committed to helping them grow and excel in their careers. Explain to them that you want to take on more of a mentoring and coaching role, and help them identify development opportunities that match their long-term career goals. Commit to holding everyone equally accountable to the highest performance and teambuilding standards, starting now. Does that sound like something you can do? [Yes.]

Great. In light of my recommendations, give some thought to how you want to launch this "new you" initiative. I'd like to meet with you in the next few days, so you can let me know how you plan to approach these leadership offense and defense strategies with your team, and what the results might look like over time. I'll be by your side as we move down the road together on this. I see this process as an important part of your career development, and I want to help you strengthen your reputation in this critical area of leadership and employee retention. Sound fair? [Yes—thank you.]

Future lessons with Louis can focus on fine-tuning his leadership practices regarding delegation (as a developmental exercise), time management, motivation and engagement, succession planning, and other critical individual and team performance factors. At this juncture, what's important is that the stage is set for resetting expectations around leadership, communication, and teambuilding—the "Big Three" that can make or break a leadership career by fostering stability and retention to stem turnover and talent flight. Congratulations for successfully resetting Louis's expectations surrounding these three pillars of management success.

SCENARIO 78

Lack of Leadership—Failure to Partner Appropriately with Human Resources

As an effective leader in any organization, it's important for you to understand the importance of maximizing your relationship with your company's human resources team. After all, when done right, HR can be an incredible resource—both for strategic partnering on business issues as well as for confidential, off-the-record discussions about your own future career plans. Even so, when viewed the wrong way, HR can represent yet another barrier to getting things done the way you want. It's important, therefore, that you establish a relationship with HR that can help you better manage your employees.

Since HR is a class in almost every MBA program, you must understand that the HR discipline, broadly speaking, is about managing and motivating people and maximizing employee productivity. As such, it's a portable skill that needs to be explored and honed throughout your career. What many managers fail to realize is that working with and through HR can significantly mitigate or even eliminate your personal liability as a supervisor in certain situations.

The Solution

When conducting coaching conversations with your leadership team members about the importance of partnering with HR, highlight three key points, as follows:

HR IS ON THE FRONT LINE, BY YOUR SIDE

Keisha, for HR to be effective, it must be on the front end of employee interventions. Line managers greatly appreciate when they can go to HR for guidance and support on handling potentially adverse or hostile employment actions, and managers find a true ally who will partner with them and have their backs. On the flip side, nothing is more frustrating to HR than having to fix a people problem once it's reached a crisis point. HR's purpose in our organization is to support management in making the best people decisions for the company. Does that make sense? [*Yes.*]

One area where HR can provide you with invaluable support is in the employee relations (ER) arena. Supervisors hate having to discipline or terminate staff members or engage in the "progressive discipline" steps that precede a termination for cause. As a result, it's not uncommon for managers to delay the inevitable with underperforming employees and avoid confrontation, hoping that the problem will fix itself. As is usually the case, problems continue to build until some final straw breaks the camel's back, and then managers explode into crisis mode and want the employee fired immediately. Way too much drama!

Keep in mind that HR doesn't want to be seen as an obstacle to management. And one could argue that one of HR's key responsibilities lies in insulating supervisors and companies from employees' bad actions. When HR first learns of a manager's desire to fire someone at that crisis point, its only recourse is to examine the case's merit from a legal standpoint. It starts by pulling the employee's personnel file, to see what kind of paper trail exists. More often than not, HR finds little, if any, progressive discipline (that is, written and final written warnings) that can help justify a termination for cause.

When that's the case, HR has no choice but to nix the termination because there's no paper record to support it. The only solution that HR can offer is to begin the progressive discipline process from scratch by composing a first written warning. Unfortunately, that makes HR appear to be the "red tape" machine that stops you from taking the action steps you feel are necessary and warranted to keep your operation running smoothly. How much easier it would have been if HR had been involved earlier in the process: With prior warnings documented and substandard annual performance reviews on file, this final incident that escalated the situation to crisis mode could have indeed justified a clean termination decision with minimal fear of legal recourse. Do you follow the progression here? [*Yes.*]

HR CAN INSULATE YOU FROM PERSONAL LIABILITY

Don't inadvertently take on personal liability for issues that occur in the workplace. They don't pay you enough to shoulder responsibility that can jeopardize your home or savings. It's a little-known fact that in many states, managers found guilty of unlawful employ-ment decisions can be personally penalized up to $50,000 for engaging in what are known as "managerial bad acts" (i.e., acting outside the course of your employment scope). In fact, in some states like California, there's no limit to how much a supervisor can be personally sued for. Now tell me that's not scary!

The best way to insulate yourself from potential charges of personal liability lies in getting the hot potato off your lap and having everything blessed by HR first, before taking any type of potentially adverse action, like termination, against one of your employees. Are you clear on that, Keisha? [*Yes.*]

Remember something else: Employees are sophisticated con-sumers and often realize that the best way to protect themselves from managers' complaints about their individual *performance* is to strike first by filing complaints about their supervisors' *conduct*.

One in four managers in corporate America will be involved in employment-related litigation at some point in her career, so it's important that you remain aware of potential pitfalls that might blindside an otherwise unsuspecting supervisor. That's why I want to make sure that you're erring on the side of overcommunicating with HR regarding potential employee challenges. I don't want to inadvertently find you or our company on the sharp end of a lawsuit's spear. Does that make sense? [*Yes.*]

Great! And that's why you must immediately go to HR when you suspect there's a performance problem, or if you're going to deliver bad news to one of your team members. HR needs to be in the loop, in case an employee feels like they're vulnerable and might try to launch a "preemptive strike" against you, their su-pervisor, by filing a complaint with HR about your conduct, using terms like *harassment* and *discrimination*. Timing is everything in matters like these: If you get to HR first, then HR deals with an employee performance problem; if the employee gets to HR first, you may find yourself the target of an investigation, based on complaints about your conduct as a manager. Accountability is key, but you wouldn't be the first manager in history to step on a landmine due to a lack of awareness about the dreaded preemp-tive strike. Can you see my logic here? [*Yes.*]

DON'T WALK ALONE

In my experience, line managers avoid HR like the plague. But that's not how we want to partner with HR here at our company. The old mantra "Keep it inside the family" is still alive and well in corporate America, especially since many managers believe that if they can't handle a problem in their group themselves, they'll be perceived as weak. Nonsense! As a line manager, you need support in resolving people issues and maximizing staff performance. Your partnership with HR, when forged early in your time at the company, will provide you with key strategic advantages to insulate you and our company from charges and challenges that arise in the employment litigation arena. Are we on the same page? [*Absolutely!*]

Wonderful! I appreciate your support with this, and it's an important enough matter that I wanted to share my feeling with you early in your journey with our organization. Partner with me any time you need help, keep me in the loop, and encourage your employees to meet with HR if they ever have any concerns. They don't need to stay within the "chain of command," so to speak, and they can speak with HR any time. We'll find out about a problem together when the timing's right, and it's no harm, no foul if people want to speak with HR before coming to either of us. What's important is for all leaders on my team to know how to maximize the HR resource from day one. Thanks for meeting with me about this.

Well done! You just taught your newly hired or recently promoted leader an important lesson about HR's role that's in both her and the company's best interests. A simple message of "HR is our partner, and there's nothing to be afraid of" is a critical learning step for any leader. Mapping out the specific benefits significantly helps in making HR a trusted partner and go-to resource, especially before signs of trouble surface.

SCENARIO 79

Unacceptable Skip-Level Findings for Directors and Above

Many organizational leaders are aware of problematic departments with chronic performance and stability challenges. Yet few senior executives take time to conduct "skip-level" meetings, where they have an opportunity to bypass their midlevel managers and speak directly with members of their extended (i.e., nonmanagerial) teams. For example, if you're a corporate vice president and wish to speak with your department members who report to the director, you can hold one-on-one meetings with the manager and the supervisor, and small group meetings with the rest of the team—analysts, coordinators, administrative assistants, and the like.

It's best to be fully transparent about this, and yes, staff members may feel uncomfortable about sharing their feedback with their boss's boss. But these meetings are healthy and should be ongoing to ensure full transparency and access to senior management. In cases where constant performance and conduct challenges weigh negatively on team performance and where turnover is rampant, these skip-level meetings serve a more immediate and critical purpose. If they result, as you suspect, in ongoing complaints about the director's poor communication, leadership, or teambuilding abilities, then talking this out directly will help set the record straight, reestablish your expectations as the corporate vice president, and accord workplace due process by addressing the problem, the timeframe in which to fix it, and the consequences of inaction.

The Solution

When your findings are of serious concern, appropriately set the tone for meeting with the director by getting right to the point:

As you're aware, David, I opted to conduct skip-level meetings, so I could hear directly from the staff members of both you and others who directly report to me. The purpose of those skip-level meetings was to gauge the overall culture and level of employee satisfaction and engagement on our team. I was a bit taken aback by your staff members' description of your department's culture and your leadership style, which they described as follows:

1. Your department is infected with chronic negativity.
2. Your communication style is described at times as caustic, confrontational, arrogant, and defensive.
3. Your team suffers from an "overreactive grapevine," meaning that team members gossip, "stir the pot," complain about senior leadership, and criticize one another.
4. You appear to reward employees' negative behavior by pitting certain team members against one another, while encouraging others to "stand their ground on principle" and not give in.

Further, your team continues to suffer from high turnover, substandard productivity, and overall disengagement.

In the past, when I've asked you for your input regarding the status of your team, you always seemed fine with the state of things and told me that everything's okay. Yet you haven't shared any of these findings that I'm now getting directly from the team members. That leads me to believe that you're either (a) unaware or (b) hiding this from me. Which is it? [*I'm not sure; I guess I didn't want you to have to worry about this.*]

Truth be told, that's just as significant as the initial problem. How can I trust you if I feel like you're sweeping things under the rug and hoping I won't find out? Isn't it reasonable for me to assume that my first-line direct reports will share problematic issues in their group with me on a proactive basis? Should I have to go directly to your team to find out what's really going on, or would it be reasonable for me to believe that you'd tell me that there are problems, where they are, and how you plan to deal with them? [*Yes, I should be telling you what's going on in my group.*]

Overall, David, of the eight members of your team I interviewed, all but two described your leadership style as lacking, apathetic, or caustic. The majority of those interviewed stated that you not only tolerate caustic behavior—you actually model and perpetuate the negative actions that define your department's work atmosphere. Is there another side to this story that I'm somehow missing? [*No, I guess not.*]

I expect you to take this skip-level feedback very seriously. The level of commitment you demonstrate is clearly within your control. I expect you to complete a full turnaround in your commitment, engagement, and motivation levels. I want to hear what ideas you have for improving your relationship with your staff, so please schedule time on my calendar next week, and we'll review your findings. If there's any particular leadership training you feel you need in this area, let me know. I also recommend that you buy some books on what it means to be an outstanding leader.

Then again, there's another way of looking at this that goes beyond books and articles. The issues we're talking about here stem from trust and respect for others. People tend to respond in kind, so remember that what emanates from you returns to you. I expect you to instill a greater sense of respect, trust, and camaraderie in those you're privileged to lead. My next round of skip-level meetings is scheduled for early next quarter, and I expect significantly stronger feedback from your team members regarding your commitment level, communication style, willingness to help, and focus on results. Does that sound like a reasonable expectation on my part? [*Yes.*]

Good. Then make it happen.

If you commit to reengaging your team and solidifying your relationship with your staff, you'll go a long way in demonstrating your commitment to the organization and to those whom you're privileged to lead. Turning around an underperforming team is an important leadership skillset, and I'm open to partnering with you as appropriate. Please note, however, that this is your team, and you're fully responsible for its ultimate success or failure, including setting the tone and culture for team interaction and recognition. I expect you to make this a top priority from this point forward. Also, be aware that if you were to receive your annual performance review right now, you wouldn't be meeting expectations for the review period.

If you're either unable or unwilling to demonstrate total commitment and key improvements in this area, your suitability for the leadership role that you currently occupy may be subject to reconsideration and could result in demotion or disciplinary action, up to and including termination of employment. Are you clear on this point? [*Yes.*]

But now's your chance to turn the situation around. I'm looking forward to our chat next week to hear more about your ideas for improving the situation at hand.

This kind of negative feedback about any leader is serious and concerning. However, after having this tough conversation, you've set your expectations, offered to help, and scheduled multiple follow-ups to ensure that appropriate action is taken. Skip-level meetings are an excellent way for senior executives to measure the commitment, performance, and progress of their immediate direct reports. Formally interviewing extended reports (i.e., members of your team who report to your immediate subordinates) is a smart and healthy exercise in general and often the quickest and most efficient way of dealing with leaders who aren't meeting expectations and need immediate turnaround.

PART IV

CORPORATE ACTIONS

12

Corporate (Intentional) Actions

orporate actions include probationary terminations, administering written warnings, terminating employees for cause, and occasionally talking employees into leaving your company for your and their own good. In short, it's where the rubber meets the road in terms of ultimate workplace confrontations, and it's where your verbal skills and strategies will serve you best in terms of protecting yourself and your company from liability. If that sounds overly *defensive*, there's good reason: Inappropriate tactical approaches or the selection of the wrong word or phrase at the wrong time can have disastrous results in the litigation arena.

It's important to look at this in an *offensive* mode as well, however. Positioning these conversations the right way and allowing employees to proceed with their respect and dignity intact is one of the most important roles you play as a supervisor. There's a lot of power that comes with the job of manager, but a wise leader knows that it's not about power, it's about strength. And strength comes from connectedness and selflessness, as when extending an olive branch while administering a written warning or even termination. Let's look at some of the most common challenges you'll face along these lines along with strategic conversations to move things in the right direction.

Probationary Termination

Most employers realize that they have a right to terminate new hires during a probationary period. There's a little history that you need to understand about this particular topic to protect your company from unnecessary legal challenges because probationary periods are generally misunderstood. The misunderstanding stems from confusing union and at-will employees.

Historically, union contracts allow for probation periods—initial hiring periods of thirty to ninety days when companies have an undisputed right to terminate new hires at a whim. The company's only obligation typically is to notify the union of the termination because there's no obligation of due process or union negotiation. The collective bargaining agreement provides the employer with a contractual right to pull the plug pretty much at any time within that probationary period. (Of course, once the probationary period expires, the union will argue that a termination for just cause standard will apply, meaning that employees may not be terminated without appropriate written warnings.)

On the other hand, non-union, at-will employees are not governed by collective bargaining agreements and do not have a magical time window in which termination can occur without challenge. A terminated at-will employee may sue a company for wrongful termination, even if that termination occurs within the initial probationary or introductory period. Therefore, you have to be careful not to overly rely on probationary periods when terminating at-will workers: You should still vet your decision in advance through human resources or with appropriate legal counsel. If done incorrectly, the legal concept of *employment at will* may be countered by the concept of *sue at will!*

Of course, if your company hires employees at will to begin with, there's really little need for a probationary period. After all, in an at-will environment, the employee can be terminated at any time, with or without cause or notice. A probationary period allows that same relationship only for an initial thirty to ninety days. So why would a company institute a probationary period for a few months when the entire employment relationship is theoretically governed by that same premise?

The answer is simple: Companies are used to this union vestige, which continues to be passed down from generation to generation. In other cases, organizations have become enamored with the psychological comfort that probation periods provide. Whatever the reason, many employment lawyers consequently argue that there's no reason for a probation period in an at-will environment because it's overkill. More problematically, the existence of a probation period may infer that a company that allows employees to continue to work beyond their probation period may create an expectation that workers are entitled to some greater right to job security in the form of workplace due process than they had while in their probation periods.

The topic of probationary periods in union versus nonunion environments goes beyond the scope of this book. However, it's important that you understand this brief history to ensure that you handle this topic appropriately in your termination conversations with new hires. If nothing else, remember this: Terminating an at-will probationary employee still carries legal risk, and you may want to occasionally provide some form of workplace due process (typically in the form of a written warning) even to new hires in their probation periods. It never hurts to provide a written warning as a cheap insurance policy should that individual choose to sue your company for wrongful probationary termination.

The Solution

Here's how you might address the issue of probationary termination in an at-will environment:

> Jorge, I wanted to meet with you because I need to let you know that unfortunately this employment relationship isn't really working out for us. From my point of view, there doesn't appear to be a good match between your skills and our needs, and to quote a television show that was popular some years back, it's not really a "love connection."
>
> Don't get me wrong: I know you've really tried to make this successful, and we appreciate all your efforts in trying to make this work. But when a new hire in his probationary period doesn't seem to fit into the new role for any of a number of reasons, we feel it's best to separate employment.
>
> My assumption is that you may have sensed that this wasn't working for you either. Am I wrong to assume that? [*No, I know*

there were some problems, but I thought all was going fairly well.] Well, I certainly didn't mean to surprise you with this news, but we've had several earlier discussions, and I assumed that you realized that there were serious issues.

Frankly, Jorge, with new hires in their probation periods, we don't have an obligation to go through the steps of progressive discipline in the form of written warnings and the like. Although that's often the case with longer-term employees, that's not really an issue with probationary new hires. If we sense that a new hire really isn't well suited for a particular role, we tend to exercise our discretion and separate the relationship cleanly and hopefully amicably.

Again, I'm sorry it had to come to this. Is there anything you'd like to share with us at this point? [*Um, no—I guess not. It sounds like you've already made up your mind, and I'm sorry that this didn't work out.*]

Yeah, I'm afraid so. I thank you for all you've done for us, Jorge, and I'm sorry that this is the end result, but I hope you can respect our decision under the circumstances. Here is your final check, which includes pay through the end of the business day, and you'll receive additional paperwork from our human resources group in the next few days. Thank you again and I wish you all the best in your career.

It is highly recommended that you do not include any type of severance or separation pay with new hires in their probation period. Although many companies try to smooth the blow of the termination by paying out an additional week's worth of wages, a plaintiff's attorney looking to sue may very well attribute negative motives toward your benign and well-intentioned gesture. In short, your "payoff" money could be seen as hush or guilt money, paid out to entice the individual to go away quietly. No good deed goes unpunished, and many unsuspecting employers have been blindsided by such manipulative interpretations by plaintiff's attorneys.

As you can see in this example, the fact that the company has a probationary period makes it easier to explain the termination without written warnings. If your company doesn't have a probationary period, it would be just as simple to replace the probationary period concept with the employment-at-will concept—that is, "Because our employees are hired at will, we don't have an obligation to go through the steps of progressive discipline in the form of written warnings and the like." (Technically this may be true, but understand that it is very much in your company's best interests to apply progressive discipline in the majority of cases, even during probation periods. After all, a written warning, even during a probation period, can only help and will rarely hurt your case. Looking at this another way, it can never hurt to provide extra workplace due process.)

As always, remember to treat the individual with dignity and respect, remain available should he have follow-up questions or requests, and keep the tenor and tone of your conversation businesslike yet caring.

SCENARIO 81

Performance Review Bombshells: Surprising Employees with New Information at the Time of the Annual Appraisal

Why even present this scenario? Everyone knows that annual performance reviews should never introduce new information, especially if it's negative. That's not fair to the employee and should be avoided at all costs, right? Yes—and the example below should only be used on rare occasions where new information has to be introduced during the annual performance appraisal. It should be delivered with a sincere *mea culpa* from the manager, for letting the matter progress so far before addressing it. But sometimes this is necessary, when addressing longstanding problems that have gotten way out of hand for extended periods of time. Let's agree to take a gentle approach in addressing the issue, but reestablish go-forward expectations while delivering long-overdue feedback.

The Solution

Communicating expectations and providing performance feedback is something that should be happening all year long—even all *day* long in a typical, healthy working relationship. Many companies formalize a midyear or quarterly review process to ensure that workers are updated with regular feedback on a consistent basis, so the annual performance review is a culmination exercise, not an opportunity to spring new—and potentially surprising or disappointing—information on a subordinate to justify a substandard performance review score that negatively impacts their merit increase or bonus.

But even if it's intuitive that employees shouldn't be blindsided during the annual performance appraisal, it still happens on occasion, which is why we need to address it. New managers may have differing expectations from prior leaders. Or current supervisors realize they've been permitting poor behavior or substandard performance for too long, or perhaps inflating grades for fear of upsetting or demotivating the individual, only to have human resources or a member of senior leadership instruct them to "put their foot down" and stop the behavior or address infractions once and for all. In many ways, the annual review serves as a hard-stop wakeup call, a command to take an objective look at someone's performance or behavior and provide accurate and sometimes difficult feedback. So, it stands to reason that occasionally some new and potentially negative information may need to be interjected to addresses performance or conduct concerns.

Bear in mind that it's generally considered the supervisor's fault for not communicating more effectively by raising the issues at the time of occurrence, so there's a shared sense of culpability. That's a fair compromise. Here's how such a conversation might sound:

> Oliver, as we open this discussion about your annual performance review, I want you to know that my goal here isn't to surprise you with new information, but I'm afraid that's necessary in this case, because certain issues have become detrimental to your reputation and to our ability to execute effectively as a team. Before we begin walking through the details on the evaluation I've prepared, I want you to know that you won't be meeting expectations for this review period. But I also want you to know that I'm holding myself accountable for not sharing problematic issues with you at the time they occurred, and I apologize to you for that. From now on, I'll commit to immediately bringing problematic issues to your attention.
>
> However, it's time to share the concerns formally in writing and to set our expectations on a go-forward basis. The annual review gives us the opportunity each year to recalibrate and set a new course going forward, because it's a hard stop in providing feedback and setting the record straight.

Several of the issues and concerns outlined in this performance review weren't addressed at the time they occurred during the performance period. Even so, that doesn't detract from their significance. In preparing for this meeting and in reviewing the documentation with human resources and departmental leadership, we determined that you're not meeting overall performance expectations in your role, and we've reflected that at the end of the document.

First—and I'm not making any excuses here—most managers hope a problem will fix itself over time. I'm no exception there. And they say that the path of least resistance is avoidance, and I'm guilty of avoiding potential confrontation in your case. But before we address the individual performance categories and overall score at the end of the review, I want you to know that I sometimes find it difficult to share feedback with you. From my vantage point, I often feel like you're defensive, you're quick to assign blame for something gone wrong to someone or something else, and you don't appear to assume responsibility when roadblocks get in the way, or issues fall through the cracks.

That overt defensiveness makes it difficult to share feedback with you at times, and again, I'll commit to taking on that responsibility going forward. But I'd also like you to reflect on why I may be feeling that way as your supervisor, and whether other members of our team may sense a similar feeling of walking on eggshells when partnering with you.

In any event, let me walk you through this review. I'd like to read it in its entirety before we revisit and address each individual category with you, so you have a better sense of the broader picture. Will that be okay? [*Yes.*] Great. Then, once we've discussed the entire appraisal, we can go back to each performance category to discuss your feelings about the score I've awarded or anything else I may have missed. . . .

Yes, this sounds harsh and isn't an easy message to deliver. But it's not enough to say, "Surprises should never happen during the performance review" and end the story there. Surprises should be the exception, not the rule; but sometimes issues like this surface at the time performance feedback discussions are under way. It's never easy to issue a negative document that will be permanently codified in the individual's personnel file. But occasionally, and with agreement from your senior leadership team and human resources, this type of approach may be necessary to correct the record and reset future expectations.

Special Note

If your employees are governed by a collective bargaining agreement, the union contract may stipulate how this situation must be handled in terms of the "step" process being followed. In addition, you should look closely at your organization's past practices to see how matters like these have been handled historically and to explain any potential deviations.

SCENARIO 82

Performance Review Bombshells: When a "Meets Expectations" Score Is Issued in Error

Grade inflation occurs more frequently than you might think, and companies have to find smart ways to clarify the record and ensure that employees have clear go-forward expectations when errors are identified after the fact. For example, if an employee received a verbal, written, and final written warning in the performance year but then was mistakenly awarded a "meets expectations" score, which was identified after the individual received an annual merit increase, what's an employer to do?

It would be great if all frontline operational leaders held "calibration sessions" with their bosses in advance of holding performance review meetings with their teams, to discuss overall scores and challenges for each employee on the team. That would likely catch the problem before any written communication is shared with the employee. Likewise, it would be wonderful if your HR department had an opportunity to read the performance review drafts before those appraisals were shared with each employee, as the inflated overall score would likely be flagged. But in reality, few organizations engage in calibration sessions or have HR look over performance appraisal drafts in advance of the review meeting. Therefore, on a practical basis, employees occasionally receive passing performance review grades that should actually show that they didn't meet expectations for the performance review period.

The Solution

You'll likely want to correct the record with a memorandum of understanding that states that the annual performance appraisal score awarded was incorrect, due to the reasons you outline in your conversation. In doing so, you'll not only clarify the record in terms of the failing score—you'll also have an opportunity to reset expectations regarding the final written warning remaining active, the individual's job remaining in jeopardy, and the manager's willingness and availability to help. That approach will clearly place the company in the best light possible, should you later need to terminate the individual's employment despite the inflated annual review score.

In a situation where you've already assigned a grade of three out of five ("Meets Expectations"), communicated it verbally and in writing to the employee, and awarded a merit increase, your best approach will be to honestly address the error, both verbally and in writing, and then commit to being more careful in the future with providing feedback that reflects the individual's performance and conduct record more accurately. Your conversation might sound like this:

Alyssa, the first reason why your annual review should have reflected that you didn't meet performance review expectations in the calendar year was because of the final written warning you received in November for substandard job performance. As you know, that final written warning had resulted from a written warning in September and a documented verbal warning in August.

In addition, there's a second reason: You received discipline for a separate matter in the first quarter of last year, related to excessive tardiness. When we looked at the record, you were on two separate planes of discipline during the performance year, and one of those areas—performance—actually resulted in a final written warning. When we were reviewing this year's performance review results, the inconsistency jumped out at us immediately, so we needed to bring this to your attention as soon as we found out. I also have a separate memorandum of understanding that I'll share with you in a moment, which will be attached to your annual review to clarify the record. And of course, I'll give you a copy after this meeting.

We realize that you were issued a merit increase two months ago, and we're not planning to ask you to return the money. Likewise, we'll allow the merit increase to remain intact going forward, since this grade inflation error wasn't your fault. In fairness, though, depending on how you perform this year, it could affect your merit increase next year. I just want you to know that information, in a spirit of full transparency. Does that make sense? [Yes.]

Okay, then the terms of the final written warning are still in place. The disciplinary consequences remain the same, my commitment to supporting you however I can is still here, and we can move forward with a more consistent performance track record. My apologies for the error in assigning the grade incorrectly, and I commit to paying more focused attention to any issues I learn of that might impact you either directly or indirectly.

How are you doing so far this year? Do you have any concerns about meeting the terms outlined in the final written warning, and is there anything I can help you with right now to help you succeed in your role from this point forward?

Clarifying the record both verbally and in writing is the goal. Of course, it's up to you whether you choose to do so with or without rescinding the merit increase that was received several weeks or several months prior. Just keep in mind that in situations like these, allowing the employee to benefit financially from the company's error shows the organization to be wise, transparent, and constructive, which is always a key goal when dealing with someone who may be terminated in the not-too-distant future.

SCENARIO 83

Correcting for Grade Inflation Across Your Department, Division, or the Entire Company

Correcting for grade inflation across an entire enterprise is no easy feat. When everyone is graded as a superstar (e.g., five out of five, meaning they exceed expectations), how do you bring the entire population down to a more manageable and realistic score that legitimizes your performance-management program? The good news is this: Launching a new performance appraisal system that focuses on individual performance and team achievement, as well as the behaviors and conduct that create a healthy workplace, isn't as hard as you think, as long as the communication and go-forward expectations are clear and precise. Let's assume that at your organization, the annual performance review has become a paperchase where managers award everyone fives, indicating that they're all superstars. In such cases, broad-brushing scores across the paper canvas does little to help individuals build performance muscle, set and achieve goals, or otherwise stand out from their peers. Instead, you'll want to reset expectations surrounding the way you grade performance in general and, more specifically, how you intend to assign scores in the future.

Grade inflation—not an uncommon management *faux pas*—typically occurs when managers either dedicate little time to the performance evaluation process or attempt to avoid confrontation by not holding others accountable. In those circumstances, your CEO or senior management team may want to ratchet down scores to reflect a more accurate and realistic assessment of individual and team performance. The scorecard below comes from a book I wrote with Winston Tan, *The Performance Appraisal Tool Kit: Redesigning Your Performance Review Template to Drive Individual and Organizational Change* (AMACOM, 2013). Let's see how this rollout of a new system might work.

The Solution

To spice up the process and create true differentiators in terms of assigning performance grades, you move from a three-tier grading system (e.g., exceeds, meets, and fails to meet performance standards) to a five-tier system that looks more like this:

> 5—Distinguished Performance and Role Model: Clearly and consistently demonstrates extraordinary and exceptional accomplishment in all major areas of responsibility. Others rarely equal performance of this caliber in similar roles.

4—Superior / Highly Effective Performance: Performance is continually and consistently superior and regularly goes beyond what is expected. Performance consistently exceeds expectations.

3—Fully Successful/Effective Performance: Performance consistently meets the critical requirements of the position, and the individual continually performs at the level expected.

2—Partially Successful Performance / Needs Improvement: Performance does not consistently meet or occasionally falls below what is required of the position; improvement in specific areas is required.

1—Unsuccessful/Unacceptable Performance: Performance fails to meet minimum expectations for this role, and immediate and sustained improvement is mandatory.

Your discussion with your employees might proceed as follows:

Team, it's time we take a more realistic look at our performance review program. This year we're announcing some changes that we think you'll all like. My first comment is that the scoring program is going to change, and scores of fours and fives—exceeding expectations—will likely be lowered to better reflect reality. We realized that we award so many fives that we're missing the point of the exercise: Employees can't all be fives across the enterprise year after year. But lowering those five scores down to fours and threes will require a lot of communication, and hopefully, some positive inputs to offset what some of you may feel is a takeaway. After all, no one wants to see their scores go down.

This change is being implemented companywide, so there's no reason to feel bad if some scores decrease this year. I just want you all to be prepared individually, because we're being asked to scour our teams with a steel-wool brush, and it's not an easy exercise.

First, we're employing a new grading system with five grading points. Instead of three overall score categories, we're moving to five, so we can more accurately distinguish between performance levels. As the revised grading shows you, to receive a score of five, you have to be a top performer in class, exhibit role-model behavior, and basically be ready to promote into your supervisor's job right now. That's a high standard to meet, and few five scores will likely be assigned. We'll discuss the rest of the scores in a moment, but by fine-tuning the meaning of "exceeds expectations," we'll automatically gain an advantage in distributing scores more evenhandedly across the organization.

Second, we want you to know that beginning this year, we're going to invite you all to assess your own performance using a newly introduced self-assessment tool. It's not mandatory that you do this, but we're going to encourage all of you to engage in your own evaluation by providing examples of your performance throughout the review year. We'll ask you to focus on your achievements and accomplishments that made our company a better place this past year—linked to increased revenues, decreased costs, or saved time. We're looking forward to delegating this all-important exercise to you so that you can promote yourselves and your achievements proactively and ensure that your supervisors have the most up-to-date information about your overall performance, achievements, and behavior.

Third, we're going to engage with you about a month after the reviews are concluded, to establish performance goals for the upcoming review year. We'll help you define your goals and the measurable outcomes, to ensure you've achieved them. Finally, we'll ask all staff members to schedule quarterly follow-up meetings with their supervisors, to make sure that they're on track to meet their goals. Those quarterly touch-base meetings will give you opportunities to discuss any unforeseen roadblocks, potential changes in your plan, or even amendments to your original goal.

We're looking forward to partnering with you on this, and don't worry if it seems like a lot right now. We'll walk you through this every step of the way, and we'll mark this year as the new year in becoming a performance-based employer, meaning that our pay-for-performance culture will be taken to the next level.

When done right, switching up your performance-management program can be an incredible culture changer. Whether you seek to get away from "serial rankings" (where everyone either meets or exceeds expectations), this sort of modification can escalate your organizational performance to the next level. Combined with some of the performance appraisal template samples you can find in *The Performance Appraisal Tool Kit*, for example, this kind of program can help you focus on your organization's top priorities, your company's stage of growth—start-up, growth, mature—or your key workforce composition—hourly/union, exempt/professional, and so forth. It's definitely worth the conversation!

SCENARIO 84

Administering Disciplinary Warnings

For employees who are outside of the probationary period window (if your company has such probationary periods), it is clearly in your organization's best interests to administer disciplinary warnings for performance- and conduct-related infractions before proceeding to termination. Your company will likely be held to a for-cause standard to justify its decision to terminate a worker, and as many judges and arbitrators will tell you, if it's not written down, it never happened.

There are two ways to administer warnings: First, you can draft the warning, meet with the employee, and give him the document so you can both discuss it. Second, you meet with the employee, explain that you intend to give him a written warning assuming nothing he is about to say changes your mind, lay out your concerns, listen to his side of the story, and then decide whether a warning is appropriate.

Both approaches are valid, but I highly recommend the latter whenever possible. It shows that you're a reasonable employer who doesn't rush to judgment before hearing the entire story. More important, it treats the worker with dignity and respect so that even if a written warning is the ultimate result, the individual will have had an opportunity to defend himself. There's an additional benefit to listening to the employee before administering the warning: If the employee shares information that you feel should be included in the warning, you can draft the warning like this:

When I asked you why you felt it was necessary to . . . , you stated . . .

Again, incorporating the employee's feedback into the written warning itself demonstrates your reasonable approach to investigating the matter thoroughly before reaching a conclusion. And assuming that the employee had no good reason to do what he did, it allows you to strengthen your case in writing.

Can there be times when a warning is drafted and administered without gaining the employee's feedback first? Yes. But this should be the exception rather than the rule. For example, if you have a no-fault absenteeism policy and employees receive warnings once they attain a certain number of incidents of unscheduled absence, then administering a warning at the time of your initial conversation may be appropriate. Specifically, if a fifth incident of unscheduled absence occurs—regardless of the reason—and your policy dictates that a first written warning should be issued under your company's no-fault system, then giving the warning at the onset of the meeting may be justified. Then again, in cases of "no-fault" attendance control policies like this, remember that you're still obligated to remain aware of the possibility that an occurrence of unscheduled absence or tardiness may fall within the purview of the Family Medical Leave Act, the Americans with Disabilities Act, or state-specific paid sick leave laws that can negate the disciplinary action. So it's still typically better to talk first (whenever possible) and issue the document second rather than doing both simultaneously.

The Solution

When you have to administer a written warning and want to learn the employee's side of the story, open your dialogue this way:

> Hannah, I called you into this meeting to discuss a situation that has come to my attention that's very important. I need to let you know up front that I want to hear your side of the story before any decisions are made, but unless I receive a compelling explanation for what's occurred, you could very well end up being disciplined for this, most likely in the form of a documented warning.

Be careful with your upfront reference to a "written" warning. Until you know the employee's side of the story, the document may be at the verbal, written, or final written level. For example, if this is a serious conduct infraction or a repetition of a prior offense, then your discussion may end up with a suspension or even outright termination. So don't refer to a "written" warning in your initial dialogue, and use the term "documented" warning instead. That may avoid confusion if a more serious company response like a final written warning or suspension actually results.

> Here's what I've heard: Dennis Smith, our head of finance, told me that you "stormed" into his office this morning and banged your hand down on his desk in anger, accusing him of negligence and referring to him as incompetent. This was witnessed by Jamie Lee, the senior financial analyst, who was present at the time. Clearly, this description of your behavior concerns me because, regardless of the nature of the business issue, such a response would be highly inappropriate.
>
> First, you should have told me about this as soon as it happened so that I wouldn't be blindsided by the finance people involved. Second, though, I need to hear your side of the story to see if this description of your conduct is accurate and if you feel you've behaved inappropriately. Please let me know your side of the situation at this point.

That's a straightforward setup that states your case fairly and objectively. It also names the individuals who were involved and who witnessed the occurrence. Assuming that Hannah has little to say in her own defense, your written warning may be drafted as follows:

> When I asked you if you did indeed bang your hand down on finance director Dennis Smith's desk in anger, accusing him of negligence and referring to him as incompetent, you stated that you had "momentarily lost your cool" and wanted to apologize for your actions. Although your remorse and intention to apologize are appreciated and encouraged, your behavior nevertheless violates our company's expectations regarding appropriate communication and respect in the workplace. If you ever again shout at a supervisor, coworker, or company visitor; slam your hand down in disgust or in an effort to intimidate the other party; or engage in any conduct that could be perceived as threatening, intimidating, condescending, or disrespectful; further disciplinary action, up to and including immediate dismissal, could result.

See how it works? Your verbal conversation allows the employee to have her day in court, so to speak, and share her side of the story. You then incorporate her explanation into the written warning, documenting your willingness to hear both sides before making a judgment, and then state the clear consequences should such disruptive behavior occur again. Clean, simple, and to the point, your verbal discussion dovetails very nicely into your written warning.

SCENARIO 85

A Final Written Warning as an Alternative to Outright Termination for Senior Managers

Many employers jump to termination too quickly, often out of frustration or because of the proverbial "last straw." But before you rush to outright dismissal—even for vice president- and director-level employees—consider a final written warning instead. First, the final written warning buys you security in knowing that you've accorded the individual with workplace due process—a key factor that, when missing, can lead to lawsuits for wrongful termination and discrimination. Second, the final written warning gives your human resources or administration officer an opportunity to negotiate a settlement on the company's terms, because the final written warning serves as leverage. Third, a final written warning is a better option than a "take-it-or-leave-it" separation package because you, the employer, have little if any leverage when it comes to "packaging someone out," meaning the employee can negotiate upward, since there's little motivation or downside risk that is forcing the individual to accept your offer.

The caveat to the final written warning option is that the employee may opt not to leave the company if your negotiation is unsuccessful. In that case, you'll at least have the final written warning to fall back on should problems continue. But don't be surprised if the individual begins a clandestine job search, even if he refuses to resign with some sort of separation package—senior-level managers almost always begin a job search for fear of the other shoe dropping. Either way, they'll typically exit the organization in a relatively short time once they realize the company is actively documenting the performance problems that have been "suffered" in the past, when senior management didn't address them.

The Solution

Here's the scenario: The CEO and the vice president of operations want the director of construction gone. The problems have gone on too long without being addressed, the work backup is significantly impacting operations, and worst of all, the director is throwing the newly hired vice president (his boss) under the bus, blaming him for issues that clearly lie with the director. While the CEO's gut instinct was to terminate immediately after a new piece of bad news surfaced about a large-scale project that's been significantly backlogged, the vice president of operations and the vice president of human resources convinced the CEO to go with a final written warning instead. (Note that the director is a ten-year employee, diverse, and over forty.)

Once the final written warning is issued by the vice presidents of operations and human resources, the vice president of human resources holds a follow-up meeting with the director of construction the next day that sounds like this:

> Tony, yesterday we issued you that final written warning for misconduct and insubordination, regarding your ongoing public comments about the vice president's incompetence and your willingness to see him fail and ultimately be fired. We likewise issued it for the ongoing performance challenges you've been experiencing, as evidenced by the backlog of projects that are holding up our sales team from closing their business transactions.
>
> I know you don't want to risk losing your job after putting ten years into the company, because that could certainly complicate your future job search, and while I can't promise anything, I can ask for a separation package for you that would mirror what you'd get if your position were being eliminated—twenty weeks of pay plus continuation of benefits and outplacement services. In addition, we wouldn't contest your unemployment.
>
> But that's strictly up to you. I'll support your decision whether you opt to remain with the company under the final written warning or request a separation package. I just want you to be aware of your choices and not feel like you have no options. You

do have to be careful, though, because any further actions on your part that could be construed as insubordination or substandard job performance could result in immediate termination, and there won't be a separation package as a safety net. Why don't you sleep on it, and let me know tomorrow what you decide and whether I can help with that separation package option?

No promises, no threats of any kind—just a presentation of options that allow the individual to resign with dignity. You also might want to emphasize that the separation package isn't a negotiable item: You're making your best offer up front, and it reflects what the package would be if this were a layoff (which it's not). No muss, no fuss, and a helping hand to bridge the gap to the individual's next role at some other company. This is a smart strategy when your employee is longer tenured and protected in multiple categories. It's amazing how much leverage a final written warning can give you—especially when the individual has had no prior disciplinary documentation and only outstanding performance reviews on file.

Special Note

The separation agreement that you offer should include a release of all claims, including age, race, and other protected areas. For a sample separation agreement template that would assist you in cases like this, see my book *101 Sample Write-Ups for Documenting Employee Performance Problems: A Guide to Progressive Discipline and Termination, Third Edition* (AMACOM, SHRM, 2017).

SCENARIO 86

Administering Decisionmaking Leaves

One of the greatest challenges to supervisors and managers lies in turning around workers when their performance doesn't quite rise to the level of a written warning but is detrimental nonetheless. A formal written warning will probably appear to be too heavyhanded, but when numerous verbal notifications don't seem to get the results you desire in terms of altering a subordinate's performance or conduct, then a once-in-a-career decisionmaking leave may be just what the doctor ordered.

First, let's define the term: A *decisionmaking leave,* or *day of contemplation,* is a paid day off where an employee is granted the opportunity to rethink her commitment to working at your company. Unlike a formal suspension, it isn't necessarily a step in your company's documented progressive disciplinary process. Also unlike a traditional suspension, the employee's pay is not docked for the time away from work. The worker actually gets paid to stay home for a day and mull over whether working for your company is the right long-term career move for her. (It also provides a healthy dose of what it feels like to be unemployed!)

If this sounds like too lenient a strategy that lets the worker benefit from being bad, don't be too quick to judge how effectively this tool can actually work. Here's why: Adult learning theory will tell you that when you treat people like adults, they will respond in kind. Unlike formal discipline, which tends to punish workers formally for substandard job performance or inappropriate workplace conduct, decisionmaking leaves are more subtle. More important, they don't negatively impact the worker's take-home pay, so there's no element of resentment toward the employer or embarrassment for having to explain to a spouse or family member why the paycheck is less that particular week.

This element of holding people accountable without negatively impacting their personnel file or payroll tends to catch people off-guard, because problem employees, like problem children, are often expecting negative attention for their bad behaviors. Thrown into this new "adult" paradigm of responsibility and accountability, workers tend to respond like adults, and their assuming responsibility for the problem—or, at least, the perception of that problem—often works to effectively shift their mindset and fix the problem.

The Solution

Let's say, for example, that you've (fortunately or unfortunately) inherited a new employee in your unit who happens to be the CEO's nephew. Now let's also assume that Junior demonstrates a bit of an entitlement mentality and tends to name-drop his relationship to his uncle. At first, it's a bit awkward but then it becomes downright uncomfortable. Worse, it's soon followed by excessive tardiness, absenteeism, and substandard work performance. Your first reaction is to speak with your supervisor and human resources to make sure you're not going to commit career suicide by facing this problem head-on. Your second issue will be how to explain this to the CEO in advance of initiating your intended action. Assuming, though, that you've got a comfortable level of support from senior management to mentor and redirect this young pup, your numerous verbal attempts to improve the situation may require a documented next step.

Clearly, you don't want to formally write up the CEO's nephew if you can avoid it—and besides, you don't really feel it's necessary at this point. After all, he may be a bit spoiled and suffer from an entitlement mentality, but he has a number of positive attributes and you genuinely like him. You just want the behavior to change and the performance to improve, not only for your and your staff's sake but for the good of Junior as well.

Again, assuming you've got senior management's buy-in to approach and handle this potentially career damaging predicament, introduce the concept of the decisionmaking leave before initiating any formal, written warnings like this:

Gary, we've had a number of conversations and coaching sessions to discuss some of the perception problems that might exist in terms of your performance and conduct. We initially addressed your overmentioning your relationship to our CEO to people you came into contact with, which, as you know now, sometimes intimidates some of your coworkers. Then we discussed your tardiness and, following that, your excessive absenteeism. Now I'm noticing that a number of projects are falling through the cracks, and some of my peers are starting to question how reliable you are and whether you can be depended on.

I don't want to give you a formal written warning because I feel that may only demotivate you. But I am going to place you on what we call a *decisionmaking leave* for a day, and I'll explain how that works. First of all, today is Tuesday, and tomorrow I'm going to ask you to stay home. I'm paying you for the day tomorrow, so you don't have to worry about your paycheck being impacted, and I want you to know that this is a once-in-a-career benefit that you should use to your advantage.

While you're at home, I want you to give some serious thought as to whether you really want to work here or not. If you come back to work on Thursday morning and tell me that you'd rather resign and look for work elsewhere, I'll be totally supportive of your decision. But if you come back to work on Thursday and tell me that you really want to keep your job, then you'll have one additional assignment to complete while you're away from work tomorrow.

Now remember that I'm paying you for the day, so here's your homework: If you decide to return to work on Thursday morning with the intention of keeping your job, you'll need to prepare a letter for me on Wednesday convincing me that you assume full and total responsibility for the perception problem that exists in terms of both your performance and conduct.

You'll need to convince me in writing that you recognize why there may be a perception problem and again convince me in writing that the problem will be fixed and that we'll never have to address these issues again. I'll hold onto that letter—keeping it outside of your personnel file for now—but with a clear under-standing that if you violate the terms of your own agreement, then you may end up firing yourself.

I'm considering this a very serious exercise and something that could be an incredibly important turnaround point in your career development. Now tell me what questions, issues, or concerns you have about this decisionmaking leave that you'll be taking tomorrow.

The value of this paid leave is that it forces career introspection and self-critical insight without the traditional trappings of formal pro-gressive discipline. The worker won't walk away thinking, "I can't be-lieve my boss gave me a written warning and is docking my pay. She's a terrible supervisor." It's much more about, "Wow, I guess she's taking this pretty seriously. I know I won't get a written warning or get my pay docked, which is good. I just can't believe that she said that she'd accept my resignation when I'm back on Thursday morning and that she'd be supportive of my leaving the company. Ouch, I guess I'd better be good, and I hope my uncle doesn't find out about this!"

It's in shifting the traditional disciplinary paradigm that a day of contemplation provides the most value. When workers are disciplined, they're *angry*, and anger is external, so the problem is someone else's fault. When they're held accountable without formal discipline, they feel *guilty*, and guilt is internal. That's always where you want to be when dealing with your subordinates because that's where problems get fixed once and for all.

In addition, understand the significance of the record you'll have created: The particular element of due process will read to a jury or judge *not* as:

> Irresponsible company failed to communicate the graveness of the situation and did little to help the employee improve.

but as:

> Responsible corporate citizen did its duty in every way to help proactively rehabilitate the worker and communicate the severity of the problem but the employee refused to respond.

Special Note

Decisionmaking leaves can be a very effective tool but may provide little value when the individual's performance problem has to do with excessive absenteeism. If the individual is having a difficult time getting to work every day, then giving her more time to spend at home to think about getting to work probably isn't necessary. In addition, if your employees are covered by a collective bargaining agreement, then an unpaid suspension may be part of the formal progressive disciplinary process, so adding a paid leave to an unpaid leave may not be necessary or make much sense. In any case, don't expect the union or an arbitrator to recognize this day of contemplation as a replacement for any formal step(s) in the disciplinary process outlined in the union contract.

SCENARIO 87

Termination for Cause (in Conjunction with Progressive Discipline)

Let's assume you've provided an employee with verbal, written, and final written warnings as outlined in your company's policies and in accordance with past practices. You've also spoken with human resources or outside legal counsel to ensure that your termination is on solid and legally defensible ground should the individual pursue post-termination litigation activity, and you've received the appropriate approvals to move forward with the termination. What do you say and, more important, how do you say it?

The Solution

One good thing about according employees with workplace due process in the form of progressive discipline (i.e., written warnings, decisionmaking leaves, unpaid suspensions, and the like) is that the ultimate termination shouldn't come as too much of a surprise. True, individuals may feel that they've turned their performance around and reached an acceptable level and may feel surprised by your decision to terminate. However, even in times of disagreement about the ultimate decision to terminate, the individual should be aware that there's a serious problem and that his employment is in jeopardy of being lost.

When opening your conversation, be direct, caring, and get to the point right away.

David, I'm calling this meeting to let you know that I'm afraid we're going to have to separate your employment today.

This is a much nicer way to phrase what's happening. "Separating your employment" says the same thing as "terminating you" or, heaven forbid, "firing you," but in a much kinder way that allows the individual to retain dignity and self-respect.

As you know, we've been going through a number of interventions with you regarding your overall performance on the job, both via verbal and written notices, and I'm afraid that we've made the decision to go our separate ways.

I know you've been trying to meet the expectations outlined in the notices you were given, and I appreciate that. Please don't think that we see this as a lack of trying on your part. It's just that there comes a time when we realize that our interventions are not really sustainable in terms of turning around an individual's performance, and it becomes best to separate employment.

I thank you for all you've done for us. I'm sorry it had to come to this, but I hope that in your heart of hearts as you think of this, you'll realize this is probably the right thing for both sides. As a company, we want to act as a responsible corporate citizen and do our best to make our workers successful. Equally as important, we don't want to see someone constantly fighting an uphill battle just because the job's needs and that individual's strengths really aren't in sync.

Therefore, we're making today your last day with us, and we've got two checks for your regular work hours through the end of the business day today as well as for your accrued but unused vacation. Although unemployment is determined by the state rather than by our company, we don't intend to contest your claim for unemployment insurance at this time.

You'll hear from human resources in the next few days regarding continuing your medical and dental insurance through our company's COBRA program, and I want you to know that if you think of any questions or need anything, you should feel free to call me or our human resources department at any time.

In addition, David, we want to handle this respectfully. Although we'd like you to leave the premises shortly, will you want boxes to pack up your personal materials? If you're not comfortable doing that now, we can arrange for you to come back and pack up or we can simply do that for you and courier your items back to your home later today. Also, would you prefer to leave quietly, or would you like to say goodbye to some of your coworkers before you leave the office?

Finally, just a few more thoughts. When you return to your office, your computer will be disconnected from the company network. Please understand that we do that in all cases when someone is being notified that their employment is ending for whatever reason.

Also, once you pack up your personal items, you'll want me or someone in human resources to check your boxes before you leave. That's for the company's good as well as for your own: If something goes missing after you leave, you won't want someone to say, "Oh, David must have taken that." If that were to occur, you could simply respond, "No, Paul checked the four boxes that I filled before I left, and he confirmed there were no confidential or proprietary materials in them."

I know this is a lot of information coming at you at once. Are you okay at this point? Do you have any particular questions that we can answer for you? [*No.*] Thanks for everything you've done for us, David. I wish you all the best in your career. How much time do you think you'll need to pack up your desk and say goodbye to your friends? [*Twenty minutes.*] Okay then, I'll let our security folks know that you'll be leaving no later than thirty minutes from now. Thanks again and all the best.

At that point, the employee may leave or meet with human resources to conduct a formal exit interview. This is the time when the company will collect the employee's ID badge, cell phone, laptop computer, office keys, and any other outstanding items. Likewise, that's the best time to ask if the employee is owed reimbursement for outstanding expenses and to make arrangements for payment.

SCENARIO 88

Convincing an Employee to Leave Voluntarily When There Are No Progressive Disciplinary Warnings on File

Convincing underperforming employees to leave voluntarily may seem like a daunting task, especially if you haven't administered progressive discipline in the form of written warnings or annual performance reviews stating that the individual isn't meeting company expectations. However, employees with bad attitudes, entitlement mentalities, and poor work habits will often remain with a company for fear of change or out of principle. You can't force them out, and they won't let themselves be removed until they're ready.

So what's an employer to do when there's been no record of discipline created and the idea of starting that process now seems counterproductive because of the hard feelings that exist? The best solution from an employee relations standpoint may be to broker a peace where both parties can walk away from the working relationship with their dignity and respect intact and options at their disposal.

Note as well that meetings such as this typically require a third-party facilitator. First, if you are the immediate supervisor and are part of the problematic interpersonal relationship with the disenfranchised employee, any attempts that you make in terms of talking the person into leaving his job may be seen as insincere or self-serving. More important, whatever is shared with the employee in a meeting like this could later be interpreted as *constructive discharge*, a legal concept akin to wrongful discharge, except where the employee resigns rather than gets fired. (In such cases, an argument is made that any reasonable person would have resigned under those same intolerable circumstances.)

So before you lash out and create a record that could appear to be an ultimatum—"Either you resign voluntarily or we'll terminate you"—make sure that you've planned your discussion well and have another member of management present to act as a witness to disprove any claim that you might have told the employee that she wasn't welcome there anymore and had no future with the company.

The Solution

Here's what such a discussion might sound like:

Michelle, I've asked Paul from human resources to join us for a meeting because I wanted his help to support us through the difficult time we're having. You've worked as my assistant for almost two years now, and I know that I've had a difficult time holding back in showing my frustration on a number of occasions. I've shared with you on and off that I felt like I've had to do a lot of work myself that you should have handled, and I've also sensed your frustration with me. I assume responsibility for letting the relationship deteriorate and get to this point, and I apologize to you for that.

In fairness, though, I don't believe you're as engaged and dedicated to this role as you were two years ago. Am I fairly on the mark here? [*Yes.*]

Okay then, is it safe to say that you'll accept partial responsibility for the problem, seeing that it takes two to tango and that you may have also acted less than ideally in certain situations? [*Yes—I can see your point to a degree.*]

Most individuals will respond honestly when an olive branch is extended in terms of admitting to their own shortcomings. However, even if the employee refuses to agree with these points and shows no sign of shared accountability for the problem, continue along with the dialogue as outlined.

So if we're both frustrated at the situation and a bit miffed with each other, let's lay down our shields. The truth is that there's enough work around here to sink a battleship on a day-to-day basis. When you add interpersonal friction to the equation, it becomes very difficult, to say the least.

Sometimes it's fair to say that it just isn't a right fit, and I'd like you to consider something: Would leaving now on your own accord allow you an honorable exit strategy? Or would exploring other opportunities outside the company while you are still employed make sense for you at this point in your career?

If so, I've already talked with Paul (from HR), and we would be willing to allow you to begin interviewing at other companies while you remain employed with us. I know it's easier to find a job when you're employed than when you're unemployed, but the challenge is getting the time off to interview without making your boss suspicious. In this case, we could keep this whole thing confidential, and I'll allow you to interview on company time as long as you promise that our work continues to come first and that you give me twenty-four hours' notice of an upcoming interview.

However, I also need to be very clear about something: This is strictly up to you. If you would like our support to either resign on your own terms now or to begin looking for other work, then we'd be happy to help you. If not, that's okay too. In the latter case, we'll do everything we can to help reinvent our working relationship and start anew. We just want to give you these options so that you don't feel like you have no choice but to continue in a job that you don't like. That's a lose-lose outcome for everybody, and truth be told, this is something you and I should have addressed a long time ago.

There's no need to come to a decision now. Feel free to think about this, sleep on it, and let me or Paul know how you feel about it in a day or so. And, of course, you can speak with Paul one-on-one in human resources at any time to discuss the matter confidentially. Thanks for coming in and meeting with us to discuss this, and let me know whenever you're ready to pick up the conversation.

This velvet glove approach requires that you make yourself vulnerable to some degree. By admitting your own shortcomings and your role in the problematic relationship, you inject humanity into the equation. In addition, you're honestly and openly letting Michelle know where she stands, which is always a good thing. And that's where the healing can begin: When people are treated respectfully and see others making themselves vulnerable, they will often (even if begrudgingly) respond in kind. And although delivering a message like this can be confrontational, it's therapeutic because these words have needed to be spoken for a long time. After all, most people would prefer to hear directly where they stand rather than have to divine by their manager's actions that they're really no longer wanted.

So confront, don't avoid. Have a witness present, and respect the individual's ultimate decision to resign, launch an agreed-upon job search campaign, or commit to reinventing the working relationship. After all, no matter how angry employees are at their companies or supervisors, they will more than likely come to realize that fighting an uphill battle makes no sense. When angry people are treated respectfully, their anger dissipates. And when the anger is gone, they feel less inclined to stay with your company on principle. They may leave quietly on their own terms, without all the drama and histrionics that have plagued your relationship up until now.

On a practical basis, you'll likely find once this cathartic conversation has taken place, the individual's anger will dissipate, and she'll probably find work elsewhere within three to six months. That's good for her, good for your company, and good for the remaining staff members. It will also eliminate any serious threats of post-termination litigation that might have arisen had you acted too quickly in terminating her without progressive discipline on file or had she stormed out one day in anger, only later to claim constructive discharge.

SCENARIO 89

Negotiating a Separation Package When There Are No Progressive Disciplinary Warnings on File

The previous example demonstrates an open and honest way of handling a very common yet dangerous situation at work: Encouraging an employee to leave the company when there are no progressive disciplinary warnings or substandard performance reviews on file. It relies on good faith, honesty, and a willingness to make yourself vulnerable for the problematic situation at hand.

But what happens if the individual in question is a minority, over age forty, or pregnant? All of a sudden alarm bells ring because you realize that there is significant liability if matters are handled incorrectly. In cases where legal protections apply—disabled employees or workers who could argue retaliation for having gone on record against the company or against their supervisor—additional measures are often needed before such a conversation takes place.

The advice of qualified legal counsel is absolutely required before you engage in discussions like the one that follows below. Still, it's important that you draft your ideas and suggestions and provide them to your legal counsel as a starting point. This way both you and your lawyers will be in agreement as to what's going to be said, how, when, where, and in front of what type of witness (again, typically human resources, labor relations, or some other member of your company's administration or operations team).

The Solution

Let's use the same example as Scenario 88, and even the same dialogue up to a certain point: You're an executive who is having ongoing performance and conduct problems with your administrative assistant. You two don't really get along or like each other, you get on each other's nerves quite often, and you look at the world totally differently.

However, you were remiss in documenting the problems you've had with her work performance and behavior in the past, and now you're wondering how to address your olive branch discussion about her (1) resigning outright, (2) agreeing to look for work elsewhere while continuing her employment, or (3) totally reengaging and recommitting to you.

I know this third option may not be what you want, but you have to be sure to offer it clearly and with commitment. This is no time to railroad someone out of your company, especially since you've been remiss in holding up your end of the bargain: Had you documented the performance and conduct problems when they occurred in the past, you wouldn't be in this situation right now.

Your lawyer will need to determine the strategy for your discussion based on the merits of the particular case. A potential age discrimination claim may not be terribly daunting if you hired this individual when she was over age forty or if your workforce has a large percentage of older workers. On the other hand, if the individual can make a claim for mental stress based on comments you've made about her "nuttiness" or "mental instability" in front of witnesses, you may have an ADA claim that could cost your company dearly.

Remember that the Americans with Disabilities Act protects mental as well as physical impairments, whether the individual has such an impairment or is merely regarded as having such an impairment. One-off comments about someone's mental condition can indeed trigger ADA ramifications. You don't want your company to become a footnote in the case law books of how sharp the ADA's teeth can be in terms of awarding damages!

So let's pick up the conversation where we left off earlier:

Okay, then I just want to raise a consideration for you to ponder: Would leaving now on your own accord allow you an honorable exit strategy? Or would exploring other opportunities outside the company while you are still employed make sense for you at this point in your career?

Before you answer, I'll also throw one more idea out there for you to think about, Michelle. We could consider putting together what we'd call a "separation package" for you. A separation package is different than a severance package, which comes into play only when a position gets eliminated. We wouldn't be eliminating your position and would plan to backfill it after you left, but sometimes employees feel more comfortable with an incentive of sorts to move along in their careers, and if it's something you'd like us to consider, it could be an option. [*Well, what would this separation package look like?*]

Before we scheduled this meeting, Paul from HR and I spoke with our finance group because we thought you might ask us that very question. We would typically model it on the severance formula, even though we're not calling it severance. Under the severance scenario, an employee is eligible for two weeks of severance pay for each year of service. As a two-year employee, you would be eligible for four weeks of severance.

However, since it's a separation package and not severance, we don't have to strictly follow that exact formula. Therefore, rather than offering one month, we would offer you a three-month package. We'd continue your pay as if you still worked here (we call that "income continuation"), and we would pay your COBRA costs so that your benefits wouldn't cost you anything for that three-month period. In essence, you'd be making more in "separation" mode than you do as an active employee because as an active employee you have to pay for your benefits yourself.

We wouldn't contest your unemployment at the end of the three-month period, so you should have no problems receiving unemployment from the state.

In exchange for all this, though, we would ask you to sign a release, which is a hold harmless agreement confirming that you waive your right to sue the company for any disagreements or other issues. In essence, the three months of continuous pay serve as legal consideration for your signing the release. To make the contract valid, we have to give you something in exchange for your signing the release agreement. That something is called *consideration*, and the three-month package would constitute that consideration.

What's important for you to remember, though, is that this is all strictly up to you. We'll accept whatever decision you make. If you were to tell us that you'd rather remain employed and give our relationship a new chance, I'll make the good faith commitment to meet you halfway. If you decide that you'd rather remain employed and look for another job on company time, so to speak, we'll be okay with that as well, as long as you keep us as your priority and always give us at least twenty-four hours' notice of interviews so that we can arrange for backup support. And if you decide that you'd rather accept a three-month separation package in exchange for a release, we'll be fine with that as well.

There's no need to come to a decision now. Feel free to think about this, sleep on it, and let me or Paul know how you feel about it in the next few days. And, of course, you can speak with Paul one-on-one in human resources at any time to discuss the matter confidentially. In fact, you're more than free to discuss it with an attorney to make sure you understand your rights.

Again, we want you to handle this however you see fit and not feel any pressure to rush to make a decision, okay? [*Okay.*] Thanks for coming into this meeting and discussing this with us today.

Mission accomplished: You offered a compelling package for a two-year employee, and by proffering a release in exchange for this separation package, you'll have provided your company with ultimate downside protection. More important, you'll have handled the matter professionally, respectfully, and without drama.

13

Corporate ("No-Fault") Actions

o-fault actions are often the most difficult to explain to employees. After all, they're no one's fault. They're simply the result of doing business in an economy that sometimes can be erratic and unpredictable. Layoffs, department closures, and plant relocations are simply the fallout of global competition in a changing business world.

In fact, it's arguably easier to terminate someone for cause than to lay them off. Why? Because with a termination for cause, the employee can at least see it coming and arguably had some ability to avoid the outcome. That's not the case with layoffs, where positions are eliminated, and the people occupying those positions are then let go, often without much warning or notice.

However, if you see yourself as a coach, consultant, facilitator, and networker who is willing to help your displaced worker, you may just lose some of that panic feeling that goes along with letting people go due to downsizings. Simply see yourself as their champion and initial support network. After all, it does eventually happen to almost all of us, and the goodwill that you spread at this point for others may very well come back to your aid at some point in your own career.

Of course, if your company offers its displaced workers outplacement services, then the outplacement provider will do all those things and more. It's important that the laid-off individuals understand that you're not simply sending them packing without an action plan, safety net, or follow-up support system. In short, be there for your staff members when they are most vulnerable, and know that you're helping them through a traumatic time in their careers.

For instance, you might want to provide them with copies of their performance reviews so that they can show them to prospective employers as a reference. Provide them with information regarding unemployment insurance coverage and benefits continuation through COBRA. Remain in touch with them, if for no other reason than to listen to their issues and needs. If possible, extend the company's Employee Assistance Program (EAP) services to the displaced workers and their families, should the need arise for more in-depth counseling. With that type of dedicated attention, most workers can refocus on their future rather than bemoaning their past.

SCENARIO 90

Layoff: Position Elimination—LIFO

LIFO is the accounting term that refers to "last-in, first-out," meaning that the last person hired will be the first person let go during a business slowdown. This is actually the easiest conversation to have because the layoff is simply a matter of tenure and seniority and has little or nothing to do with individual performance, personal style, or popularity.

The Solution

Open up your conversation with the impacted worker using a straightforward yet caring approach:

> Belinda, in an effort to reduce costs, we are restructuring our business, and that will result in the elimination of a number of positions in our company. Unfortunately, your position has been selected, and I'm afraid we're going to have to lay you off. You're the last person hired in our department, and as a result, you're the first person to be impacted by the layoff. Does that make sense? [*Pause.*]
>
> Today will be your last day of work with us, and we have information to share with you regarding your severance package, COBRA, and unemployment insurance. I know this is a lot of information coming at you at once, and I'm so sorry to have to relay this message to you, but before I go any further, I want to stop here and see how you're doing. Are you okay? [*Pause.*]

Just so you're aware, a number of other positions are being eliminated throughout the day.

You're under no obligation to define that number more specifically. If three, thirty, or three hundred people will also be laid off, you're probably best off keeping that confidential at this point. Otherwise, the impacted worker may slip and inadvertently start a gossip chain that makes its way through your entire company like a lightning bolt that day. The day after the layoff (or possibly at the end of the notice day) is the best time to fully inform the remaining employees of the reductions in force that took place. This way, people can come together with information and facts that will help them begin to heal from the loss.

Out of respect for the other people involved, I'd ask that you say as little as possible today to other employees. We'd prefer to tell the affected employees ourselves because we want to avoid people hearing about this through the grapevine if we can help it. In addition, I know that some people prefer to leave quietly while others want to say goodbye to a few close friends. We'll respect whatever decision you make. How do you think you'd like to handle that?

Also, Belinda, will you need help packing up your desk? Can we get you boxes, do you need a lift home, or is there anything else you could think of where we can assist you with your move? Finally, I just want to thank you for all your hard work and dedication for the past two years and say I'm so sorry for what you're going through. You've made it a better place around here, and I'm personally going to miss working with you. Thank you for all you've done for us.

Special Note

Many management consultants recommend avoiding saying you're sorry. After all, they reason, saying you're sorry is an admission of weakness and guilt, and this is simply a business decision. It's not your decision, so there's no reason to say you're personally sorry.

Nonsense! What's critical about communicating with employees is that you treat them with respect and convey your feelings adequately. If people are treated with dignity, they will typically respond in kind. If your company lays off workers due to a reduction-in-force, then don't let that last impression be cold, distant, or formal. It's okay to say you're sorry that this is happening to them. Don't let anyone walk away from your company saying to themselves, "After years of giving my heart and soul to this company, no one even bothered to say thank you for all my hard work or sorry that this had to happen."

Remember, when employees walk away feeling underappreciated or taken advantage of, they're more inclined to look for ways to sue. When, in comparison, they feel they were treated fairly—even though they don't like the outcome of your company's decision—they're more inclined to come to terms with the layoff as a fact of business and get on with their lives.

SCENARIO 91

Layoff: Position Elimination—Lack of Qualifications

Understand that layoffs may not be purely a matter of eliminating a particular position; sometimes individual performance does play a role. On the one hand, if an entire department is going to be outsourced, then all employees in that area will typically be laid off. These are straightforward reductions in force that are fairly simple to present and explain. On the other hand, if one secretarial position is going to be eliminated and there are four secretaries in a particular department, then management has the responsibility of developing a "Peer Group Analysis," which serves to evaluate the pool of candidates and select the *least qualified* individual from within the group. In such cases where there are comparison pools, management typically needs to look at all four employees' overall qualifications: performance reviews, tenure, disciplinary history, attendance records, education, special skills, certifications, and the like. At that point, one of the four will be selected for layoff based primarily on documented performance and the "fit" factor. How you pose your presentation in this situation may be a bit different than in Scenario 90.

The Solution

Under the circumstances, expect a reasonable employee to challenge you in the heat of the moment. After all, panic typically sets in at the time of notice: How will I continue to pay my mortgage? What's going to happen to my health insurance? How will I make ends meet? Once the employee learns that her peers will be retained, however, and that she's going to be the only one let go, escalation of frustration may result. So let's look at how to present this information in the most supportive and constructive manner possible, realizing that you won't want to disclose too much information to confuse the impacted worker:

> Laura, in an effort to reduce costs, we are restructuring our business, and that will result in the elimination of a number of positions in our company. Unfortunately, your position has been selected, and I'm afraid we're going to have to lay you off. This is such hard news to deliver for me because you're such a hard and dedicated worker, and I'm sure this comes to you with a great amount of surprise. [*Pause.*]
>
> Today will be your last day of work with us, and we have information to share with you regarding your severance package, COBRA, and unemployment insurance benefits. I know this is a lot of information coming at you at once, and I'm so sorry to have to relay this message to you, but before I go any further, I want to stop here and see how you're doing. Are you okay? [*Pause.*]

Assuming she gives you the green light to continue, proceed with your conversation as follows (not mentioning the fact that she's the only one of four secretaries to be laid off in your department):

> Just so you're aware, a number of positions are being eliminated throughout the day. Out of respect for the other people involved, I'd ask that you say as little as possible today. We'd prefer to tell the affected employees ourselves because we want to avoid people hearing about this through the grapevine if we can help it. In addition, I know that some people prefer to leave quietly while others want to say goodbye to a few close friends. We'll respect whatever decision you make. How do you think you'd like to handle that?
>
> Also, Laura, will you need help packing up your desk? Can we get you boxes, do you need a lift home, or is there anything else you can think of where we can assist you with your move? Finally, I just want to thank you for all your hard work and dedication

over the past two years and say I'm so sorry for what you're going through. You've made it a better place around here, and I'm personally going to miss working with you. Thank you for all you've done for us.

Once the initial head rush is over, the employee may want to leave quietly or say goodbye to friends and peers. If the employee chooses to leave quietly, encourage her to do so. Follow-up conversations that night and in the next few days will help you place the pieces of the puzzle together for her, especially in terms of the specific answers to questions that she may develop.

However, the employee may respond with questions on the spot, which is also reasonable under the circumstances. Examples of such questions and appropriate responses might include:

Question: Why was my position chosen for elimination?

Answer: It was a business decision. Please don't take this personally; when a reduction in force occurs, *positions* are eliminated. The *people* who are attached to those jobs then get laid off. It's the hardest thing a manager can do. Eliminating positions is so difficult because you realize that people's lives will be interrupted. That's why I'm so sorry that this is occurring.

Question: Who else is being laid off? Am I the only one in our department? Why me?

Answer: Laura, I can't share who else is being laid off in the department at this point. We haven't spoken to the other individual(s) yet, so I'd ask that you allow me to hold off on answering that for now.

or:

Yes, yours is the only position in our department that's being eliminated. Again, please don't feel that you've disappointed anyone. I want you to know that you're rehirable once the hiring freeze is lifted. For now, though, understand that we had to eliminate one head count, which is why your position was impacted.

Question: How can that be? Who's going to do all the work that I do once I'm gone?

Answer: That was part of the pre-layoff analysis that we performed, and I want you to know that we're very aware of all the work that you do. I'm afraid we'll have no choice but to divvy it up among the remaining staff members. Travis is here from human resources to discuss some of the details related to your severance package and other important benefit details relating to this layoff.

Question: Wait. You can't lay me off and keep Rachel. I have more longevity than she does!

Answer: I recognize that. I want you to know that we did indeed consider tenure in our decision, but it wasn't the only factor. I'm not in a position to provide more details at this point. Just know that tenure was one of many considerations. Are there any other questions that I can answer for you?

Special Note

As you can see, these conversations can get uncomfortable. As this example demonstrates, it's certainly okay to tell someone that they're going to be the only one laid off in the group. But it's probably not a good idea to lay out the criteria you used in selecting who would be retained versus who would be laid off (i.e., tenure, performance appraisal records, technical certifications, and the like). Similarly, it's *not* okay to justify the reasons for your overall conclusion in selecting Laura for the layoff versus other members of the team.

In short, the actual analysis behind the decision is for the company and its lawyers to know. No one else, including the impacted employee, should be made privy to the details supporting the company's ultimate decision. If this sounds cold or secretive, it isn't meant to be. The reality is that sharing too much information with a highly charged employee may result in the worker misinterpreting what you tell her or hearing only what she wants to hear. Even if you feel a burning desire to share all the details that you're aware of—refrain! Too much information can be a bad thing when, seen in a vacuum, the larger picture is lost.

SCENARIO 92

Layoff: Position Elimination—Union Bumping Privileges

Union layoffs pose a different twist to the layoff process. Although union contracts differ, the basic concept that unions espouse is that tenure trumps all (unless the company can prove otherwise). In other words, all else being equal, those with the most longevity should be protected, while new hires with little tenure remain at risk.

If your employees are governed by a collective bargaining agreement that contains language regarding "union bumping privileges," then understand that the union contract is attempting to create a systematic process for defining seniority protection according to a preset formula. Typical language in a union contract may read:

An employee without sufficient seniority to remain in his/her classification in the department may exercise seniority rights to displace a less senior employee:

1. *(a) Within the same department in a lower classification,* provided that, in the Employer's reasonable judgment, the employee seeking to displace has substantially the same or better work-related skills, qualifications, abilities, performance record, disciplinary history, and attendance record as the potentially displaced employee, or, if no such positions are available,
2. *(b) Outside the department in the same classification,* provided that, in the Employer's reasonable judgment, the employee seeking to displace has substantially the same or better work-related skills, qualifications, abilities, performance record, disciplinary history, and attendance record as the potentially displaced employee.

You can see from the language here that whereas the union will argue for seniority-based selection, the company will argue for merit-based selection in order to retain the most talented individuals—not just those who have been around the longest. Let's look at how it works, and more important, what you may need to say to handle someone who is "bumped" as a result of a union contract's bumping provisions.

The Solution

The sample language from the contract looks at both movement within and movement outside of the impacted employee's department. Let's say you work for a university where the position of Clerical Specialist II is a covered classification in a union contract with these preset bumping provisions. If your administration department is required to eliminate one position, and that position is a Clerical Specialist II, then you would look at the least tenured individual in that role. (We'll call him Charlie.) You do a quick analysis from paragraph (a) and see that there is no one else within the department in a lower classification (e.g., Clerical Specialist I) who could be laid off instead of Charlie. Therefore, you then look to paragraph (b) to see if other Clerical Specialist IIs in other departments may have less tenure than Charlie. With HR's help, you develop a list of all Clerical Specialist IIs throughout the entire university system based on tenure, and you learn that there are six workers in other departments at the university whom Charlie could potentially displace because he has more tenure.

When it comes to union bumping privileges, you have to conduct a Peer Group Analysis (again, with the help of HR or your labor relations group) of each of those six people, making note of why or why not each employee is potentially "bump-able." You remove some people from the list because they have specialized skills and others because they work the graveyard shift, which has its own training requirements, and you then realize that one other person, Barbara Jones, who currently works in the operations department, could be laid off instead of Charlie.

Therefore, although a position is eliminated from the administration department, Charlie bumps into Barbara's job in operations. The net result is a position elimination in administration and a staff replacement in operations. (After all, although Charlie's position is now gone, he gets to bump Barbara out of her role in a different department because she has less tenure than he does.) As Barbara's supervisor in operations, your meeting with her might sound like this:

Barbara, I called you into this meeting with me and union steward Michael Shanahan to let you know that in an effort to reduce costs, we're restructuring our business, and that will result in the elimination of a number of positions in our company. Unfortunately, your position has been selected. Being in the union, you're unfortunately the least-tenured Clerical Specialist II on campus, and as a result, I'm afraid you'll have to be laid off.

Today will be your last day of work with us, and we have information to share with you regarding your severance package, COBRA, and unemployment insurance benefits. I know this is a lot of information coming at you at once, and I'm so sorry to have to relay this message to you, but before I go any further, I want to stop here and see how you're doing. Are you okay? [*Pause.*]

The employee may respond with questions or challenges on the spot that you'll need to be prepared for, which might include:

Question: I've heard that layoffs were in the making, but not in our area. Operations is so busy and doing so well. I just don't understand why I'm being laid off. People have been talking about union bumping privileges. Is that at play here?

Answer: Yes. The union contract looks at tenure according to classification, both within and outside the department. The least-tenured union member on campus is at the most risk because the union looks to protect members according to tenure with the university.

Question: So what's happening to my job? Is it going away, or is someone else getting it?

Answer: Actually the job that was eliminated is in administration. The person who's in that position, Charlie Rosen, will be transferring into your position here in operations. His tenure, in essence, allows him to "bump you" out of the role you currently hold and transfer into it himself.

Question: How can that be? Why have I been paying union dues and initiation fees—just to make my job *less* secure?

Answer: I'll invite your union steward to answer that one, Barbara, since she's here with us. [Defer to union to respond.] Alternative: In a way, I'm afraid that your lack of tenure puts you at risk in terms of job security according to the union contract. Union bumping privileges protect tenured union members but at the expense of the less tenured. I'm so sorry for how this is affecting you, Barbara.

Your role here is not to protect or defend the union, per se. Understand, however, that the impacted worker may express a number of negative feelings toward the unforeseen consequences now at hand because of her union membership, and you'll need to be an empathetic ear on the one hand while helping her focus on the new challenges that lie ahead in finding other, suitable work.

Just be careful not to jump on the bandwagon in terms of putting the union down or otherwise launching into a union bashing campaign with the displaced worker. Yes, you need to provide her with factual information regarding the nature and terms of her separation. But these are tough situations for all, and sensitivities typically run high. Simply respect the individual's emotions and avoid any temptation to assign blame.

SCENARIO 93

Layoff: Position Elimination—Department Closure

Laying off individuals is really tough; eliminating entire departments is excruciating. Companies eliminate departments for any number of reasons–outsourcing, offshoring, corporate consolidations, and mergers with competitors being the primary culprits—but whatever the reason, the group meeting is particularly heart wrenching.

The Solution

When calling an entire department into a group meeting, be clear and direct in your communication while demonstrating empathy for those who are being displaced. Allow as much time as necessary so that you can answer all initial questions. Have a support network on hand, such as HR, outplacement, or other service providers who will support the group going through transition. Likewise, have packets of materials customized and ready for each individual.

Your opening statement might sound like this:

Good morning, and thank you all for coming to this meeting. I've got some very sad news to share with all of you, and if you'll please allow me, I'll get right to it. I'm afraid that our entire department is being eliminated as part of a larger corporate re-structuring effort, and the transition will officially begin now. Your employment won't end today. In fact, we're hoping that you'll all agree to stay aboard with us for the next ninety days, which will help you build momentum in launching your job search and also entitle you to a "stay" bonus at the end of the ninety-day period. We'll talk more about that in a few minutes.

Right now, though, I need to tell you how sorry I am for what's occurring. Some of you may be aware that because of international competition, the demand to lower costs has simply skyrocketed in the past year. Payroll is the largest expense on our company's operating statement, and many of our competitors have already offshored positions in customer service and compliance to benefit from lower payroll costs overseas. I'm afraid that it's now our turn to move in that direction.

I know some of you may feel angry and betrayed by this, and you certainly have every right to feel the way you feel right now. These trends in outsourcing and offshoring are very problematic in general, and I want you to know that the company didn't reach this decision without a lot of forethought and consideration of how this would impact workers' careers. However, the cost of not going through with these actions could jeopardize the entire com-pany, and it was only under such circumstances that we came to the conclusion that this was our only way forward.

Now I know this is a lot of information coming at you at once, and before we go any further into these discussions, I just want to take a breather and give you time to digest all this. [*Pause.*]

Be sure to provide time after your initial introduction to allow em-ployees to vent. Too much information too quickly will leave people bewildered and dazed. There is a natural rhythm to delivering group news, and part of that process must allow time for the information to sink in and for people to voice their feelings.

Once the initial concerns and frustrations are vented, your next focus should be on answering questions and providing information. Expect employees' queries to focus on the work being abandoned as well as the insurance benefits available for those who are about to be laid off. There's no such thing as a dumb question at times like these, and giving employees carte blanche to pose any questions in a stream-of-consciousness format gets everyone talking, which is healthy.

With the initial questions addressed, invite everyone in the room to open their layoff packages so that you can review the contents together and out loud. Read the highlights of all forms included in the package, as this will trigger additional questions. Follow this question-and-answer format until the mass of queries subsides, and of course, don't be afraid to say you don't know an answer to a question but will research it and follow up as soon as possible.

Introduce the outplacement counselor, if one is available, and allow that individual or team to conduct a short presentation on the benefits of outplacement services in terms of speeding up people's job search, updating résumés, conducting mock interviews, and giving displaced workers access to industry resources and networks that wouldn't otherwise be available to them.

If your company chooses not to use an outplacement firm to aid those who are about to transition, consider asking your human resources department to schedule a résumé-writing workshop and also edit and upgrade everyone's résumé on an individual basis. Additional workshops regarding job change, interviewing, and job search strategies will also be well received.

End your initial meeting on a positive note of aid and assistance, and plan follow-up meetings either with the entire group or with individuals so that they can benefit from the dedicated attention that is so important at times like these. In short, be there for your people when they need you most, keep them informed about updates and changes as they occur, and be sure that their needs are met both from a professional (job search) and personal standpoint.

SCENARIO 94

Layoff: Position Elimination—Plant Closure (WARN Act)

If your company has one hundred or more employees and intends to lay off a significant number of workers, the Worker Adjustment and Retraining Act (WARN) may require you to provide sixty days' notice in advance of the layoff action.

First, a note of caution: WARN can be particularly difficult to decipher, so you'll definitely want to discuss any intended layoff actions with qualified legal counsel. Further, some state WARN laws, such as in California, have different triggering requirements, adding to the need to discuss this with legal counsel. Sometimes companies fail to provide the appropriate notices under WARN, making themselves vulnerable to significant damages. At other times, companies mistakenly issue WARN notices even though they're not required. Therefore, legal analysis prior to any intended group layoff action should always occur. Consider it a cheap insurance policy for your company's benefit.

Strictly speaking, the federal Worker Adjustment and Retraining Act may govern the notification requirements and obligations of a layoff when you plan to close an entire plant or lay off workers en masse. WARN applies to businesses that employ (a) one hundred or more employees, excluding part-time workers, or (b) one hundred or more employees who in the aggregate work at least four thousand hours per week, excluding overtime hours.

If your company plans to enact a reduction in force that results in an employment loss at a single worksite during a thirty-day period for the lesser of (a) at least 33 percent of the employees and at least fifty employees (excluding part-time workers) or (b) at least five hundred employees (again, excluding part-time workers), then WARN obligations may apply. Are you confused yet? Even if you're comfortable interpreting the language of the act, consider that if layoffs are planned over a six-month period rather than a ninety-day or thirty-day period, WARN may not apply. Ditto if employees at different work sites or employees of separate and identifiable business units within the same physical site are being laid off.

If this sounds like legal mumbo jumbo to you, you're not alone. The point to remember is that qualified legal counsel may be able to help you structure company layoffs to avoid meeting WARN's notification thresholds. In addition, WARN has sharp teeth: Penalties for failing to provide appropriate notice to displaced workers may include back pay for up to sixty days, the costs of employees' benefits for that period, and fines not to exceed $500 for each day of the violation.

The Solution

Let's look at how you might structure your group notice if WARN does indeed apply to your company:

Good morning, and thank you all for coming to this meeting. I've got some very sad news to share with all of you, and if you'll please allow me, I'll get right to the point. I'm afraid that our entire plant is being closed down because our company is closing this division of its business, and the transition will officially begin today. Your employment won't end today, however. We're giving you all sixty days' notice not only so that you can help us wrap things up at the facility but also so that you can have additional time to prepare your résumé, initiate a job search campaign, and have enough time to care for your personal and professional needs.

A federal law known as the WARN Act—WARN stands for the Worker Adjustment and Retraining Act—asks companies that are closing plant facilities to provide those soon-to-be displaced workers with sixty days' notice to get their lives and careers in order. We're happy to oblige as that law is something we'd want to do in any case.

Right now, though, I need to tell you how sorry I am for what's occurring. Some of you may be aware that because of international competition, our industry has suffered seriously in the past few years and is getting smaller every day. As much as the senior management team has tried to keep the company profitable and heading in the right direction, and despite all your hard work and dedication over the years, we have no choice but to close our doors.

I know some of you may feel angry and betrayed by this, while others feel a profound sense of loss. Whatever your initial reaction, you certainly have the right to feel the way you feel right now. I mean it when I say I'm so proud of everything we've accomplished together, but it's time for us to work together for this last, critical mission. And I want you to know that we've prepared a number of benefits and resources that will help you through this unforeseen transition period in a number of ways. However, we'll talk more about that in a few minutes.

For now, I know this is a lot of information coming at you at once, and before we go any further into these discussions, I just want to take a breather and see how you're all doing. [*Pause.*]

Your conversation at this point will naturally turn to answering employees' questions, outlining the programs you've established to help them through this transition, and discussing some of the material terms of their layoffs (for example, severance benefits, COBRA, outplacement, unemployment insurance, and the like). As in Scenario 93, be sure to end your initial meeting on a positive note of aid and assistance, and plan follow-up meetings either with the entire group or with individual departments so that they can benefit from your dedicated attention and commitment to helping them through this trying time.

Of course, the bigger the plant, the more difficult your ability to provide one-on-one dedicated attention. However, even when time and resources don't allow for that level of care, you can still be there for your people when they need you most. It's critical that communication and contact don't fall off after the initial announcement. Instead, keep your people informed and up to date by practicing MBWA ("Management by Walking Around") and having a physical presence whenever possible. After all, when you signed up for a career in managerial leadership, it was by design a career defined by wins and losses. Be sure that your leadership shines just as brightly when you're facing the losses that come with the territory, even if your own position is scheduled to be eliminated along with those of your coworkers.

SCENARIO 95

Follow-Up Discussions with Survivors
After Layoffs Occur

Downsizing, right-sizing, outsourcing, offshoring, restructuring, reductions in force—there seems to be no shortage of acronyms and euphemisms for shedding people in corporate America, which seems to expand and contract almost like an accordion these days. And maybe that's understandable seeing that payroll-related expenses still show up as the highest cost on a typical corporate P&L statement.

Up to now in this chapter, we've focused on how to address the individual worker or workers who are impacted when their positions are eliminated. It is equally as important to address the survivors on your team who will be called on to assume the remaining workload and who will simultaneously have to come to terms with the loss of friends and peers in a post-layoff environment.

The Solution

After an individual member of your team is laid off due to a position elimination, meet with the remaining members of your team either that day or first thing the following morning to openly address and acknowledge what has occurred.

> Everyone, I called this meeting right now to let you know that we've unfortunately had a position elimination in our department, and Laura has been laid off. Some of you may have seen her before she left yesterday, and others of you may be learning about this for the first time.
>
> I know it's pretty shocking either way, and I wanted to bring us all together to discuss this. First, I want you to know that Laura handled the news very professionally and with a lot of class, as she does in so many things in her life. It was a shock to her, no doubt, but I explained that position eliminations happen to all of us from time to time and have almost become a rite of passage these days, which she understood. We're also able to assist her in her job search by offering her outplacement services, which will help her update her résumé, give her access to jobs and company profiles that are proprietary, and even enroll her in a number of workshops that will help her hone her interviewing and résumé-writing skills. In addition, she qualifies for a severance package that will help her navigate this unexpected change in her career plans.
>
> I want to answer your questions, but I've got a few points that I'd like to make first:

1. Laura is rehirable immediately, and should something change where we could hire her back, we'd be very happy to consider that.
2. We've treated her with respect and dignity, and she responded in kind, so we're all on good terms. Therefore, there's no need for walking on eggshells or otherwise feeling uncomfortable if you see her.
3. The company has no plans to lay off anyone else in our department or elsewhere after today. Just so you know, though, there were other layoffs in different parts of the company yesterday as well. It's important that you realize that the plan was to get these things over all at once so that the remaining employees wouldn't have to worry about additional waves of layoffs impacting them.
4. We'll all take a close look at Laura's responsibilities as they'll need to be divided up among the rest of us. That doesn't need to happen today, though, and you can give some thought to that in the next few days.
5. Remember that any calls from prospective employers or headhunters need to be forwarded to human resources. It's not appropriate for any of us to share references, good or bad, because of our company's privacy policies. As is always the case, please don't feel guilty if someone asks you for references and you have to refer them to HR. We've given Laura (and everyone else impacted by yesterday's layoffs) copies of their performance reviews so that they can share them with prospective employers as evidence of their strengths and weaknesses. Now, all that being said, let's discuss some of the questions that you have.

This is a professional way of handling messages about individual position eliminations because it answers the immediate questions that people have (e.g., "Will Laura be well taken care of?" "Is my job in jeopardy now as well?") and also outlines your expectations regarding references and other policy and procedure matters.

What would be different about your conversation, however, if a group of individuals was laid off instead? Group layoffs tend to produce greater ill will toward the company, and that resentment may show itself in demonstrations of anger, defiance, or apathy. In such cases, your role as a manager will be to refocus your team on the bigger picture and not allow them to get lost in all the angst that comes from such sudden trauma in the workplace. In addition to covering the previous five points, add the following closer to your announcement meeting:

I sense some anger and resentment out there, and that's to be expected at times like these. But remember that sometimes you have to change your perspective in order to change your perception. In other words, look at the situation from a different perspective and you may experience its results very differently.

For example, don't forget that—yes, you've worked very hard for this company for many years—but the company has kept our families fed and roofs over our heads for just as many years. And as much as I'm going to hate to see us getting along without the four members of our team who were just laid off yesterday, we're still obligated to earn a good day's pay for a good day's work. That means that our production goals and our productivity targets still need to be met. However, we'll get that done in a more flexible manner than has been done in the past. In short, I want you to know that I'm still onboard and fully engaged and willing to help you in any way that I can. I'd like you to consider joining me in looking at this sad situation as something that we can all learn and grow from in terms of being there for one another. Please give that some thought over the next few days as we all look to rebuild in light of our loss.

Focusing everyone on the fact that the company has kept you all employed and helped send your kids to college is an important reminder at a very stressful time. Answer the group's questions honestly and openly but refocus them on what's important, which is that they're all still employed and have a job to do. The company is relying on them more than ever. And you need their support to let the healing begin and to reinvent yourselves as a group in light of this new and unexpected challenge. You may just find that the surviving employees demonstrate a greater appreciation for their jobs in addition to a loss of any entitlement mentality that may have crept into the culture over time.

14

Summary Offenses (Immediate Discharge)

Terminations for first-time offenses are always challenging for managers. While most supervisors assume that written warnings are the norm before terminating someone, not all offenses in the workplace are subject to progressive discipline. If someone steals from your company, the organization has the right to terminate immediately, even for a first-time offense. In fact, failing to do so could make your company appear irresponsible and set a dangerous precedent in terms of your ability to terminate future thieves. After all, it doesn't make much sense to give someone a written warning after they steal cash from the register stating, "If you ever steal cash from the register again, you'll be terminated."

As you might guess, employers have a significant amount of discretion to move to summary (immediate) dismissal for *conduct*-related infractions like stealing, fraud, embezzlement, and gross insubordination. When it comes to *performance*- and attendance-related transgressions, employers are typically expected to go through all the normal steps of progressive discipline as accorded under company policy and practice.

This chapter addresses the tough conversations that are necessary when faced with cases of summary, or immediate, dismissal. In all cases, act reasonably and responsibly and avoid demonstrating contempt or "throwing them out on their ear." Let cooler heads prevail, even at times when you're exceptionally angry and disappointed.

Of course, you also have the right to look into pursuing the individual legally for post-termination reimbursement to the company, but that should be discussed with legal counsel. At that point, you'll need to determine whether any collection action on your part will be worth the expense of pursuing it and balancing that opportunity cost against the lesson you wish to give the perpetrator on principle.

Finally, note that "You're fired!" is not a nice way to end anyone's employment as it deprives the person of respect and dignity. Although you may feel that the employee has forfeited any right to respect and dignity by his egregious actions, keep in mind that firing people on the spot is best left for reality TV. When you suspect that a summary dismissal may be warranted, it's typically best to send the employee home with pay on an "administrative" or "investigatory" leave so that he is off the premises and you have the time to investigate your intended action more thoroughly.

Terminating the individual over the phone while he's at home can then take place, which provides you and your company with more safety while allowing feelings of anger and resentment to subside. Besides, you'll make a much better record for the company if you place the individual on paid administrative leave before rushing to judgment, and courts and juries favor that type of corporate wisdom and restraint.

SCENARIO 96

Employee Theft

Employee theft is a multibillion-dollar business, with estimates ranging from $50 to $400 billion per year in US companies. And of course it comes in so many forms: retail theft of clothing and apparel, funneling and diverting accounting funds away from the company and into a personal bank account, absconding with old computers that were meant for corporate donations, and even pilfering company charity donations and writing them off as if they were your own donation for tax purposes.

Whatever the form, employee theft should be addressed swiftly and definitively. Of course, you'll always want to hear and document the employee's side of the story before initiating termination proceedings. Just remember that even if you've caught the misdeed on tape and have witnesses willing to sign statements of testimony, you absolutely want to listen to the employee's side of the story to ensure workplace due process. Strange things happen in the workplace, and sometimes what you see isn't necessarily "what is," especially if someone is being set up.

Let's assume an employee who works as a janitor decides that he wants to take home a dozen computers that have been tagged for donation so that he can sell them for parts. The worker comes to work on a Saturday, let's himself into your building, and loads his pickup truck with a number of Macs and PCs that your company was planning on distributing to local schools. Unfortunately for the janitor, he doesn't realize that the building's surveillance monitoring system runs 24/7, and the security department is able to figure out first thing Monday morning who absconded with the computers.

The Solution

When you, the janitorial department head, are asked into a meeting with human resources and security to watch a tape of the employee driving away from the building with the computers, you first ask yourself why on earth he would have done that. Then you wonder if he was acting on someone else's instructions (for instance, the information systems department) to remove that company equipment. You also wonder where all those computers are right now, since they were removed from the company property on Saturday, two days ago.

You meet with the employee and open up the conversation this way:

> Mike, we have something important to speak with you about. There were about twelve computers in the information technology department that were tagged to be donated to local schools. However, they're missing, and IT isn't aware of their whereabouts. Do you know where they might be?

Assuming Mike responds that he has no idea, then simply cut to the chase and lay the foundation for your argument:

> It's funny you should say that. We have footage of you leaving the building in your pickup truck on Saturday morning at about 11:00 a.m. with a dozen computers in the flatbed. We could show you the video if you'd like. We need to know what's going on, though, Mike. Did you remove them from company premises

with someone else's permission, or did you do that on your own volition? And where are those computers currently?

Assuming that Mike suddenly can't remember anything, including his driving to the company on Saturday, letting himself into the building and the IT storage area, loading up the truck, and then driving off, then state the obvious:

Mike, in light of your not being able to account for the missing equipment, even though we show you on film removing it from company premises, we can only assume that you stole it. Please understand that you can be terminated for stealing and that we can pursue the return of the equipment legally. What am I missing, Mike? I want to give you every chance to explain what's going on so that I'm not missing any important facts or assuming anything.

And lo and behold, Mike has no answers. He begins to cry and apologizes for his actions. He confirms that he only took them because they were going to be given away anyway, and he makes so little money as a janitor that he needs to earn extra money to make ends meet. Besides, he reasons, a large and successful company like yours wouldn't necessarily need the money from the computer proceeds that he needs just to get by. At that point, after you've given him a chance to explain himself and also jotted down his "defense" and justification for his actions, you explain that he's terminated.

Mike, I'm very disappointed that you chose to go this route. You've worked for our firm for two years, and I'm sure you realize that this was patently wrong. As a result, we're terminating your employment, effective immediately. We'll need you to leave the premises right after this meeting. We'll then cut your final checks and courier them, along with any personal belongings that you have back at your desk, to your home later today. Is there anything else you'd care to say at this point? [*No. I'm sorry.*] Thank you for apologizing, Mike, and please take the opportunity to think about this and learn from the mistake you've made.

Plain and simple and without a lot of fanfare, this termination meeting is handled professionally and efficiently. Afterward you can determine how to retrieve the stolen goods or press charges if they're permanently lost.

Time Card Fraud

Time card fraud is a tough one: Employees often don't realize that it's not necessarily subject to steps of progressive discipline and can be interpreted as a summary offense. Depending on the nature of the incident, its severity, and the number of times it has occurred, a company has the discretion to terminate once the offense is discovered. It helps very much if the company has a timekeeping policy that states that violations are not subject to the progressive discipline process and will result in immediate discharge.

To be clear, not every incident of time card misrepresentation must result in termination. For example, if an employee showed on her time card that she worked until 5:00 p.m. one day last week but actually left the office at 4:00 p.m., that would probably be best addressed by a short discussion stating that you expect people to carefully log when they clock in and out (especially if it's a first occurrence).

However, certain infractions should be interpreted as summary offenses. For example, assume that two nonexempt clerks go to lunch every day together at noon. However, when it comes time to return from lunch at 1:00 p.m., only one returns but does swipes on two separate time cards—one for herself and one for her coworker. Others in the department soon catch on to this little game where every other day, one of the two employees takes a two-hour lunch while the other swipes back in for the first. These coworkers then report this fraud to human resources so that a "sting" operation of sorts can be set up: HR and security make note of the time the employees swipe back in from lunch, and the supervisor also tracks when both individuals actually return to their desks.

The Solution

When the time cards are submitted, you notice that the first employee, Cindy, shows consistently that she took lunch from noon to 1:00 p.m.

every day the week before. Not surprising, the second employee, Sarah, shows time cards that reflect the same misinformation.

You first call Cindy into your office, with either human resources or security present, and ask the following:

> Cindy, I need to speak with you about something that's come to my attention that's very important, and I've asked Ashley from Human Resources to join us because this could be a potentially serious offense that could result in termination. I need to ask you about your lunches and your time cards last week. Was anything recorded inappropriately or inaccurately?

Cindy looks at you questioningly and states that, to her knowledge, all is accurate. You then clarify that coworkers witnessed her extending her lunch beyond 1:00 p.m. every other day that week, and you show her the time card report that reveals the falsifications.

Cindy ultimately admits that she was engaging in that game, apologizes for gaming the system, and then responds with shock when she is told that this is a terminable offense. She fully expected to be given a warning instead. You respond as follows:

> Cindy, time card fraud literally steals time from the company. Yet the old adage "time is money" is relevant and real in this case: Time is a proxy for money, and stealing time is the same as stealing money in the workplace. We don't provide progressive discipline to employees who engage in theft of any sort, and I'm afraid we'll have to terminate your employment, effective immediately.

When you later call the second employee, Sarah, into your office, you find that she committed the same wrongdoing. Both employees' assumptions that they would only be disciplined rather than terminated if they were caught has little bearing. The standards that you uphold and the precedent-setting decisions to support them establish the *practice* that your company adheres to, which many employment lawyers will tell you is just as, if not more, significant than the *policy* you have written in your company handbook.

SCENARIO 98

Threats of Violence in the Workplace

Generally speaking, companies have little discretion in responding to threats of violence. That's because once the company is put on notice that one employee is threatening another, the company has an affirmative obligation to protect the threatened employee and provide for a safe and secure workplace. Should the company not take the threat seriously and injury or death results, the company could find itself liable for a host of violations, including negligent hiring, negligent retention, negligent infliction of emotional distress, and other tort claims.

Let's assume that a nighttime security guard, Alma, threatens her supervisor, Denise. This comes in the form of a verbal threat where Alma tells Denise, "If this happened outside of work, I'd beat the sh-- out of you."

When questioned about the occurrence, Alma admits that she made the claim and added that "she would be only too happy to take matters into her own hands." You find out that Alma and Denise have known each other personally and disliked each other intensely before either started working at your firm. Supervisor Denise did not make a counterthreat; she simply reported Alma's threat to human resources.

The Solution

Now that you've completed the investigation and heard directly from Alma that she did indeed threaten Denise and also repeated her threat in your presence, you have little discretion not to terminate immediately. In this case, you might want to educate Alma about the nature of threats in the workplace.

Alma, I don't know the history of your relationship with Denise, and I also didn't know that you both knew each other before you joined the company. You explained why you made the comment, and I understand that you feel that Denise doesn't respect you. Truth be told, though, if you had any problems with Denise, you had the option of reporting the problem to your department head or to human resources. However, you didn't have the option of threatening to "beat the sh-- out of her."

I assume you realize that this would probably get you terminated, both for threatening your supervisor and for insubordination. Does it shock you to hear me say that? [*No.*] Alma, you need
to understand something that's very important: Companies no
longer have the discretion to retain employees who make direct or
even veiled threats. This was definitely the case of a direct threat,
but in a world where workplace violence gets so much attention
and where lawsuits can be so punitive, companies just can't
afford to take the risk of retaining anyone who makes threats of
physical violence or bodily harm.

Okay then, we do indeed need to move to termination under
these circumstances. I want to thank you for your service up to
now and ask you to leave the building premises without returning
to your desk or visiting Denise. We'll forward your final checks
plus any of your personal belongings to your home via courier.

Alma should be escorted off premises by security at this point, to
ensure the safety of her supervisor, Denise.

SCENARIO 99

Sexual Harassment

Sexual harassment may be a summary offense or it may be subject to
progressive discipline. As you can imagine, it depends on the nature of
the individual's conduct, the egregiousness of the offense, and myriad
other factors. In Chapter 8, we addressed sexual harassment findings
that generally did not rise to the level of immediate dismissal. In our
current scenario, we'll address a situation that does require summary
termination.

Let's assume you're the COO of your company and learn that the
administrative assistant in the operations department just came in to
human resources crying and saying that she's been "forced" to sleep
with the vice president of operations for the past three months. The
assistant tells human resources that she never wanted to develop an in-
timate relationship with her department head but felt that if she didn't
comply, she would face retaliation and ultimately dismissal. This is a

typical case of quid pro quo harassment where sexual favors effectively become a condition of employment.

The Solution

When you're faced with this type of claim, get immediate help from your human resources department in addition to qualified legal counsel. These cases pose unusually serious legal threats to your company and should be guided by an attorney behind the scenes.

It's not uncommon for the supervisor to defend himself by arguing that the relationship was consensual. The problem, of course, is that you'll be facing a he said–she said situation where you (or a jury) can't know the truth, so the victim's allegations become the standard of judgment. In short, there's very little defense that a company could proffer if one of its supervisors engages in sexual relationships with a subordinate, which is why a defense attorney needs to be involved early on in the game.

In this example, with HR present (or with another member of your management team), your meeting with the department head (we'll call him Mark) might open like this:

> Mark, I needed to meet with you because something's come to our attention that requires immediate resolution. Dana, your assistant, apparently went to human resources this morning claiming that the two of you have been sleeping together for the past three months. Clearly, I can't just take her word for it without hearing your side of the story as well, so would you please let me know what, if anything, is going on here?

As is often the case, Mark responds that they have indeed fallen in love and developed a physical relationship. He also states that he was planning on disclosing that to you, his supervisor, but hasn't had a chance yet and has been thinking about how to best present the information. However, Mark assures you that the relationship is consensual and that he hasn't engaged in any inappropriate behavior.

You then remind Mark of his obligation to report such romantic relationships that develop between supervisors and their subordinates immediately under policy and procedure guidelines. Mark acknowledges that he was aware of those requirements but that the relationship has really been on again/off again for the past few months, and he wasn't really sure if it would become serious in any event.

Finally, you inform Mark that Dana came to human resources in tears that morning stating that she feared retaliation for rebuffing Mark's advances that weekend. This Mark clearly denies, stating that this is all being taken out of context.

Your response should be very straightforward and direct: Place Mark on administrative, investigatory leave while you continue your investigation:

> Mark, I have no choice at this point but to place you on inves-
> tigatory leave with pay while I look further into this. I wanted
> to meet with you this morning to confirm that these events did
> indeed occur, which you've verified. However, I've got to let you
> know that your arguments that you weren't sure if this relation-
> ship would last or how you would notify me don't excuse your
> serious violation of company policy. I also need to let you know
> that this may result in your immediate termination. I'll know more
> once we've had a chance to vet this with outside counsel. Please
> leave the premises and wait at home for my call.

Don't be surprised if your attorney recommends that Mark be terminated immediately for breach of company policy and failure to disclose a romantic relationship with a subordinate. Mark's immediate termination will help mitigate the harassment case that your company may face from the subordinate because it demonstrates that your company took the issue seriously and remedied it immediately on learning of the problem. Your call to Mark that night might then sound like this:

> Mark, it's Paul. I need to let you know that we're exercising our
> right to terminate your employment for breach of trust and failure
> to follow the company's policies that are clearly outlined in the
> policy and procedure manual and employee handbook. We'll have
> someone from human resources get in touch with you in terms of
> collecting your laptop, company ID, and the like. Do you have any
> questions that I can answer for you at this point?

Companies have little reason *not* to terminate under circumstances like these. Be sure to document the time of your call to Mark as well as his response—both in terms of what he says and the tone of his voice.

Your attorney will then advise you whether a written letter of termination would be appropriate under the circumstances.

SCENARIO 100

Insubordination

Insubordination is a conduct infraction that stems from one of two things: (1) intentionally disregarding a supervisor's explicit directive or (2) demonstrating extreme disrespect for a supervisor, either in private or in front of others. Your knee-jerk reaction to an insubordinate subordinate may be to respond in kind (for example, by cursing back at someone who hurls profanities at you or by terminating the person on the spot in front of his peers.)

In reality, though, insubordination may be subject either to progressive discipline or to summary discharge. A lot will depend on the circumstances surrounding the event, the employee's prior history with the company, and in the egregiousness of the offense. Don't rush to judgment: If immediate termination is the ultimate result, it would be better to make it a quiet and low-key event with the employee waiting at home while on investigatory leave rather than a "shoot-out at the O.K. Corral"-style conflagration in front of the whole staff.

In fact, when an employee appears to blow up and spew expletives at a supervisor in front of the rest of the staff, your best bet as the supervisor will be to end the meeting, dismiss the rest of the staff, and ask the employee to meet with you in private in your office. If you have a human resources department onsite, ask that a member of the HR team join you to moderate the meeting. After all, no matter how much you pride yourself on your objectivity and fairness in managing others, once you're a participant in the game, you can no longer play the role of referee and mediator. You'll need an objective third party to do that, and human resources or another member of the management team can join you as the arbiter of the dispute.

The Solution

In the case where a subordinate "calls you out" in front of the rest of your team, meet with your company's HR representative or some other third party as outlined previously and explain exactly what was said, including the language and tone of the message, whom it was said in front of, and what other body language was involved. Explain that you'd like their help at this point in terms of meeting with the offending employee and determining an appropriate company response.

For example, let's assume you were holding a staff meeting and one of your team members suddenly stood up and exclaimed, "This is bull----! We shouldn't have to do this again. We're being asked to do double work because of your f---ing incompetence. If you knew what the hell you were doing as a supervisor, none of this would be necessary, and I'm sick of it!"

Explaining this to the third party and then inviting the employee into your meeting, you could calmly open up the conversation by asking:

> Joe, I explained to Marlene from human resources what happened in the staff meeting. I wanted to invite Marlene to meet with us, though, so that she can provide an objective evaluation of the whole situation. I told her how I recalled your outburst happening, but I'll leave it to Marlene to take it from here and learn your side of the story. I'll leave you two alone at this point. Marlene, please let me know where things stand after you've concluded your meeting with Joe.

Marlene then meets with Joe, learns that he indeed said those things in a fit of rage because he believes that Paul is an incompetent manager, and then receives an apology from Joe for acting out of line. Regardless of Joe's about-face, she places him on paid administrative leave and sends him home.

She later explains to you that the company has no choice but to terminate Joe for gross insubordination and explains that she will terminate Joe over the phone this afternoon. Yes, precedent should be reviewed (i.e., how your company has handled similar situations) in addition to Joe's tenure with the company and protected status (e.g., age, race, and so forth) as well as any potential claim for retaliation based on prior events. Assuming, however, that you've never publicly humiliated Joe or engaged in similar behavior, you should be safe to terminate.

Let's assume that Joe calls you the next morning to apologize; in that case, you might want to consider accepting his apology and explaining:

> Joe, I don't know where all the anger is coming from, but you need to know that such behavior can't be condoned in the workplace. I haven't seen this type of reaction from you under other circumstances, but understand that a company doesn't have any discretion to waive termination for displays of gross misconduct. I was embarrassed, humiliated, and exceptionally disappointed that you chose to express your frustrations the way you did in front of the whole team. I hope you never do that to another supervisor in your career, and I hope that no member of your staff ever blindsides you that way.
>
> In addition, just so you know, we'll be very respectful of your privacy as far as the other staff members. I'll hold a meeting with them today, letting them know that you're no longer with the company, that we've treated you respectfully, and that any phone calls from prospective employers or headhunters looking for references will be referred to human resources, where only your dates of employment and last title held will be shared.
>
> Finally, because this is not typical of your ordinary workplace demeanor, we as a company don't intend to contest your unemployment. That means that whatever you tell the folks at the unemployment insurance office in terms of why you left the company won't be disputed. In fact, we won't even return their call.
>
> I wish you well, Joe, and I'm sorry things had to end this way. I hope that you can come to terms with whatever caused this outpouring of emotion in the workplace and will be able to avoid incidents like this in the future. Human resources will call you with more details regarding your separation from the company. Take care.

Notice that despite the employee's inappropriate behavior, the supervisor never escalated his feelings in public. Instead, he handled matters privately with the employee in front of a third-party witness. The fact that the supervisor didn't react emotionally had significant bearing on the ultimate outcome of the case. If the supervisor had sunk to Joe's level and engaged in a shouting match, then immediate dismissal may have been more difficult to justify.

Again, let calmer heads prevail, let respect rule the day, and remember that it's all about the record. When facts speak for themselves and they're very black and white, the company will have much more discretion and latitude to terminate as appropriate.

15

Special Circumstances

The special circumstances outlined in this chapter don't easily fit into the other categories in this book. However, as you read through this chapter's topics list, you'll learn how to address some very practical, yet taxing, discussions that revolve around compensation conflicts and wage and hour challenges. Whether employees are asking for a raise based on their internet research, won't be getting a merit increase or bonus based on poor performance, this chapter will keep you ahead of the discussion curve.

It stands to reason that you'll need to know how to move threatening employees off your premises safely. Investigatory administrative leaves allow you to do just that, preserving the individual's dignity while continuing his pay, so that you can conduct a fair and unbiased investigation. If termination becomes necessary upon completion of your investigation, the employee will already be off-premises, and you'll have time to alert your security, operations, and front desk reception areas with instructions not to allow the individual access to company property. Note that in all these cases, the impacted employee will be treated with dignity and respect. In addition, company benefits, like an Employee Assistance Program (EAP) or mental health plan, might be extended beyond the individual's separation date to provide for additional support for the ex-employee and her family members.

Again, the beauty of these verbal discussions is that little preparation time will be needed, thanks to having this book on hand. And you'll likely find that anticipating employees' reactions to various types of special circumstances will help you navigate them very successfully and with very little turbulence because of your proactive and open communication style.

SCENARIO 101

Compensation Conflicts—Dealing with Raise Requests Based on Internet Research

Compensation will always be an emotional subject. Employees constantly wonder if they're being paid fairly, whether they'll get a promotion, and how compensation gets determined in the first place. After all, a number on their paycheck tells them that their time and effort is worth a certain amount, and it's understandable that people remain curious about what their contribution could garner elsewhere. As a result, it's critical for managers to navigate these critical conversations with care.

Dollars will always be limited. Salary ranges, budgets, and internal equity considerations act as regulators to any worker's pay rate. While salary usually ranks fourth—behind recognition and appreciation, leadership, communication, and career engagement—when polling workers in employee engagement surveys and exit interviews, it's still a significant swing factor that helps workers justify whether they should remain with their current employer or pursue employment elsewhere. Thanks to online resources that collect salary data from workers at particular companies and in specific industries, employees often come to a compensation meeting "armed" with what they see as concrete, objective data that proves they're currently undercompensated for what they do and the contributions they make. Don't let that throw you off: You've got resources at your disposal to dispel the myth that all data on a salary website is accurate and reliable.

The Solution

When faced with such data, patiently explain that self-reported data from the internet is just that—self-reported data. There's no way of confirming the data integrity, since no organization or compensation consulting firm is vetting the data that's posted.

The goal of your discussion isn't necessarily to disprove the employee's findings. After all, many people mistakenly believe that if something is published on the internet, then it's legitimate. Instead, use this as an opportunity to explain how compensation decisions are made and what considerations determine an individual's base salary. There's nothing like open and honest discussion regarding matters near and dear to the heart, so begin your conversation as follows:

Nelson, I hear you, and I appreciate your sharing this with me. I want to take this opportunity to walk you through how this works in most organizations, not just ours. Compensation discussions are tricky, and there are more considerations than meet the eye. Still, now's probably a good time for this discussion, since you've researched this on your own and are hoping to make a compelling case for an increase in your pay. Sound fair? [*Yes.*]

Okay, first off, not to challenge the data you've learned online through your research, but generally speaking, when you're looking at salary-focused websites, you're asked to report how much you earn in exchange for data from the larger group of participants. Does that sound about right? [Yes.] Okay, so when you report your salary data, you're entering information that really can't be vetted by any official source, like a compensation consulting firm, for example. It's simply self-reported data that's then aggregated and reported outward. Can you see how those websites function? [*Yes, that makes sense.*]

In our world, we handle salary data differently. We rely on aggregated market data from three published and well-known surveys, developed and updated each year by prominent compensation consulting firms. Those firms don't just pull in raw data—they separate the data by industry (for-profit vs. nonprofit, manufacturing vs. service, and the like), by company size (small, medium, large, and super-large), by location (urban vs. suburban vs. rural), and there can be other factors as well—domestic vs. international, union vs. nonunion, etc.

Anyway, we have a salary structure program that reflects our company's specific needs and that breaks down jobs into a salary grade structure that covers every position in our organization, from CEO on down. What's important to remember is that the salary survey data that we use isn't the only factor. First, the salary grade has a range with a minimum, midpoint, and maximum. That's the broadest cut of data. Second, we have budgets that we work with. For example, each department tracks its salary data as part of its annual budget, and payroll is usually the largest item on a company's profit and loss statement, so any changes are measured carefully.

Third—and this is most important—we look at what's known as "internal equity" when we slot employees and new hires into the range. Generally speaking, that means that we look at our current employee base and measure years of experience, education levels, technical skills, and whatnot, and we then make sure that each employee fits well in that salary band. In other words, each employee's salary—or their position within the salary range—is based on the individual's proficiency level and performance.

In essence, Nelson, the salary range is a broad data point, but placement is governed by the budget and internal equity considerations. Those two data points are more important than the range itself, because they're more tailored to our specific compensation program. Querying a salary search platform on the internet simply helps you determine the broad range for a particular position, which is the least useful of the three elements that we consider. Also, because that information is self-reported, not regulated by a third party, and typically makes no tie-in to company size, location, or geography, it tends to confuse people because it's not tailored to our market.

I wanted to walk you through all this because I want you to understand what magic goes on behind the wizard's curtain, so to speak. But there's really no magic at all—it's more about math than anything else.

I'll do more homework by sharing this with human resources, to ensure that we're at market and paying you fairly in your role. I don't know what that outcome will look like yet, but I'll get back to you within the week. Regardless of the outcome, I appreciate your sharing this with me, and I want you to know that it's very important to me that we manage this thoroughly and responsibly. Is there anything else I can do for you in the meantime? [*No, but thanks for the explanation and for looking into this for me.*]

In good faith, a logical next step would be to review Nelson's salary with human resources, to ensure you're paying competitively. If you are, then follow up with the employee and explain that he can rest assured that the company believes he's paid competitively relative to his peers and the market as a whole. If you're not, then consider awarding a salary adjustment immediately or at the next merit cycle, where a lump-sum increase may be awarded or where the individual can be placed on a "salary plan" (i.e., a series of budgeted increases at six-, twelve-, or eighteen-month intervals to bring his position to market).

SCENARIO 102

Compensation Conflicts—No Annual Increase Due to a Low Performance Review Score

Of all the performance reviews you do for your team during any given cycle, this is the one you're most likely saving until last. That's reasonable—we all put off conflict or potential conflict for as long as we can. Failed performance reviews frequently lead to low or no salary increases or bonuses. To do otherwise could undermine the integrity of your performance-management program.

For instance, awarding a "Does not meet expectations" overall score, accompanied by a 3 percent merit increase, could cause a plaintiff's attorney at some point in the future to argue: "My client didn't realize his job was in serious jeopardy of being lost. Sure, he failed his annual review, but he received the same merit increase as everyone else on the team, and money speaks louder than a paper appraisal. By terminating him under those circumstances, you denied him workplace due process because he had no indication that his job was on the line. . . . " And from such arguments stem wrongful termination claims that can later be attached to discrimination, harassment, and retaliation charges, which all carry the potential for punitive damages.

No doubt about it: informing an employee that there will be no annual merit increase or bonus because of a failed performance review is a tough conversation. Your approach becomes all the more important, and of course, much of your conversation will be driven by the reasons for the failed overall score at the end of the review.

The Solution

Of course, a lot depends on whether the failed review was due to substandard job performance or inappropriate workplace conduct.

In cases of gross misconduct or egregious behavior, it might be easier to fail the employee for the review period. Employers have a lot more discretion with conduct to "skip steps" in the progressive discipline paradigm, for example, by terminating for a first offense like theft, fraud, or embezzlement or issuing a final written warning for a first offense like harassment or bullying. In such cases, failing the employee for the entire performance year may be warranted, to demonstrate the seriousness of the matter or the severity of its impact on your organization. For example, if you issued a final written warning for an investigation that surfaced serious sexual harassment allegations but couldn't quite justify outright termination due to missing facts or witnesses or the employee's long-term tenure relative to a first offense, then the failed review—and zero merit increase—ties in well with the final written warning in a case where the employee was lucky not to have been fired.

With performance challenges, it can be more difficult to fail an employee on the review and issue no merit increase. Why? Because the employer likely and reasonably had opportunities along the way to bring problems to the employee's attention, so the individual could turn around her performance. By not saying anything at the time and then hitting the employee all at once during the annual review, the employer's action can seem vindictive or retaliatory, and it's not an unreasonable argument to say that the problem was with the supervisor more than with the worker.

In any event, gain guidance from your supervisor, human resources, or qualified legal counsel when failing an employee on the annual review and awarding no merit increase or bonus. In the example that follows, we'll look at the situation outlined above—failed annual review because of a one-time case of egregious misconduct that could otherwise have resulted in the employee's termination. In this case, the employee is a solid performer overall but engaged in an incident of misconduct that resulted in a final written warning. As such, seven of the eight categories in his performance review, like productivity, customer service, and quality, met or exceeded expectations. But one category—teamwork and respect in the workplace—almost resulted in a summary termination and warranted a final written warning, even though it was a first-time event. Here's how that conversation might sound under those circumstances:

Jose, before we go into detail regarding your annual performance review, I need to let you know that you won't be meeting expectations for the year, because of the incident that occurred last June and resulted in a final written warning. Further, you won't be eligible for a merit increase or a bonus this year because of the failed performance review. I wanted to open with that, so you have a framework for our discussion today. May I proceed? [*Yes.*]

As you'll recall, and as I shared with you at the time, we seriously considered terminating your employment in June. I won't rehash all the details, but generally speaking, because of your long tenure with the company and your clean record leading up to that event, we opted not to separate your employment. But this review covers the entire performance year, and the event that led to the final written warning occurred within that timeframe.

Further, you'll see when I share this document with you that you performed well in seven of the eight categories. However, the one category that you failed—teamwork and creating a friendly work environment—was enough to justify a failed overall score at the end of the document.

We don't average the individual categories to come to the final score at the end of the review. Each category is weighted, and anything relating to conduct, behavior, or ethics outweighs anything else in the scorecard. Does that make sense? [*Yes.*] That's why your overall score demonstrates that you didn't meet expectations for the review period. Are you clear on that? [Yes.] Okay, then let's discuss the other seven performance categories first, since those are unrelated to that June event and focus on your performance and productivity. . . .

In a situation like this, it would be best if you'd notified Jose in June, at the time of the final written warning, that he wouldn't be meeting expectations for the entire review year when his annual performance appraisal would be due. That would help take the sting out of the message above. But one of the key rules regarding performance reviews is to evaluate the entire performance period and not to get caught in what's known as "recency error"—the rater's tendency to allow more recent employee performance or conduct to outweigh the performance over the entire rating period. In short, the annual review score should reflect the year's overall performance and conduct record, and a year in which the employee could have been fired should be met with a failed performance review, for the sake of a consistent record.

SCENARIO 103

Compensation Conflicts—Denial of a Raise Due to Budget Considerations, Internal Equity Challenges, or Being "Red Circled" at the Top of the Salary Range

What do you say when one of your employees meets with you to convey that she needs and deserves a raise, when your gut screams that a raise isn't even close to being possible? Aside from the fact that the employee's performance may not be as stellar as she thinks, there will always be reasons why an out-of-cycle raise or promotion may not be warranted: budget restrictions, peer-to-peer pay competitiveness, or simply being paid at the top of the salary range. These are all fairly common issues in the compensation world, so let's address all three one at a time.

The Solution

Budget limitations are the number one reason why companies can't award out-of-cycle or special raises to employees. Payroll tends to be the number one or number two expense on any organization's profit and loss report, so managing payroll dollars becomes a critical budget responsibility. Some organizations are not prone to pay salary increases because their budgets are already stretched, and being honest with the worker while combining realism with optimistic alternatives is your best path:

> Setche, I hear you. I understand why you're asking for a raise even though it's not performance review time, and I think it's good that you're asking. If you don't fight on your own behalf, others typically won't either. I appreciate the content you've provided in this spreadsheet that justifies a salary increase in your mind, but I'm afraid I can't support your request right now.
>
> The truth of the matter is, we've already been told that due to budget restrictions, there can be no out-of-cycle increases during

the budget year. I know you're aware that payroll is often the number one expense on a company's P&L, and we're no exception. Our CEO has made it clear that holding the salary line is critical throughout the year, and I've looked into your request with both human resources and finance and got the same answer: not at this time.

Now I want to move the discussion in a different direction: career development. Money is a critical factor for anyone in the workplace, which is understandable. But not all companies have the wherewithal to award salary increases or promotions or to create new headcount during the fiscal year. What I'd personally find of equal value is if my boss would be willing to sit down with me to discuss how to prepare for my next move in career progression—either here at XYZ Company or elsewhere. I'm willing to do that with you.

Your performance has been very strong, and you know that I go out of my way to recognize you and communicate my appreciation for all the hard work you do. Don't get me wrong—I don't want to risk losing you for lack of awarding you a raise, but it's simply not an option, and I don't want to mislead you or give you false hope. If you choose to remain with us, we can look at using the company's tuition reimbursement program to help you grow and develop in your career, we can consider rotational leadership assignments, we can have you spearhead critical projects, or we can help you build a better work-life balance. I'll need your thoughts and insights to determine what that might look like.

But in a spirit of full transparency, I don't see a possibility of awarding a salary increase this fiscal year outside of the merit increase cycle next June, and that likely won't change next year either. So we have to be realistic and make the most of what's available to us and what will help you feel like you're growing and thriving in your role, despite the fact that we can't award you a raise right now.

An internal equity challenge is yet another reason why a salary increase may not make sense. Internal equity is the comparison of employees' salaries based on their merits—prior experience, technical skills, education and certifications, and the like. You wouldn't want to pay a new hire more than your existing staff, for example, if the new hire has fewer years of experience or lighter professional credentials. When corporate recruiters extend offers, they benchmark the new hire's skills, knowledge, and abilities to those of the existing staff and "slot" them into the lineup to ensure the integrity of the pay structure.

No matter how well someone with a master's degree is performing, for instance, you probably couldn't pay them more than a coworker with a PhD. Likewise, if a three-year operating engineer on your team is running circles around his peers who all have ten years of average tenure, then you're likely not going to pay the newcomer more than the rest of the team. There may be exceptions of course, but any exceptions can be disastrous because once the senior folks find out the new guy is making more than them, they'll likely initiate job searches. In short, you don't want to promote one worker and lose three as a result. Here's what your discussion might sound like:

Imani, I understand why you feel justified in asking for a raise. You've been performing exceptionally well and helping to turn around our department in many ways, and I hope I've been successful in demonstrating my appreciation for all that you're doing. Asking for a raise is a healthy thing, and I have no problem whatsoever in your meeting me like this to make a case for yourself. I respect that, and I'm hearing all that you're saying.

There's a "however" in this though. When we consider pay matters, we always look at what's known as internal equity. It's a concept that requires employers to slot workers into the salary lineup based on their prior history, current performance, education, licensure, technical skills, and similar criteria. Currently, you're paid fairly relative to your peers. I've had the chance to review this with our compensation people, and they reviewed the entire team for pay equity. If we were to bump you up to the level you've requested via this increase, we'd run into what's known as "salary compression," where pay of a more junior employee either matches or exceeds the salary of more qualified or more senior workers.

It's not a matter of what's in the budget or how broad the salary range is. It's really a matter of where the worker sits within the range relative to those with higher or lower credentials. In short, to award you a raise, we'd need to award raises to certain other individuals who have more tenure and higher credentials than you, and we're not in a position to do that.

I want to be clear, Imani: Your contributions are valued, and we appreciate your achievements and your high level of productivity. But unfortunately, we're not able to award an increase unless you can promote into a new, higher-level role. That being said, I'd like to discuss your career goals and how we can help you with professional development. At any time, an employer may not be able to meet your requests for a promotion or a raise, but they should always be willing to help their top performers get ahead in their careers, whether that's through further education, more challenging responsibilities, or greater leadership responsibilities.

If you're game, I'd like to explore that with you more, but I don't do so to deflect from your original request—only to realistically set your expectations about how we determined that a pay increase isn't in order, while also focusing on career and professional development as a healthy alternative. In short, I don't want to lose you or risk demotivating you, but you have to realize that there are limits to what employers can do at any given time. I've always found that honesty, transparency, and trust are the healthiest way to approach these types of discussions, and I'm willing to do my part in helping you get ahead in your career even though I don't have dollars to offer you at this point.

When employees are "red circled" at the top of their salary range, it basically means that until the entire salary range goes up, the worker is maxed out and can't really have any further increases to the base salary. In a way, that's a good problem: it means they're being paid as high as the company will allow for their position. In many cases, that also means that they're high relative to the overall market (where the midpoint of the salary range comes close to mimicking the market). Here's a gentle way to explain this concept, along with some healthy alternatives that might help diffuse some of the anger or disappointment that comes with finding out that there's no potential for a higher salary in the current role:

Li Min, I appreciate you meeting with me regarding your request for a salary increase. I had a chance to discuss this with our human resources department, and I'm afraid that we won't be able to award you an increase because you're already at the top of the salary range. Did anyone ever share that information with you before? [*No.*] Okay, let me explain how that works.

Salary ranges at our company and pretty much at all companies are built around data points, known as minimums, midpoints, and maximums. Those salary data points indicate, as you can guess, the competitive rate that the market pays for similar skills and capabilities. Once you're at the maximum of the salary range, your salary is frozen until the entire range moves up. In your case, your current salary is already at the maximum, so there's nowhere to go until the entire range shifts upward.

We have no plans to do that in the near future, because our compensation studies tell us that we pay competitively in your discipline relative to the rest of the market. Also, I was able to confirm with human resources that we can still award you pay increases in the future, but they'll be paid to you as a lump sum, and they won't be added to your base salary rate. That's a fairly common way of handling situations like this: we want to continue to recognize your efforts, but we can't exceed the maximum of the salary range.

So yes, you'll still get a salary increase, but it won't be added to your base salary, meaning that it won't impact the value of your benefits package, including your 401(k) contribution rate. To begin "baking in" increases to your base salary, you'll need to promote into a higher classification, meaning that you'll need a new role with a higher salary grade. While we don't have any openings right now that you could promote into, we can begin discussions about how you can prepare for an opportunity like that when one becomes available. Of course, I can't guarantee that you'll be promoted once a higher-level position becomes available—I don't have a crystal ball—but preparing for that next step is a healthy exercise that focuses on your professional and career development, which I'm happy to help you with, if you're game.

In each of these scenarios, you've treated the individual with respect, you explained the logic behind your response, and you offered an alternative path—career and professional development—that could help refocus the individual's efforts. That's always the wisest approach when raises and promotions aren't currently available. Just remember that if you make such a commitment, you'll be responsible for setting the stage for career and professional development talks. It may be as simple as asking the employee to identify what he would like to pursue and then scheduling quarterly meetings to measure progress. But it must have a concrete action plan and professional development focus to ensure ongoing employee engagement and satisfaction—especially for your highest-demand contributors.

SCENARIO 104

Compensation Conflicts—When Employees Inflate Their Worth While Drafting Self-Reviews

Many companies encourage employees to have input into their annual performance reviews by participating in the process and preparing self-evaluations with individualized input. Generally speaking, that's a healthy way to engage employees, save managers' time, and make the annual evaluation process a shared exercise. Some companies accomplish this by distributing the appraisal form itself to employees and asking them to complete it prior to the review meeting. Other organizations encourage employees to provide feedback without necessarily sharing any type of formal feedback template to capture results and goals. In my book *The Performance Appraisal Tool Kit: Redesigning Your Performance Review Template to Drive Individual and Organizational Change*, cowritten with Winston Tan, we recommend something in between—a simple form that helps employees structure their thoughts around achievements, areas for development, and future goals. Employees who are asked to provide their own performance review input tend to appreciate the respect demonstrated for such an important annual exercise. Consider issuing a simple questionnaire two weeks in advance of the review that asks employees simple questions like the following:

1. Address your overall performance track record and accomplishments for this review period. Highlight any achievements that may have increased revenue, decreased expenses, or saved time. How would you grade yourself in terms of overall productivity, quality, communication, and teamwork?

2. What can I do as your supervisor to support you in terms of your own career growth and professional development?
3. What are your performance goals for the upcoming review year? What are the measurable outcomes to ensure that you'll have reached your preestablished goals?

Under most circumstances, employees will share a realistic assessment of their historical performance and future goals. After all, many workers tend to be harder on themselves than their boss will ever be. That places you into the role of mentor and coach, rather than authoritarian and unilateral decisionmaker, which is where you'll always want to be. But every once in a while, you get someone who has an inflated self-worth, and how you handle that conundrum speaks volumes about your ability to directly address differences in perception.

The Solution

On occasions where your assessment of an employee's performance or productivity differs significantly from the individual's view of self—whether during performance review season or at any time during the year—try structuring your questions and comments as follows to help realign expectations and bring the individual back to reality:

Shamus, I've reviewed your self-evaluation, and I appreciate your going through that exercise for me. However, I wanted to meet with you before we sit down to conduct the actual performance review because I have questions about some of the comments that you included in the self-review tool.

Let me start this way: The self-assessment tool doesn't ask you to assign a numerical grade to your overall performance, but if it did, and on a scale of one to ten with ten being highest, what grade would you assign yourself? [*A ten.*] Okay, why would you feel that score is the most appropriate to reflect your performance and contributions over the past year? [*Because I'm the only one who really does anything around here. I honestly feel like I carry the bulk of the workload, and I don't want to miss the opportunity to bring that to your attention in preparation for my annual review.*]

Fair enough. Now, using the same scale, what score would you think I'd assign to you if asked for a number off the top of my head? [*I'd guess a nine or a ten.*] And that's why I called this one-on-one meeting. Would it shock you if I told you that I saw you as falling somewhere between a six and a seven? [*Yes, it sure would.*] Then let's discuss what this looks like from my vantage point as your supervisor.

There are many times, Shamus, when you do perform like a ten, but what I've witnessed and what I've overheard others mentioning was that you can come across as arrogant and condescending at times. I don't see you consistently building camaraderie and team spirit by involving others appropriately, asking for feedback, and helping others grow and develop in their own careers. And I also think that you're quick to accept praise that rightfully belongs to the team, but tend to place blame on others when things don't go as expected.

Yes, it's true that I think you can be an excellent performer at times and that you have moments of brilliance, but that sometimes comes at the expense of others and not to other's benefit. Let me give you an example. Back in August, do you remember how you were called out and recognized for completing the due diligence assignment for Company X that garnered positive accolades all around and was completed two weeks before deadline? [*Yes.*] I saw that truly as a team effort where everyone supported you in your lead role. When you were publicly acknowledged for the data we provided and our recommended acquisition plan, your acknowledgment focused on *you*—not on the rest of the team behind the scenes that helped you achieve your goal.

That was a chance for you to share the glory and pass along the recognition and appreciation for what we accomplished as a team. First, even if you did 99 percent of the work, and the rest of the team only contributed 1 percent, it would have been gracious of you to include them. Second, and more important, you couldn't have completed your due diligence assignment without everyone being on board and contributing to the effort. It took an enormous amount of coordination and communication to make that come together so well. And that coordination and communication came from me, not from you. Therein lies the problem.

I'm not criticizing you here for the Company X due diligence. You did an excellent job with that assignment, and everybody knew it. But you missed an opportunity to share the gratitude and build the team. Even if everyone knew that you were the main driver, your willingness to share the spotlight and acknowledge your peers would have been well received. Instead, people likely thought, *There goes Shamus—hogging all the glory for himself again.* I don't know if anyone literally thought that or said that to anyone else, but you get my point.

As your boss, I'd be doing you a disservice if I didn't take this opportunity to share this kind of feedback with you. I know it can be difficult to hear that your boss thinks you're a seven when you feel like you're knocking it out of the park, but in this instance, it's not your performance that's holding you back—it's your behavior. If you truly want to get ahead in your career and set a realistic goal for yourself for the upcoming year, focus on leadership and teambuilding. Understand how to motivate and engage those around you. Don't assume that you're the only one doing all the work or that others aren't keeping up with you.

Let me tell you why. Even if you were the top-performing analyst on our team or within the entire company, there will always be someone on your heels. Guaranteed. New generations of analysts graduate from excellent universities with bright, shiny MBAs in their hands, and sooner or later, you'll be outperformed, outmaneuvered, and outflanked by the competition. By that time, you'll be older. Your value to your organization—this firm or any other—won't be in your ability to perform as an individual contributor. It will be in your ability to lead, to build strong teams, and to harmonize those teams to conquer all sorts of problems—not unlike what my role was in the Company X due diligence project.

What do you want people to say when they hear the name Shamus Kennedy? How do you want them to complete the sentence: *I know Shamus, and he's. . . .* What three adjectives will follow your name as you grow and develop in your career and transition from individual contributor to leader and executive? I have to share with you, Shamus, that you're not where you need to be yet. You've got a good amount of professional development ahead of you, and this is a career inflection point. The question you need to ask yourself is, are you willing to pivot? And am I the right person to help you get there?

I'm happy to serve as a career mentor and coach for you. I'm happy to help you focus on that transition from individual contributor to corporate leader. But you have an inflated sense of self at times, and you're not building up those around you by making it a friendly and inclusive work environment. In reality, I expect you and everyone else on my team to practice selfless leadership—to help develop and grow those *around* you. This way you'll learn how to eventually grow and develop those *beneath* you as you progress within your own career and climb the corporate ladder. But don't let any perceptions of arrogance or condescension hold you back. Your job from this point forward is to get work done *through* others—not *despite* them—and to carry them along the way on your path to success. That's what leadership is all about, and that's what I expect from you going forward.

If that sounds like the kind of relationship you want to have with your current boss and it likewise sounds like where you see your career going over the long term, then I'm here and happy to help. Honestly, though, if you don't think you can or want to meet these expectations, then this may be the wrong team for you at this point in your career. It'll be up to you to pursue different teams in other leagues, if garnering all the praise and accolades is more important to you than building up those around you.

So, this is why I called the meeting, and now you know what I want you to reflect on. And for the sake of clarity and transparency, this is what I see as your next career move and a way to truly earn a score of nine on your annual self-review. What questions can I answer for you at this point? [*Nothing right now, but you've given me a lot to think about. Thanks for the candid feedback.*]

And there you have it. A "take him down a notch" discussion that injects reality and future expectations into a potentially critical reflection point in this individual's career. As a rule, beware of those members of your team who seem to think that they do all the work and deserve all the kudos for the team's efforts. Whatever the nature of your discussion—performance, productivity, conduct, ethical behavior, and so forth—use the "scale of one to ten" exercise as a starting point. Make your case for your score, and then point out the wisdom in your argument (i.e., why it's best for the individual's longer-term career and professional development). With a structured argument like that, few will have difficulty understanding your performance assessment and motives behind the meeting. Then it will simply be a matter of their business maturity and awareness as to whether they wish to gain from your wisdom or look to some other source for their career development.

SCENARIO 105

Terminating Employees Who Are on Investigatory Leave

Whenever an employee makes direct or veiled threats of violence and you believe you have a legitimate cause for concern, placing that individual on an investigatory leave may make sense. First, you'll want to remove the employee from company premises for safety's sake. Second, you'll want to conduct a thorough and impartial investigation, and the employee's presence may compromise your objective fact-finding efforts.

The Solution

Your conversation with the employee at the time you place him on an investigatory leave must be calm and caring yet firm. For instance, your discussion might sound like this:

> John, we need to talk. Your comment about people knowing that they shouldn't bother you or else. . . . Well, let's just say that in today's age of workplace violence, we have no choice but to interpret that very seriously. Tapping the bullet on the desk, which you admitted to doing, spooked a number of people, and rightfully so.
>
> Therefore, I'm going to have to ask you to go home for the rest of the day. We're considering this to be what we call an "investigatory leave" so that we could look into things on our end without you here to influence the outcome of the investigation. No worries about your pay: You'll be paid for the rest of the day and until we've had a chance to complete the investigation on our end. You'll simply continue to be paid as if you were working as normal.
>
> However, I need to let you know, John, that depending on the outcome of the investigation, this may result in discipline, up to and including dismissal. I just want you to know that up front

because, again, we're taking this all very seriously. For now, it would be best if you left the building and waited at home for my call. I'll plan on giving you a call by 4:00 this afternoon. Are you clear on what I'm telling you?

John's response at that point may be, "Oh, Paul, I didn't mean anything by that. I was just kidding. You know that. I wouldn't ever threaten to hurt anyone. I just happened to have that shell in my shirt pocket, and I tapped it rather than a pencil without thinking." Still, you may very well feel that his threatening behavior was unacceptable, especially in light of the record that could be created:

1. Employee threatens that no one should bother him today.
2. Employee taps a live piece of ammunition on his desk when he makes that statement.
3. Employee later tells human resources that he was only joking.
4. Human resources allows employee to return to work.
5. Incident of workplace violence against coworker occurred at 5:00 p.m.

Of course it's the possibility of that fifth point that concerns you.

In questioning the staff about John's overall behavior or if any threats have been made before, you learn that John has indeed made similar threats to his coworkers. And they're especially concerned because John is known for keeping hunting rifles in the trunk of his car and goes shooting at a rifle range after work every night.

Assuming that you've vetted your findings either through your company's HR department or through qualified legal counsel and agree that termination is appropriate, you would then call John at home and explain the following:

John, it's Paul. Is it a good time to talk now? [*Yes.*] Okay, grab a pencil so that you can take some notes. We spoke with senior management about how to handle this, and it looks like we'll need to part ways. I can't say I disagree with their decision, John: In today's day and age, any possible threats of workplace violence are taken so seriously. Therefore, in our internal records, we'll have to reflect this as a termination for cause. I want you to keep a few things in mind, though.

First, you'll continue to be paid through tomorrow. We'll draft your final checks for straight-time pay plus any accrued but unused vacation. We'll courier the checks to your home by the end of the day tomorrow, and we'll also include any personal belongings that are still at your desk. We'll have to deactivate your badge on our end, but I'll ask you to mail it to me, along with your office keys and your cell phone. Finally, John, for safety's sake, I have to inform our security team that you aren't to have further access to the campus without my specific approval. I know this is a lot of information, but I want to make sure that you've got it all. Is everything clear so far? [*Yes.*]

There's one more thing: I can't know if that threat was real or a passing joke, but John, please don't do that at any other company where you work in the future. I'm afraid they'll have no choice but to interpret it the way we're doing so today, and obviously I wouldn't want you to have to go through this again. Know how much we appreciate all your hard work over the past year and a half. And I'm sorry for this outcome. But again, I hope you could understand why this is a reasonable response on our part under the circumstances.

Special Note

Whenever you find yourself in a situation where your corporate attorney recommends terminating an employee while out on investigatory leave, be sure to take notes outlining your counsel's advice. If possible, have your attorney email you her recommendation so that you've got a written record before you take any action.

That's important for two reasons: First, many employers who become "spooked" by employees making veiled threats of violence jump the gun too quickly and terminate without completing a thorough investigation. Second, you'll want your written record to demonstrate that you (1) investigated the situation thoroughly and objectively and reached a reasonable conclusion in a timely manner and (2) relied on qualified counsel before initiating any action.

Your written record will help avoid or significantly minimize any potential claims for wrongful termination or mental disability discrimination that could be raised under the Americans with Disabilities Act. What courts and juries look for is that the company acted reasonably and responsibly, and you'll clearly have met that standard by placing the individual on investigatory leave and then documenting your findings and legal conclusion before taking action.

In fact, you might want to keep a timeline in your notes of when the complaint was made, when the investigation took place, when the attorney was contacted, and when the employee was informed of the decision to terminate. Take notes of the employee's response over the phone as well. Such a written record can serve as evidence of your proper handling of this situation. More important, you'll demonstrate your care and concern for providing a safe workplace for your employees. Remember this: In the world of employment litigation, you can be sued by both sides. The terminated employee can sue you for wrongful termination and disability discrimination, for example. And (heaven forbid) your employees or their survivors could sue you if that employee ever acted on any of those threats and injured or killed anyone.

The question you have to answer for yourself is, *which lawsuit would you rather fight*: the one from the threatening employee for wrongful termination, or the one from your employees who put you on notice that they were concerned for their safety in light of a coworker's threats but were injured nevertheless because you failed to act on their complaints? Sometimes the world of people management becomes difficult to navigate. However, you'll more than likely find that defending yourself from one employee who's threatening a wrongful termination lawsuit is much easier to justify than a potential lawsuit based on workplace violence from your injured workers.

SCENARIO 106

Verbally Accepting an Employee's Resignation

If you're thinking, "This is an interesting conversation with which to end the book," then you're not alone. All of our other scenarios are concrete examples of challenging workplace situations that need to be verbally addressed to set the employee on a different course of action. Once they resign, though, then they're done, right? I mean, you don't have to literally *do anything* once you've gotten a verbal resignation, do you?

Interestingly enough, this issue trips up many unsuspecting employers. When a problematic employee resigns, don't start doing the jig in the hallway just yet. You're not quite as "done" with him as you may think. First of all, ask for the resignation in writing. That helps people come to terms with the fact that they're really leaving. More important, it will help you fight an unemployment claim should the ex-worker file and tell the nice folks at the unemployment office that he was laid off.

Second, what if the employee rescinds his resignation within the two-week notice period? Do you still have the right to say, "Sorry—you're out!" or do you have to give him his job back? The short answer to this quagmire scenario is that it depends: You would think that you have every right to rely on the individual's notice of resignation and end his employment on an agreed-upon date. The key legal question, however, becomes "How did you, the employer, *act in reliance* upon that notice?" If you did nothing—neither post the job nor begin interviewing candidates nor extend an offer to someone to replace this person—then your refusal to give the employee his job back could subject you to a wrongful termination charge.

The Solution

The lesson here is that whenever a problematic employee gives you two weeks' notice, take immediate action to fill the position being vacated by posting it internally, running an advertisement, and reassigning work to other staff members. Think of it this way: If you do nothing, you could lose a lawsuit saying you had no right to prevent that individual from rescinding his resignation. On the other end of the spectrum, you could hire someone (or come as close as possible to it) in that two-week interval, and that would be the most foolproof way of avoiding any potential liability.

Here's what your conversation might sound like:

David, I understand you're resigning, and I accept your two-week notice. I'm glad that you're excited about the new opportunity that's awaiting you, so congratulations. We normally ask for resignations in writing: Would you be able to prepare a resignation letter for me? [*No. I don't like putting things like that in writing.*]
  Oh, that's interesting. Well, okay. I'll have to draft a short memo to you then saying that I accept your resignation, effective

May 10, and that I wish you continued success in your career. Does that sound reasonable? [*I guess.*]

Also, I'd like your help with something. We'll need to post the opening internally and advertise for it as well, and I'd like your help in updating your job description and helping me draft an advertisement. No one knows your position better than you do, and I'd like to discuss your suggestions tomorrow. [*Sure, I can work on that.*]

If it's a particularly contentious relationship, then you may not want to ask the individual to involve himself in this process. However, under less extreme circumstances, asking the individual to do the legwork to prepare the written materials to find his replacement saves you time and gives you both a chance to work together on this final project.

Finally, I'm planning on reassigning some of your existing work-load to other members of the team, so I'd like your recommendations along those lines. Can we discuss that tomorrow too? [*Sure.*]

Okay, now I know what you're thinking: If this hasn't been an ideal hire, why am I being so nice to this individual once he's given notice and, more important, involving him in finding his replacement? Well, there are a few practical reasons. First, it's always better to "play nice" at the finish line. You have nothing to gain by being anything less than courteous, so do the right thing and let the last impression for both sides be positive. That allows David to walk out with his head held high, and when that's the case, there is far less chance of lawsuits.

Second, allowing him to help in updating his job description, job posting, and workload reassignment makes him aware that you're *acting in reliance* on his resignation. That means if he changes his mind a week from now (when he's only one week into his two-week resignation period), you can respectfully let him know that the position has already been posted, candidates are lined up to come in and interview, and his peers are already handling part of his work.

That should be enough to convince him that he can't have his job back just because he's changed his mind about leaving. More important, it will protect you legally should he decide to pursue the matter in court. It's just a smart and practical strategy and insurance plan any time you're dealing with someone who gives notice.

Special Note

Of course, in many instances, you may choose to retain a well-performing employee who rescinds her resignation, but you have to be careful about setting an unwanted precedent: In the future, it could be argued that if you allowed one employee to rescind a resignation, then you'll have to allow others to do so as well. Therefore, you shouldn't develop an active practice of allowing such changes of heart at the eleventh hour.

CLOSING NOTE

Thank you for allowing me to walk you through some of the most challenging workplace scenarios that exist in corporate America today. Leadership development starts with communication, and avoiding conflict is a natural human response to difficult situations. My goal in writing *101 Tough Conversations*, like many of my other books, was to help you understand not just *what* to do but *how* to do it. And how to phrase things constructively so they don't make people defensive is an art as much as a science.

My final advice is simply to use yourself as a barometer: Would you feel comfortable if your supervisor spoke to you about a particular performance or conduct challenge the way it's outlined in this book? If so, adapt the proposed language to fit your own style, but remember that leadership, communication, and teamwork are the highest-order "soft skills" that will help you stand out from the competition and develop a reputation as a "favorite boss," so everyone will be looking for an opportunity to join your team and work for you.

Further, outlining these topical conversations gave me an opportunity to share the leadership wisdom that I've been fortunate enough to learn from excellent mentors of my own throughout the years. Hence, this very special book is an opportunity for me to pay it forward. I hope you can accept the book as the gift it was meant to be. In all you do, remember the simple rule: *What you want for yourself, give to another.* That's enough to help you navigate your career and your life successfully. Life, like leadership, is simpler than we sometimes make it, and I hope *101 Tough Conversations* provides you with the tools and opportunity to grow and develop your teams by focusing on accountability and productivity. If so, you'll be giving others a very special gift of your own, and so the circle continues. . . .

—*Paul Falcone*

INDEX